Honolulu-Whalemen's Paradise

Galápagos

Off-Shore Grounds

N

1. *Essex* sunk by whale
2. Henderson I.
3. Chase rescued
4. Pollard rescued

1

5

3

2

4

6

5. Mocha Dick killed 2 men
6. Mocha Dick killed 2 men
7. "Young Gentleman"

7

Harry Spiel   1955

Yankee Whalers in the South Seas

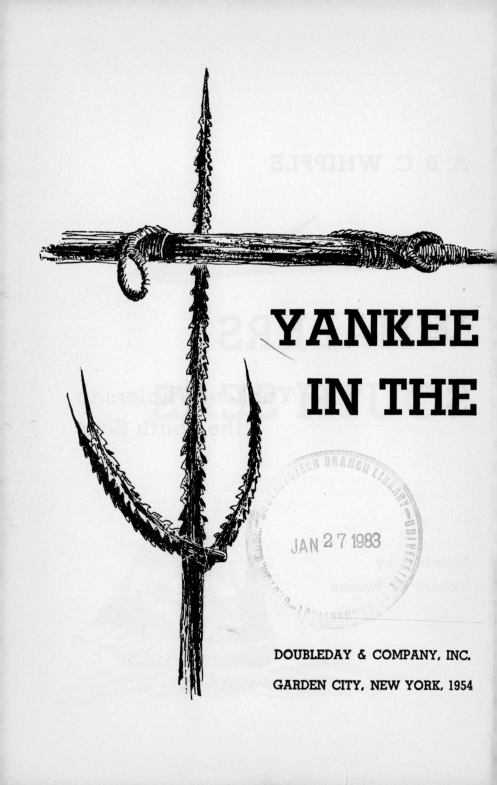

YANKEE
IN THE

DOUBLEDAY & COMPANY, INC.

GARDEN CITY, NEW YORK, 1954

A. B. C. WHIPPLE

WHALERS
SOUTH SEAS

Drawings by
Richard M. Powers

Library of Congress Catalog Card Number 54-7313

Copyright, 1954, by A. B. C. Whipple
All Rights Reserved
Printed in the United States
at the Country Life Press, Garden City, N.Y.
Designed by Alma Reese Cardi

The author wishes to thank *Life* magazine for permission to use the part of Chapter 1 which originally appeared in that magazine under the title "Three-Month Ordeal in Open Boats."

Preface

These are tales of great men. The whalemen of New England were a part—the important part—of one of the great industries of the world. And their part in that industry was one of history's most hazardous occupations. The beast they sought out and killed, the whale, was bigger than any creature that has ever swum the oceans or walked the surface of the earth. The weapons they used were harpoons and lances as small as javelins, and their whaleboats were just a little more than twice the size of a canoe. The only limits to their searchings, through baking calms and crashing storms, were the limits of the seas at the ends of the earth. Off over the horizon they went, chasing, killing, and cutting up whales for as long as four or five years before they came home. In 1851, in his novel *Moby Dick*, Herman Melville characterized the Nantucketer; but he was talking about every Yankee whale-man:

"Let America add Mexico to Texas, and pile Cuba upon Canada; let the English overswarm all India, and hang out their blazing banner from the sun; two-thirds of this terraqueous globe are the Nantucketer's. For the sea is his; he owns it, as Emperors own empires; other seamen having but a right of way through it. Merchant ships are but extension bridges; armed ones but floating forts; even pirates and privateers . . . but plunder other ships, other fragments of the land like themselves, without seeking to draw their living from the bottomless deep itself. The Nantucketer, he alone resides and riots on the sea; he alone, in Bible language, goes down to it in ships; to and fro plowing it as his own special plantation. *There* is his home."

Melville singled out the Nantucketer as his symbol because at the time this little island community was synonymous with whaling. He might as well have been speaking of the whalemen of New Bedford and New London, of Edgartown and Sag Harbor, of Mystic and Fairhaven, and dozens of other towns along the New England and Long Island coast. For all the Yankee whalemen, no matter where they came from, spent a large part of their lives on the water, not using it as a highway, but living on it and from it. They went twisting and plunging across the Gulf Stream, down through the "Roaring Forties," around the sleet-swept, treacherous point of Cape Horn and out across the Pacific Ocean, there to harvest the sea as nonchalantly as a farmer would his back lot. The whalemen lived on the rolling hills and valleys of the deep, more, in fact, than he did at home.

It took a particular kind of courage to say good-by to wife, sons, and daughters, knowing you would not see them again for at least three years, maybe five. And during the long absence the whaleman lived in more danger than if he had gone off to war; it was a rare whaleship that came home with more than two thirds of her original crew. Yet the whalemen who survived usually rested only a month or two before setting forth on another five-year hunt. Captain Benjamin Worth of Nantucket, for example, was a whaleman for forty-one years. During that time he lived a total of six years at home.

The whaleman covered the Atlantic and Pacific oceans as no

explorer had or could hope to—tracing and retracing his course to the top and the bottom of the world and across the oceans to the edges of the sunset and the dawn in his ceaseless search for whales. The names of dozens of islands commemorate those skippers and the whaleship owners who sent them out—Gardner Island, Starbuck Island, Mitchell Island. If the U. S. Government had had the foresight in the Pacific that it had in the American West, we would not later have had to win back from the Japanese many islands that were discovered by American whalemen in the first place.

There was only one other mariner in a class with the whaleman: the sealer. He too sailed off on long voyages away from home. He too made discoveries—even including the continent of Antarctica. But the main business always was whaling and sealing. The oil and whalebone and sealskins these men brought back from their long cruises were put to a hundred different uses all over the world—in lamps and corsets, soap and perfumery, caps and sewing machines. And sometimes the prize was well worth the chase; a skipper who was lucky enough to return with a hold full of sperm oil and some spermaceti when the market was good had a cargo worth nearly a quarter of a million dollars and a captain's share large enough to retire on for the rest of his life.

But this book is not a history of the whaling industry. This is a book for amateur fans of maritime history like myself, not for the scholars and historians. It is an account of the adventures of the whalemen themselves, the courageous fortune hunters who made Yankee whaling what it was. Some of them were too cruel, some too kind. Some were amiable, some ornery. There were brave men and cowards, honest men and thieves, closemouthed men and accomplished liars. There were figures of somber tragedy and comic-opera humor, quarter-deck tyrants, and forecastle strategists of rebellion. There were renegades who led cannibals against whaleship crews; and there was a castaway who became one of America's most effective ambassadors of good will among the natives. There were foremast hands who went over the side at the first glimpse of a green, tropical island; and there was another who walked home from the Arctic Circle in a heroic attempt to save his shipmates. There was a mate who saved the lives of a boat's crew at the extreme risk of his own; and there was a harpooner who led what was probably the bloodiest mutiny in maritime history.

There were cannibals who became obedient and skillful harpooners and devout Christians. There were shrieking, blue-black devils who swept down on a becalmed whaler to slaughter everyone aboard. And there were cannibal chiefs who sheltered shipwrecked whalemen, one going so far as to offer his own life to save that of his young white friend.

And the women—prim New England wives who went right along with their captain husbands and did more than their share of the ship's work; languorous island girls who would do anything for a white man; a native girl who rescued a whaleman from oblivion on the beach and gave him back his self-respect; an American girl who fooled a whole forecastle full of whalemen, no small achievement in itself.

Did any other ships carry such varied crews?—old veterans who couldn't spin a simple yarn in less than three hours; little boys and girls living in the captains' cabins with their mothers and fathers; imaginative cooks who could make almost palatable meals out of garbage (and who never got any credit for it, either); artisans who whittled *objets d'art* out of the tooth of the sperm whale; Quakers; heathens; and even a great author.

Finally, there was the quarry, the great mountainous mass of blubber and muscle with jaws literally as big as a barn door. Larger than a herd of elephants, wily as a trout, the whale was the fearsome central fact of the whaleman's existence. Every chase and kill was a voluntary, split-second brush with hideous death. And when there appeared on the scene a rogue white monster bent on destroying every whaleboat, the result was a series of battles between man and beast the like of which the world has never seen.

Chasing and battling the whale was almost as old as New England itself. Yankee whaling started not many years after the first settlements had become established towns. "In the year 1690," wrote Obed Macy in his *History of Nantucket*, "some persons

were on a high hill . . . observing the whales spouting and sporting with each other, when one observed 'there,' pointing to the
sea, 'is a green pasture where our children's grandchildren will go
for bread.' " They did not wait for their children's grandchildren,
or their children, for that matter. Nantucketers—and their neighbors all up and down the New England coast—were "offshore
whaling" before the turn of the eighteenth century. But as offshore
whaling increased, the whales went farther and farther to sea.
The whalemen followed them. First they went out in little sloops,
and the catch was still brought back to be butchered and "tried-
out" on the beach. Then, as the voyages grew longer, brick tryworks were installed on the decks of larger ships, great cranes
were rigged overhead, and the whaleship was born.

These were the Yankee whalers that plowed out into the south
seas, transporting the New Englanders into another world, a
world as unlike Nantucket and Boston and Salem and New London as it could possibly be. For nearly a century the Yankees
cruised this dangerous paradise. Then two men, James Young in
Scotland and Samuel Kier in Tarentum, Pennsylvania, almost
simultaneously discovered how to refine petroleum. Whaling continued for a few more years, but the great industry was finished.

Only the whalemen's stories are left—contemporary accounts
like these, tales of adventure and greed and murder and love.
In retelling them I have sometimes had to add to the spare,
laconic log or journal—dialogue where it was needed but did not
exist in the record, essential information from other sources, a
calculated guess where a puzzling gap has been left unfilled. And
while this is not a book for historians, I have had invaluable help
from many of them. In the last chapter I have tried to detail the
sources of the stories and express my thanks to those experts in
the field who were so willing to help an amateur.

With their help I have tried to convey the atmosphere as well
as the bare account without straying too far from the essentials
of the story as it was told by the participant or contemporary.
Which leads to the logical question: Are all these accounts really
true? I have made every effort to include only the stories that
are well authenticated; but I must add that in some cases the

best, or only, authentication necessarily comes from the whale-men who were there; and years of spinning yarns in a forecastle gave a whaleman a slightly different definition of truth from that held by the meticulous scholar. It is not that the whaleman was a willful liar; it is just that he was inclined to feel that absolute, hairsplitting, quibbling truth was sometimes overrated.

Remember, too, before you criticize him, that he is the hero of these stories. Try for a moment to picture yourself in his position, in a frail-sided whaleboat just about to enter the dread, boiling circle of the whale's murderous flukes. The nineteenth-century whaleman of America was a fantastic creature, a species apart from the landsman and even from the rest of the seamen. He was a far cry, too, from the hardy enough men of today who never-theless go out with motorized launches, ramp-equipped factory ships, helicopters, electronic detection gear, and even (the latest) "silent sound," a device that sends pulses of ultrasonic sound into the water to force the befuddled whales to the surface. With not one of these inventions the nineteenth-century whalemen supplied a far greater demand than there is today. There never was quite such a breed of men as the whalemen of a century ago, and there never has been since. About that there is no doubt.

Such are the men who made up these stories—the hard way, by performing the feats of courage or endurance or mischief that they recount. Great and good, craven and evil, they nevertheless were America's pioneers of the Atlantic and Pacific; the only ones who resided and rioted on the sea. *There* was their home.

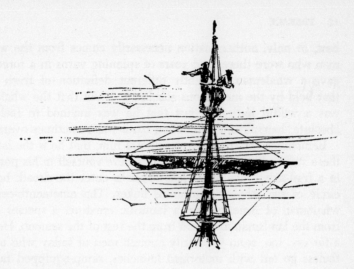

Contents

Yankee Whalers in
the South Seas

1. The doomed ship[1]

It was perfect whaling weather; a trade wind ruffled the surface of the sea and filled the sails of the whaleship, moving her gently over the rolling, even swells of the ocean. It was the morning of November 20, 1820, and the ship was nearly at the equator, in the midst of the most open stretch of the Pacific. She was a fat, round-bowed, 238-ton ship, but out here in her own boundless world of sky and water she seemed a model, dwarfed by the overwhelming expanse of sea that rolled away from her on all points of the compass—north to Alaska; south to Antarctica; east to Ecuador; west to Borneo.

From here she could sail, day after day, week after week, for more than a month without sighting the tiniest speck of land cropping up out of the enormous body of water beneath her, pulsing across one third of the earth. The whaler's course was set,

[1]A portion of this chapter appeared in *Life* magazine under the title, "Three-Month Ordeal in Open Boats" and is copyright, 1952, by Time, Incorporated.

and the helmsman hanging over the wheel held to it; but this was virtually a pretense. Actually the ship was going nowhere. She was cruising about this watery wilderness in no particular direction at all. Her goal was not some busy harbor where a waterfront warehouse awaited her cargo and civilization beckoned to her crew; her mission was not to transport goods or passengers from one port to another. Instead, her destination was any lonely patch of the Pacific that might harbor a school of sperm whales.

That could be anywhere. The whaler's mission was to search out these beasts of the sea, chase after them in boats far smaller than the whales themselves, and kill them with weapons that were to a whale what a small jackknife would be to a man. Then the grueling job of rendering the whale into casks of oil in the middle of the ocean, wherever the animal had been hunted down and killed. It was always a blood-and-oil bath, while the ship groaned over on her side with the weight of the carcass dragging on her windlass, while ankle-deep gore and grease sloshed from port to starboard scuppers, while men shouted, slid the deck's length, swam in the congealing slime, floundered about on the whale's slick back and fought to cut away the blubber and avoid the voracious sharks snapping a few inches from their feet. Then the splattering fire of the trypots on deck, as the pieces of blubber were boiled down into oil and poured into casks to be stored in the hold below. And then, far into the night, the booming sheets of flame soaring up into the yardarms as more blubber was fed to the fire and the thrashing light illuminated the billowing clouds of greasy, jet-black smoke that rolled away before the wind. Like a triumphal fire, which it really was, the "trying-out" seemed to make the spars pitch above, the sea and its sharks toss below, and the men, their begrimed faces revolving in the lightninglike flashes of the flames, dance like savages about their oily altar.

This, rather than the clean run from port to port with salt spray flying and the lee rail under, was the grisly job of the whaleship, the "floating charnel house," the "butcher shop adrift." Besides the particular whaler rolling along the Line this autumn day in 1820, there were hundreds of others separately spotted across the

Atlantic and Pacific Oceans. Like this one, they were in no hurry; it took three years, four years, sometimes five years to fill the hold with sperm oil, whalebone, and the rare and precious spermaceti. But when the whaler finally creaked back into her home port, her rigging more patches than rigging and her hull solidly encrusted with barnacles, the foul-smelling cargo below usually brought good prices. Trying-out aboard a whaleship was a holocaust of fire and grease; but the whalemen called it "greasy luck."

So on this clear, bright November morning the most important hands aboard this whaler wallowing along the Line were the men perched high in the topgallant crosstrees, ceaselessly searching the horizon for the faint, wispy spout that meant another whale, another trying-out, another row of oil-filled barrels below. Surviving records do not indicate who these men were this morning. Nor is there any way of knowing what idle, bored, homesick thoughts wandered through their minds as they stood up there, braced against the iron hoops that supported them while the masts swung them in slow circles over a somnolent sea. Certainly they had no way of knowing that the next whale sighted would be their last. For the whaleship was the *Essex*, of Nantucket Island, Massachusetts, George Pollard, Jr., master; and she was doomed.

It is not known either which of the three lookouts spotted it first—something near the horizon, off the lee bow. A tiny puff—it was little more than that—rose and blew off across the water. It could be some kind of disturbance, a fish flipping a spray into the air. It could be the kind of optical illusion, like the mirage in the desert, that tricked so many masthead lookouts who had been searching too long and too hopefully. Or it could be the real thing. Whales are animals, not fish; they breathe air, and when they sound down into the depths to feed on giant cuttlefish near the bottom, a special valve flaps over the spiracle through which they breathe. When they rise again this valve flies open as the whale exhales in a mighty gust, and the upward-shooting vapor that follows is what the whaler's lookout watched for. The tiny puff across the water from the *Essex* could be any one of a number of things, but one of those things could be a whale's spout.

The lookout kept his eye on the spot. There it went again. It looked even more like a spout this time. He took a chance.

"THERE SHE BLOWS!!"

Below him the ship erupted. From every passageway men came running, stumbling, climbing into the rigging. Second Mate Mather Joy scrambled up the ratlines as if the hull were sinking under him. What followed was a procedure that happened, almost in an exact pattern, countless thousands of times aboard whaleships all over the Pacific throughout the nineteenth century. But it never lost its climactic excitement.

Mate Joy stopped climbing just below the lookout.

"Where away?" he shouted. The lookout pointed out across the lee bow, just as the telltale spray rose again.

"Oh yes, there he is. Now wait a bit; wait until he lets go again. YES. THERE SHE BLOOOWS!"

The *Essex's* first mate was a salty, whalewise Nantucketer named Owen Chase. He came swinging up the rigging himself. "How far?" he bellowed.

"Almost at the horizon. BLOOOOWS! SHE BLOOOOOOWS!"

Captain George Pollard was still buttoning his trousers as he hit the quarter-deck. Already he was giving his orders, in a calm voice, but loud enough for every man aboard to hear and make no mistake about them. His running commentary was virtually always the same—he had issued these orders countless times before, and probably no man aboard needed to hear them in order to act. But the rapid-fire monologue spewed out anyway as the skipper seemed to race up the rigging.

"Call all hands, Mr. Chase," he said. "Stand by to run down to him. Steward, get me the glass. Sure there's only one, Mr. Joy? I don't see a thing. Off the lee bow, you say? Muster them all up, Mr. Chase. Those boats ready? Get them ready. Hustle along there, you. We've got a good day's work ahead of us. Now I see him—I think." The steward finally clambered up near enough to pass the glass to Captain Pollard, who wound an arm through the rigging and fixed the telescope to his eye.

"Don't see a thing," he mumbled. "YES! THERE IT IS! Whole school of 'em, I should say. Helmsman, keep her steady on when the lookout sings out. Little more to starboard. Little more. Keep the run of him, there aloft. Sing out when we head right. You make out more than one, Mr. Chase? Thought so. There it is again!"

Another bellow from the lookout. It was unmistakably a school of them now. "BLOOOWS! THERE SHE BLOOOWS! BLOOOOWS! BLOOOOWS! SHE BLOOOOOWS! SHE BLOOOOOOOOOOOWS!"

Pollard swung around and yelled at the helmsman. "Steady on, now!" The big ship straightened out on course and bore down on the whales, her lines whipping, her blocks rattling and her wake bubbling, as if she too had caught the excitement. The chase had begun.

Captain Pollard kept his place in the rigging as the whaler ran down toward the spouts, which seemed to increase in number as they approached. The shouting and banging died down and the men went about their routine. A crew formed up alongside each whaleboat, swinging on its davits at the bulwarks. Long, narrow, pointed at bow and stern, the whaleboats had thin board thwarts for five oarsmen, plus just enough room at the stern for a man to handle the big rudder oar and enough at the bow for another to wield the harpoon. The oars, the harpoons, the razor-sharp lances (for the kill), the wooden tubs with the harpoon line meticulously coiled in them, the knives, hatchets, water buckets, and all the other gear that might be needed were now being stowed and checked carefully by each boat's crew. Meanwhile, as much to himself as to his men, Captain Pollard kept up the monologue of every whale skipper before and after him.

"That's it [to the helm], keep her steady, there. Steady-y-y. Get those lines ready [to the boat crews]. Be sure they're fast to the irons; don't want them making off with a good iron. Look like big ones, too. Near a hundred barrels each one. There! There she breaches! Mr. Chase, stand by to brace round the yards. We don't want to run down onto them. Helm a little more to starboard, there. That's it. That's it. Steady, now. Steady-y-y. We'll lower all three boats, Mr. Chase. Confound it, wish we had the other two. Soon as they're fixed we'll most likely go weeks without a spout. Cooper [to the ship's carpenter]. When the boats are out, I want you to be careful not to get too close. Don't want to gally those critters till we're fast to them. Don't run down till I give the signal from my boat. Got that? Now. Now we're getting onto them. There, there she blows and breaches. Mr. Chase, ready with those yards. I want the main-topsail hove back. Steady at the helm, there. Steady-y-y. 'Bout half a mile off, I should think. Little more; little more. Ready?

"Now, Mr. Chase. Main-topsail aback!"

"Main-topsail aback, sir," from Chase, who was swinging dcwn onto the deck as the men hauled at the yards below and the big sail eased around.

"Helm up, there," said Pollard. "Bit more . . . more . . . That's it," as the ship came into the wind. Half a mile away the spouts of at least three or four whales could be seen clearly, even from the deck.

Captain Pollard thumped back on deck.

"Mr. Chase"—his voice was low now—"are you all ready?" With the whales only 800 yards away everyone moved about his job quietly. The atmosphere was like that of a hunter creeping up on his prey.

"All ready, sir," answered Chase.

"Hoist and swing boats!"

The blocks creaked and whined softly as three whaleboats swung down onto the water. Captain Pollard took his spread-legged stance in the stern of his boat, the end of the long steering oar cradled under his right armpit. "Remember, cooper," he spoke up at the bulwarks looming above him, "keep off till I raise the signal."

He turned to the mates, shoving off alongside him in the other two boats.

"Mr. Chase, spread the chances. We'll fan down on them. Mr. Joy, pick out your own whale. But don't let your boat get too far from the others. We want to keep spread, but we don't want to lose each other. Hear that, Mr. Chase? All right. Out oars!"

Like three elongated spiders, the boats walked across the Pacific toward the whales. Now each officer was on his own,

Captain Pollard in the "first" boat, First Mate Chase in the second, and Second Mate Joy in the third. Back on the whaler the cooper took his temporary command, with only two or three of the crew as shipkeepers, until the rest should return. Aboard the ship and in the little whaleboats it seemed exactly like every other lowering. No one had any way of foreseeing the disaster that was nearly upon them.

The boats had only closed a little more than half the distance to the whales when the big beasts apparently became aware of their hunters. With loud snorts and thunderous slaps on the water they upped their tails and went for the bottom. In his boat, holding the steering oar and facing forward, Mate Chase signaled the men to stop rowing. They rested on their oars and watched him. With their backs to the whale they could only follow the directions of the man in the stern; no one was allowed to turn and look forward. This was partly to keep the rhythm of the stroke from being broken, but also because the sight of the big animal close on had been enough to panic many a green hand. When a "greenie" got so frightened he yelled or stood up or tried to jump, the only way to quiet him immediately was to knock him unconscious with the steering oar; and in that short time the boat could swerve off course or, worse still, bump the whale.

While they waited, and Chase watched, the boat rolled gently up and over the Pacific swells. The only sound was the muffled thump of a water cask rocking against one of the line tubs and the dripping of the oar blades as they spraddled out over the water. All around them the sea was as unruffled as if no whale had ever been near the area. But everyone knew that somewhere deep below them the enormous animals were plunging, with the speed of a shark, toward the bottom—or, possibly by now, back toward the surface. The whales might be racing off in any direction, trying to make as much distance as possible under water before coming up for air. But they might also have sounded straight down and started straight back up again. So the three whaleboats sat on the sea; and the three crews waited and sweated.

In his boat Mate Chase gave over the steering oar to one of

the men and picked his way forward. Usually the man at the bow oar was also the harpooner; at the command from the officer in the stern the harpooner shipped his oar, scrambled about as quickly as he could, grabbed the ready harpoon, sighted his black, gleaming target, and heaved the big iron. The harpooner was thereupon supposed to rush aft, take the steering oar from the officer, and guide the boat on its rushing, planing "Nantucket sleighride" as the whale dashed off, pulling the boat after him. This was why the whaleman's term for harpooner was "boat steerer." The mate, relieved of the steering oar, then got forward and selected his lance. Giving his orders from the bow, he directed the shortening of the line until the boat was hauled close alongside the plunging whale, so he could thrust the lance into the animal's vitals. Chase disdained this procedure; perhaps like some other whalemen, he thought that the whole maneuver, with two men crawling past each other in a bouncing whaleboat, was clumsy and inefficient. Instead he handled both the harpoon and the lance himself. Testing the harpoon for balance, flicking his calloused thumb across its sharp, barbed point, he held the weapon, javelinlike, and watched his chance.

This was the climactic moment, the moment that occurred to a harpooner as seldom as a couple dozen times in three or four years at sea. This was what they had come halfway around the world for. This, the chase and the kill, was the payoff. As a financial proposition, it was the difference between the success and failure of the voyage. But to every whaleman it was a lot more than that. It was the biggest big-game hunt the world has ever known. No living creature on the face of the earth has ever approached the size of the whale; closest was the brachiosaurus, which had only one half the bulk of the whale. One tap from the mighty flukes of a bull sperm whale and the boat was matchwood; one chomp of the big jaw and two men could disappear into the animal's gullet like pills easing down a man's throat.

Suddenly Owen Chase tensed and arched his back. At that moment there was a sighing, whistling spout and a rush of water that made every man in the boat flinch. Chase had seen the black mass streaking up toward him a split second before it broke water; so he was ready.

The whale rose only a few yards away from the boat. From where he stood, his knee braced against the gunwale, his throwing arm raised, the heavy harpoon balanced on the heel of his hand, Chase could make out every detail of the big beast. It was medium-sized, only about twice the length of the boat. Waves sloshed against its blunt head like the sea lapping at a foundering ship. Barnacles and whitish blotches of sea lice speckled its sides. Its broad, sloping back, jet black and glistening in the equatorial sun, glided through the sea like a floating island. What made it impressive was the realization that this gigantic mass was alive. Ripples went along the side, and the great tail, almost as large as the boat itself, fanned the air. The men at the oars, well disciplined by now, did not look around. They could not see the whale. They could hear the whistling snort, the water sloshing about the big back and the whirring sound of the flukes waving in the air; they could feel the fine spray drift over them and the motion of the boat as the waves made by the whale rolled under them; they could feel the breeze stirred by the whisking flukes of the tail. They could not see it, but they could feel the tenseness of Chase as he aimed his harpoon; the line that ran back to the tub quivered as his hand closed on the shaft.

The men waited, their hands white on the oars, their rumps shifting on the thwarts. No one spoke; the black hugeness of the whale seemed to hang over them. Their eyes were fixed on the man at the steering oar; his narrowed eyes focused just off their starboard bow, as if hypnotized by the sight of the thing. In the momentary tableau every muscle gathered like a spring; everyone waited for the lunging motion of the harpoon, which would be the signal for the crazy race across the water after the wounded whale, the shouted orders from the bow, the bobbing of the boat as Chase sank the lance, turned it, twisted it, and then the showering, scalding gore as the monstrous prize rolled fin out.

Still they waited. It was probably no more than thirty seconds, but by now every man was convinced that for some reason Chase had decided to let this one go.

Then they heard the muttered "Now!" the grunt as Chase put every ounce of strength behind his throw, and the *whirrup, whirrup* as the line whipped out of the tub. Then the juicy thud as the harpoon sank into the blubbery back. And then the almost deafening *WHOOOSH!* as the animal felt the iron, followed by the rattling, sobbing intake of breath as the whale dived again.

The line streaked out of the tub, sang around the loggerhead aft and zipped forward across the water to the iron, now fast in the whale. It had been a perfect toss; already the whaleboat was starting to move. The line began to smoke as it rubbed around the loggerhead.

"Got him!" yelled Chase. "Ship oars! Watch your balance! Steady on the——"

His voice was drowned out by the crash. Before anyone saw it, the whale's big flukes struck the side of the boat. It was a glancing blow, probably nothing more than a quick flick of the tail as the whale plunged for the bottom. But it smashed a hole through the side of the boat like a fist thrust through a sheet of paper. Now, just as the boat started racing after the whale, the sea came pouring in the hole.

Chase hesitated only a moment, to be sure there was no other way. Then he grabbed the hatchet and with three rapid strokes cut through the line. The end shot out of sight beneath the water. The whale, with the harpoon still fast in its back, got away. But Chase, by chopping away the line—and risking death in the tangled, whipping mass—saved the lives of his boat's crew.

"Get your shirts and jackets off, there!" Chase yelled, already stuffing his own into the hole in the boat's side. The men kept to their thwarts, quickly tossing their clothing at Chase, who wadded it into the hole. Now only a small stream poured through. Throwing a bailer at the man nearest the hole, Chase ran aft and resumed the steering oar. "Bail for your life," he said. "Now," to the rest of the crew, "out oars and back for the ship."

They made it, with the whaleboat nearly half full of water. From the rigging of the ship Chase could see the other two boats. One, he could not tell which, was fast to a whale and planing along after it, with the other boat trying to keep close enough to help. The two were almost over the horizon, so Chase headed the *Essex* down toward them. Captain Pollard had not given his signal, but the ship would no longer frighten off the whales.

Chase had the stove-in whaleboat hauled on deck. A quick survey of the damage convinced him that he could nail a patch of canvas over the hole, lower again, and be back in the chase in a few minutes. But he had lowered for his last whale from the *Essex*. The disaster was only seconds away.

Chase was supervising the patchwork when he happened to look over the rail and see a whale break surface near the weather bow. It was about eighty-five feet long, more than half the length of the *Essex*. It spouted lazily two or three times, then sank again. The thought that it would come any nearer to the ship never crossed Chase's mind. Whales had turned on whaleboats now and then, but who had ever heard of one attacking the whaleship itself?

So Chase was bewildered at what he thereupon saw. The whale surfaced again, deliberately swung toward the *Essex*, and came at her. Chase yelled for the helm to be put hard up. The helmsman leaned into the wheel. But the ship was barely moving, and she responded slowly. Too slowly. There was a thundering smash, and the men were all but thrown to the deck. A moment later everyone could hear the water surging into the hold; the impact had opened the ship's seams.

The whale was hurt and maddened by the blow; it rolled about slowly, off to one side of the ship, shaking its head and chomping its massive jaws until the water was white foam. Chase got the men busy at the pumps. The wheezing strokes had hardly brought water up out of the hold before a man in the hatchway shouted.

"Here he is! He's making for us again!"

All Chase could see from where he stood near the helm was a white spout directly ahead of the bow. A few seconds—during which the helmsman spun the wheel frantically and Chase bawled orders and every other man aboard froze in horror—then the ponderous, crunching blow. The ship shuddered as the whale went down under her keel and disappeared.

The *Essex* staggered; water poured into her hold so fast that the pumps were useless. Chase managed to get the spare, un-damaged whaleboat taken from its rack over the quarter-deck, while the steward skittered down the companionway and back up with quadrants, practical navigators, and the captain's and Chase's sea chests. They were dumped into the whaleboat, by which time the men on deck were standing in water to their knees. They pushed the boat away from the floundering ship and jumped into it. The *Essex* groaned over on her beam ends. All this took ten minutes.

Off across the Pacific a whale had towed Captain Pollard's boat over the horizon and out of sight of the ship. Mate Joy had caught up with the captain just after the whale had broken loose. Now the two boats were making their way back toward the ship. In the captain's boat a man stood on a thwart and spied the masts of the *Essex*. Then suddenly he exclaimed, "Oh, my God!" Her masts had disappeared before his eyes.

It was a fast, suspenseful row back to the ship. When they got there, Chase and the rest of the crew were in the spare whale-boat. The *Essex* was still over on her beam ends.

For a moment or two Captain Pollard could not speak. Then, in a low, unbelieving voice, he asked: "My God, Mr. Chase, what is the matter?"

"We have been stove by a whale."

Captain Pollard immediately put the crew to work. They chopped away the rigging so the ship would right herself. She did, creaking over so that she lay just at the surface of the water, kept awash by the few remaining air pockets trapped below. With wheezing bubbles, she rocked in the ocean swells as, little by little, water leaked into these pockets. While she still stayed awash, the men chopped their way through the heavy timbers, stout oak beams that had smashed so easily under the impact of the big whale. Digging their way below, they rescued two casks of ship's biscuit, sixty-five gallons of water for each whaleboat, two compasses, a few tools, and some live turtles they had been saving since catching them at the Galápagos Islands. Then they made their whaleboats fast to the floating hulk.

The black, rolling Pacific Ocean night dropped upon them.

Some of the men, exhausted from the long, hard day they had been through since that first cry from the masthead, went to sleep immediately. Others wept like children. Chase himself could not sleep. Every time he tried to, the spectacle of the wreck floated before his eyes.

There has been more than a century of argument over the decision that Captain Pollard made next morning. But consider the dilemma he faced. The *Essex's* position at the time of the wreck was latitude 0 degrees, 40 minutes South, longitude 119 degrees, 0 minutes West, and the hulk had now drifted just north of the equator, in the center of this most open stretch of the Pacific. There were no accurate charts for most of the sea around him. A few East Indiamen had crossed the Pacific with their cargoes of China teas, but the ocean was largely unexplored. The first big clippers for the China run were not to be built for twenty years.

A hasty conference was held in the captain's whaleboat, the three officers planning their perilous voyage with the aid of their navigation tables and their own knowledge from cruising the area. To go north, Captain Pollard decided, would be too dangerous because of the oncoming hurricane season above the equator. Actually, because the *Essex* was one of the first whalers in this part of the Pacific, Pollard did not know that the hurricane season he had been warned about was a myth. Fourteen hundred miles southwest of them lay the Marquesas Islands, but the captain ruled them out. Instead, he decided, they must head south and east, hoping to find some unknown mid-Pacific island or, at worst, to survive the 3000-mile voyage to the nearest continent, the coast of South America.

The reason for Captain Pollard's decision to avoid the Marquesas was that the natives on these islands were notorious for cannibalism. As it turned out, this decision ranks as one of the great ironies of maritime history.

The three boats set out in a heavy wind, the sea breaking over them and the men bailing constantly. Mate Chase had the oldest, most beaten-up boat, so it carried only six men, while the others carried seven. The food was rationed (one biscuit and a half pint of water per man per day) for the sixty days they expected to need for the distance to South America. The twenty men in their three whaleboats settled down, prayed for fair winds and the sight of a whaleship, and steeled themselves for what they knew would be a bitter test of their endurance.

The winds increased. Chase's boat sprang a bad leak. They were able to patch it up, but serious damage had been done: the ship's biscuits were soaked by salt water. After the men ate the salty biscuits, their thirst became agonizing. Chase dared not increase the water ration. In their desperation some of the men drank their own urine. When this made them even worse, they were grudgingly given a few extra drops of water. But this bonus, Chase warned, would be their last.

On the eleventh day they killed one of their turtles, prying off its shell, in which they kindled a fire to warm the meat. They ate it, entrails and all, and rationed out the raw blood, which was gulped eagerly. This helped keep them alive for seven more days, but their strength was ebbing when, on the nineteenth day, a bad storm hit them.

They managed to drop the tiny sails they had been using, and while the seas roared up and around them in thundering mountains of foam and while flashes of lightning seemed to wrap them in flames, the men lay low below the gunwales and let the boats run before the storm. "To an over-ruling Providence alone," Chase said later, "must be attributed our salvation from the horrors of that terrible night." (It would not do for a Quaker-educated Nantucketer to credit an inanimate object more than Providence— even one of their own whaleboats, which were probably the most seaworthy craft developed since the days of the Vikings.)

Despite the violence of the storm the three whaleboats managed to keep together and afloat. But the experience of that night was enough to stir some of Chase's men to wondering if they would not do better by separating from the others. Suppose they stayed together and one of the other boats went down? Obviously, they agreed, they had no choice but to take their companions aboard the remaining boats, despite the fact that it would mean more crowding and even tinier rations.

It is a measure of how much misery really does love company that every man kept a watchful eye out for the other boats. Only later did some of them take a different view as they argued about the subject in their long, mumbling conversations. Why, these men asked, should all of them commit certain suicide when a few might be able to get through? They even muttered threats that if one of the other boats foundered and their shipmates tried to crawl over the gunwales of their boat they would beat them off. But by that time they were much nearer to death, and madness was upon them.

By the twentieth day, though the wind squalls had died, a heavy sea was still running. The seams of the boats began to open and bailing had to be increased. But the men were barely strong enough to keep it up. Someone suggested that by hanging over the side they might absorb a little moisture from the sea through their pores. When they tried it they discovered strange little clams collecting on the bottoms of the boats. Every clam within reach was quickly eaten. But the men who went over the side exhausted themselves merely by climbing back aboard.

Now that the seas were quiet, Captain Pollard was able to take an observation. He announced that the storm had driven them far off their course. The wind had gone completely, and currents were carrying them even farther away. There was no choice but to row in order to keep on course until they could get a breeze. The men went on double rations to regain enough strength for the job, and confined their rowing to the cool nights. But they found they could not keep it up for more than three hours at a time.

The temptation to seize the full allotment of food became almost unendurable; just one full stomach once more and a man could face starvation. No one threatened to take the food by force—yet. But in his boat Chase took no chances; he locked the food supply in his chest and guarded it with his pistol. At night he slept lying across the top of the chest.

Then, on the thirty-first day, one of the men suddenly squawked, "There is land!"

The crude charts showed it as Ducie Island, little more than a rocky spit in the Pacific Ocean, smaller than Nantucket. The island's sides were bare rock, and only its tiny peak showed any green. To the twenty starved, burned men in the three whale-boats, though, it looked, as Chase later described it, "like a basking paradise before our longing eyes." Yet it might be a mixed blessing. Was it inhabited? By ferocious animals? Or by the dread of all Pacific sailors, cannibals? But "hunger and thirst," Chase recalled, "soon determined us." Stumbling and clawing their way ashore, they stretched out on the firm, dry land for a brief rest. Then they explored their island.

It was uninhabited. There was no vegetation save some stunted trees, sparse clumps of peppergrass. There were a few birds, fish, and mussels to ease their hunger, but the only water came from a tiny spring on the shore, exposed for a little while at ebb tide. The men wanted to stay on the island for several weeks in the hope of signaling a passing ship. But within seven days the birds and mussels were eaten and the fish were scared away. From the fitfully bubbling spring they could only visit twice a day they managed to get a few casks of water. They celebrated a bleak Christmas on their little island, and then faced up to the problem of putting to sea again.

Which direction?

They were fairly certain that Easter Island lay 1200 miles east southeast. What kind of savages lived there they did not know. There was another possibility, one they had heard of from a Nantucket neighbor named Mayhew Folger. Twelve years earlier Captain Folger had come upon an island in this area and had been surprised to find men who spoke English. It was Pitcairn Island, still inhabited by families of the famous mutineers of the British ship *Bounty*.

But Captain Pollard decided that Pitcairn was too small to give them any hope of finding it. They would head in the other direction, for Easter Island. This was the right decision, but for reasons Pollard did not know at the time. Pitcairn had been misplaced by more than one hundred miles on the early charts, so they would certainly have missed it; and practically nothing lay between Pitcairn and frozen Antarctica. Besides, the castaways were not even on Ducie Island, as they thought. Without knowing it they were on an uncharted piece of land, later to be put on the map as Henderson Island.

So on December 27, the thirty-eighth day of their odyssey, they headed out onto the Pacific again. Three men stayed behind, unable to stand any more of the whaleboat voyage. Captain Pollard agreed that the island could probably support three, though no more than that.

By no means sure of it, he wrote out a brief account of the disaster, put it in a tin box, and nailed it to a tree, where anyone visiting the island would be sure to see it even if there were no survivors. The account ended with a few words which showed where the captain's thoughts lay as he wrote what he realized would probably be the last heard from him: "I shall leave with this," he scrawled, "a letter for my wife, and whoever finds and have the goodness to forward it, will oblige an unfortunate man, and receive his sincere wishes. George Pollard, Junior." The men staying behind on the island were not kidding themselves either. When Chase bade them good-by, one of them broke down and wept.

The three whaleboats, with seventeen men now, went down over the horizon, their tiny sails set before a light breeze, bound east southeast for Easter Island.

But by the forty-fifth day since the wreck Captain Pollard realized that adverse winds had driven them too far south. They could no longer point for Easter Island. Gloomily they realized that the best they could do was to shape a course for the Juan Fernández Islands, off the coast of Chile. They were 2500 miles from them.

On the fifty-second day the first man died. They sewed him up in his clothes, used a cooking stone for ballast and, said Chase, "consigned him in a solemn manner to the ocean."

Two nights later there was another violent storm. Like all these Pacific Ocean squalls, it came leaping at them from summit to summit of what had been gray, oily swells and were suddenly black mountains topped by flying spray. The whaleboats began to pick up speed, and were flying along before the men could claw down the sails. The wind moaned, then whined, then shrieked. The rain came in such torrents that thundering sheets of it hid boat from boat, even bow from stern. The men cowered under the force of it and scooped precious fresh water over the side, bailing for their lives while lightning magnified the waves that rushed up at them all through the night.

With dawn the letup finally came. A few of the men managed to strip off their soppy shirts and trousers, soak them over the side, and put them on again; clothing soaked with salt water is not quite so chilling. The others, unable to exert themselves that much, lay in the bottom of the boat and shook with the cold until the sun finally broke through the clouds and warmed their bony bodies.

It was when the skies cleared that Chase realized what had happened. The other two boats were not in sight. He could not maneuver well enough to retrace his course; these early whale-boats had no centerboards. But he hove to, hoping for the other two to catch up. They never did.

As the lone whaleboat with its five men made its way across the Pacific, the effects of thirst and hunger began to assert themselves. When Chase forgot to lock the food chest one night, a man stole an extra piece of biscuit. Discovered, he returned it at gun point. One night, while a school of whales rumbled, snorted, and whistled nearby, every man lay terror-stricken at the thought of the boat being playfully nudged bottomside up. But the whales kept their distance.

At times the boat drifted lazily about in circles, all steerageway lost in a brassy, hot calm. At others the sea reared so high that when the boat slipped down into a hollow the wind was blocked off and the sail hung limp, only to fill with a cannonlike explosion when they climbed atop the next crest. At night, under a tropical sky so brilliant that the stars alone seemed to light the sea, foaming hills reared up astern, swept down upon them, and, at the last second, lifted them toward the stars, rolling on past and dropping them into the valley again.

The men broke out in salt-water boils, which cracked and seared in the sun. Ulcers, made by scraping along the bottom of the boat, were kept open by the water and caked with salt. Glutinous saliva collected in their mouths. Their lips had long since swelled and cracked; now they dripped blood. Knotting, griping cramps went through their stomachs.

When the wind died, the only sounds were the creak of the little mast, the lapping of the sea against the sides and a constant, low murmur of pain. Another man died and was slipped into the sea. By January 27, the sixty-ninth day, the survivors were so weak from their ration of one and one-half ounces of food per day that no one could raise a hand to tend sail or guide the boat. "Nothing but the slight chance of meeting with a vessel remained to us now," Chase wrote later. "We gave ourselves wholly up to the guidance and disposal of our Creator."

Yet it was not until the eighty-first day that the first man went mad.

At 9 o'clock that morning Isaac Cole was sprawled in the bottom of the boat with the rest. Then a shudder went down the spine of every man as Cole suddenly straightened up and demanded a cup of water and a napkin. For an hour he kept asking for his cup of water and his napkin, while his shipmates watched him in silence, each doubtless wondering how long before he too would go mad. Finally Cole quieted, then closed his eyes. His companions struggled with the still-breathing body and managed to lay him across one of the thwarts. For the rest of the day he stayed there, groaning softly, until four in the afternoon, when he went into convulsions and died.

It was too late to prepare his body for the sea before dark. And there can be no doubt what went through the pain-twisted mind of each survivor during that night. Three days' supply of biscuit was left. Only a day or two would answer the question of who would follow Isaac Cole. But there was one way to keep alive, maybe for two weeks. The mind, even on the border line of madness, automatically chooses anything but death as long as a choice is left.

No one had the courage to speak his mind next morning until, finally, Chase himself made the suggestion. It was accepted immediately and eagerly.

"We set to work," Chase recounted, "as fast as we were able to . . . We separated his limbs from his body and cut all the flesh from the bones, after which we opened the body, took out the heart, then closed it again—sewed it up as decently as we could and committed it to the sea."

They ate Isaac Cole's heart first, then a little of his other flesh. The rest they cut in strips and hung to dry in the sun. By next morning it had begun to turn green and putrid, so they quickly roasted it over a fire built on stones from the island. Thus they were able to preserve their three days' supply of biscuit for another week. Thus too they restored some life to their starved bodies. But, whether because of exposure or the diet of human flesh, their arms and legs began to swell painfully.

On the ninety-first day Thomas Nicholson, a seventeen-year-old boy, calmly lay in the bottom of the whaleboat, pulled a piece of canvas over himself, and announced that he wished to die immediately. Chase, to whom cannibalism was possible but voluntary death was sacrilege, quietly and soothingly argued with the boy, urging him to keep his "reliance upon the Almighty while the least hope of a breath of life remained." The boy would not answer. Chase was about to give him up—when one of the men peeped over the side, gawked, wagged a bony arm, and managed a cry:

"There's a sail!"

She was the brig *Indian*, of London, and the sight of her was enough to bring the dying boy stumbling to his feet. It took more than an hour for the three wasted figures to bring their boat about and intercept the course of the brig, which waited under shortened sail for them to approach. When the little boat with the tattered spritsail came alongside, the men aboard the *Indian* could barely believe what they saw—rags of clothes fluttering on the burned, salt-encrusted bodies; eyes sunken in skull-like heads; bleeding joints where the bones were just beginning to break through the skin. The boat came straight on and bumped against the ship's side. The three whalemen did not even have enough strength to crawl over and grab hold; they simply lay there across the thwarts, emitting little animal-like whimperings of relief and delight. For days all they could eat was a watery soup made of tapioca. But they were saved.

In their little twenty-seven-foot whaleboat the three survivors had sailed and drifted almost 4500 miles. It had taken them a quarter of a year.

And what of the other two boats after they became separated from Owen Chase and his men? Beaten off course by the same head-on winds, drifting helplessly because the men could not tend sail, the two crews lost each other.

In Captain Pollard's boat the provisions gave out entirely before the first man died. After the same painful soul-searching that had gone on in Chase's boat this man too was eaten by his shipmates. So was the next man who died. Then Captain Pollard and his three remaining men found themselves in a gruesome dilemma. The human flesh had restored the survivors to life; now, with the supply gone, there seemed to be no immediate prospect of more such food.

They drew lots.

Young Owen Coffin, the cabin boy, got the short one. He was Captain Pollard's nephew, and when the captain saw the boy holding it, he started toward him, crying, "My lad, my lad, if you don't like your lot, I'll shoot the first man that touches you!" The boy hesitated a moment, then laid his head on the gunwale. "I like it as well as any other," he said. Next they drew lots to see who would fire the gun. Charles Ramsdell, who got the short one, begged Coffin to trade places. Coffin insisted it was his "right" to die for the remaining three.

"But I can tell you no more!" the captain cried as he recounted the experience a few years later. "My head is on fire at the recollection."

Coffin's body kept them alive for ten days. Then the fourth man died, and Pollard and Ramsdell divided his flesh between them. Twelve days later the two men were starving again, when they were sighted by the Nantucket whaleship *Dauphin*.

In the ninety-six days since the wreck Captain Pollard and Charles Ramsdell had sailed their whaleboat 4600 miles. Despite his condition and the contrary winds, Captain Pollard had navigated so well that they were within 2 degrees of Santa María Island, for which he had set his course.

And the third boat? None of its crew was ever seen again.

As soon as the five survivors were reunited at Valparaiso, Chile, Captain Pollard asked the U. S. Navy to send a rescue ship for the three men left behind on the island. The Navy paid $300 to a Captain Raine, of the British ship *Surrey*, just leaving for Australia, to touch at the island on his way. There the three men were still waiting, after 102 days, for the passing ship that had never come by. When the *Surrey* fired her guns, the men came running out of their shelter, shouting and jumping up and down at the sight they had given up ever seeing again—a great ship standing in toward their barren shore. The *Surrey* took them on to Sydney, where they got passage to London. One of the three was a Briton; the other two finally got home, the long way around, to Boston.

Of the twenty men who had put off from the wreck of the *Essex* eight were left. When the first of the survivors arrived off Nantucket aboard the whaler *Eagle* on June 11, 1821, a black flag rippled up to the masthead—the signal of death. But the news had already reached the island. The men were still gaunt as they stepped onto the wharf. The crowd parted for them as if cut by a scythe, and not a word was spoken as they walked slowly up the street to their homes.

Five of the eight survivors were native Nantucketers. All of them not only went back to sea again, but every one became a captain before he died of old age. The effects of their odyssey, however, were never really shaken.

Charles Ramsdell could never be brought to talk about his experience, even in his own family. He had been the one chosen by lot to shoot young Owen Coffin.

Although Owen Chase made many successful whaling cruises in later life, the terror of starvation always stayed with him. Nantucketers say he never let the smallest crumb be wasted at his table. As an old man, he made frequent trips to the market on Main Street, where he bought twice as much as he needed. The surplus he took up into his attic and secreted under the eaves.

Captain Pollard made one more voyage, only five months after his return. Within another five months his ship was on a reef, and once again Pollard set out in an open boat. This time he and his crew were picked up a few days later by a Nantucket whaler. "Now I am utterly ruined," he said. "No owner will ever trust me with a whaler again."

He never returned to sea. One of the jobs Pollard took on the island was that of fire watcher. He stood his post in a tower high over Nantucket town, like a whaleman on his crosstrees. He did not like to talk about his experience, but it is not hard to imagine his thoughts as he stared out across the rolling seas beyond the island's moors. It is no wonder that his mind began to slip as old age came on. There is a Nantucket legend that when a reporter from the mainland came out to the island to interview him on his last birthday, the reporter closed his interview with the personal remark that he was distantly related to one of the *Essex's* crew.

"You remember him, of course," he added.

"Remember him!" the old man cackled. "Hell, son, I et him!"

2. The whaleman novelist

By the time Owen Chase had been home about six months, he
had recovered from his experience. Now he could recount it in
detail without mentally flinching from the visions it conjured up
before his eyes. During the early part of the long open-boat
voyage, in the first month, when he had been able to sit up and
keep his mind about it, Chase had jotted down some rough
notes. After his recovery he got out his carefully preserved record
and used it to write a full account of what had happened. Even
then the recollection of it affected him; the account is studded
with such phrases as "many a despairing moment," "the horrors
of our situation," "helpless and wretched," "alas!" and "the blessed
vision of a vessel." But he got it all written down and a New York
publisher printed it for posterity. Although neither the publisher
nor Chase knew it, they were doing a lot more than that.

His literary labors over, Owen Chase went to sea again. Twenty years later he was still chasing whales, a captain now. And he had a teen-age son who had gone off to the Pacific himself, shipping out as a foremast hand aboard the Nantucket whaler *Lima*. It was only natural that the son would take along in his sea chest a copy of his father's book. There is no doubt that all his shipmates who could read borrowed this little book whenever there were no whales in sight. For the story of the *Essex* had, through the years, become forecastle rumor aboard nearly every whaler in the Pacific.

Young William Chase still had the dog-eared volume in his sea chest one hot July day when the *Lima* was cruising in the part of the Pacific where the *Essex* had gone down. There his ship spoke the whaler *Acushnet*, six months out of Fairhaven, Massachusetts. It was an excellent opportunity for a gam, a visit between the two captains and crews. By tradition the skippers and their boat crews visited on one ship, the mates and the rest of the crews on the other. The *Lima's* forecastle was promptly jammed with men from the *Acushnet*, clumping down the companionway to exchange stale news, tall tales of their "greasy luck," plugs of tobacco, and dirty jokes. One *Acushnet* hand who particularly caught the eye of William Chase was a black-haired, piercing-eyed young man. The visitor was on his first whaling cruise, and when he discovered that he was gamming with the son of the famous Owen Chase, he flooded his host with questions about his father's experience.

The two men talked together for a long time that day, perched on the hard bunks, rolling with the Pacific swells, listening to the droning conversation about them and the sea lap-lapping against the bow. They were still talking earnestly when the word spread that the two ships would sail in company for a few days. That meant at least another gam the next day, so William Chase dug into his sea chest and came up with the copy of his father's book. He handed it to his visitor, who thanked him effusively and promised to return it next morning. This was a historically important moment, though William Chase may not even have asked the name of his new friend. The visitor was Herman Melville; and the battered book thus became the genesis of America's greatest novel, *Moby Dick*.

Years after this chance meeting, even after he had written his novel, Melville recalled the experience vividly. "The reading of this wondrous story," he said, "upon the landless sea and close to the very latitude of the shipwreck had a surprising effect upon me." The effect was to stay, to grow on him, and to dominate a large part of his life.

So far it had been a tragically frustrating life. Herman Melville's parents had been moderately well-to-do when he was a young boy, and had provided him with a good education. But then Herman's father died. The family money disappeared as business panic swept the country. Mostly out of desperation, he went to sea, first as a foremast hand aboard a New York-to-Liverpool packet, and then as an ordinary seaman in the crew of the whaler *Acushnet*. In her grimy forecastle he rolled down across the Gulf Stream and along the coast of South America and plunged around Cape Horn into the Pacific. Here he met William Chase and read the account of the *Essex*. He was on the verge of his twenty-second birthday at the time, and the impression the story made on his young imagination was increased even more as the *Acushnet* wandered about for weeks thereafter in the same area where the big whale had rammed and sunk the *Essex*. Who knew but that, one night as the sea washed against the bow alongside Melville's ear, the same malevolent whale did not ease its bulk right under the whaleman's sleeping body?

Melville had his own worries aboard the *Acushnet*. Judging by the rate of desertions, her skipper, Captain Valentine Pease, ran a very taut ship. And the abstract of her log for this period shows that there was plenty of work to be done. Two or three times a week the loud, quavering cry rang out from the masthead, and Melville and his shipmates would thereupon clamber down into the bobbing whaleboats for the palm-blistering, back-wrenching pull toward the spout—every man putting his utmost into each heave at the long oars, while the officer at the steering oar urged, pleaded, and threatened as if this one must be the supreme effort. " 'Start her, start her, my men!' " wrote Melville later, describing one such harangue. " 'Start her like thunderclaps, that's all . . . Start her, now; give 'em the long and strong stroke . . . start her like grim death and grinning devils, and raise the buried dead perpendicular out of their graves, boys—that's all. Start her!' " Then the low-voiced cry, " 'Give it to him!' " and the line hissing across the wrists of each oarsman as the man in the stern bellowed, " 'Stern all!' " Then the boat flying through the water while wisps of smoke rose from the line's friction around the loggerhead and everyone tried to keep his balance; the old whalemen used to claim that if you shifted your cud of tobacco at a time like that you upset the boat.

And all this was simply the beginning, the preparation for the miles-long haul back to the ship, with the monster's carcass dragging its dead weight astern; and the cutting in that might take all through the night and through most of the next day. Aboard the *Acushnet* that July and August of 1841 this was completed only in time for the lookout high above them to let go his mournful cry once again. Midsummer squalls that tossed men and boats against the sides of the ship and bounced them onto the backs of the whales only added to the work and the danger. The hold was rapidly filling with barrels of oil; but so crippling was the work and so many the accidents that the *Acushnet* seemed to be proving out the time-honored slogan of the whalemen: "For every barrel of oil, at least a drop of human blood."

But even if all this had made Herman Melville begin to forget the *Essex*, he was provided with a reminder; less than a month after their first meeting, his ship spoke the *Lima* again, and he had another gam with William Chase. As he flopped onto his wooden bunk that night after his second meeting with Chase, Melville must once more have closed his eyes and pictured to himself the bloodcurdling vision: the crunching smash of the whale's head against the bow of the ship; the groan of the masts as the *Essex* heeled over onto her side; and the look on the face of Captain George Pollard when he returned and saw his ship.

After a two-day gam the *Acushnet* swung out all sail and headed off north and east, leaving the *Lima* hull down in a few hours. The grim routine set in again. But the whales began to disappear. Through the fall, the winter, and into the spring of 1842, ship after ship spoke the *Acushnet* and their captains gave the usual, cheery cry, "How many barrels?" As Captain Pease shouted back his answer, the crew along the rail realized all the more keenly that the *Acushnet's* greasy luck had gone. Instead of swelling by the hundred, her cargo was increasing barrel by barrel now.

The long run of bad luck was having its effect on Captain Pease, and the *Acushnet* was an unhappy ship. Officers became abusive, crewmen sullen, and the tension crept through the ship like a sickness. When whales were plentiful the crewmen worked until they wondered whether their backs would break; but at times like this they knew their hearts would.

That was the atmosphere aboard the *Acushnet* in the spring of 1842 when across the horizon came the whaleship *Charles Carroll*, of Nantucket. Herman Melville stood at the rail to watch the captain of the *Carroll* climb aboard, shake the hand of Captain Pease, and go below for a gam. The whispers ran along the bulwarks: This was Owen Chase. This was the man who had been first mate of the *Essex*, who had been aboard her when the whale struck, who had salvaged the few things that had made the long open-boat voyage possible, who had written the journal Melville had read a few months earlier. Years later Melville wrote: ". . . so it came to pass that I saw him. He was a large, powerful well-made man; rather tall; to all appearances something past forty-five or so; with a handsome face for a Yankee, and expressive of great uprightness and calm and unostentatious courage . . . He was the most prepossessing-looking whale-hunter I think I ever saw. Being a mere foremast hand I had no opportunity of conversing with Owen Chase (though he was on board our ship for two hours at a time), nor have I seen him since."

It is one of the many ironies of Melville's life that, although he apparently never realized the fact, this was not Owen Chase. During the previous summer when Melville had been gamming with Chase's son, the *Essex's* famous first mate had been home at Nantucket, involved in his own personal troubles. Owen Chase had sued his wife for a divorce (an almost unheard-of thing in those days), on the grounds of adultery. The divorce was finally granted by Massachusetts' Chief Justice, Lemuel Shaw, who happened to be an intimate friend of Melville and his family. Later Chase married again and went back to sea. But he was still home at Nantucket at the time Melville thought he saw him come aboard the *Acushnet*. It was an understandable mistake; Chase *had* been master of the *Charles Carroll* on her previous voyage, but he had declined the berth on this cruise because of his impending divorce. The "prepossessing-looking whale-hunter" in command of the *Carroll* that spring of 1842 was Thomas Andrews, who was indeed powerful, tall, and handsome "for a Yankee."

But the incident showed that it did not really matter whether this man was Owen Chase or Thomas Andrews. What mattered was that Melville *thought* this was Chase; and what the incident proved was that the story of the *Essex* had by now got firm hold on the young man's rich imagination. It would never let go.

The *Acushnet* rolled on along the Line, thousands of miles from the nearest spot of land, while the equatorial sun made the pitch ooze and bubble from the seams of the deck, while oily calms made even the reef points stand still, while Melville hung across the iron hoops at the masthead and scorched in the sun and tortured his eyeballs searching for the whales that seemed to have vanished from this part of the world, while the maggots multiplied in the food and the cockroaches multiplied in the forecastle and the ship seemed to become a floating hell all its own. There was small consolation in the bright tropical nights, when the men lounged against the forecastle scuttle and watched the brilliant moonlight pick out the wispy smoke from their pipes as a light trade wind swept them across the sea. Finally, in a June squall, the *Acushnet* made a landfall, went boiling past the promontory, slid into the harbor, and, her sails crackling about as the men out on the footropes clawed at them, let go her anchor in nine fathoms. They were in Nukahiva harbor, in the Marquesas, one of the most beautiful green-bordered bits of paradise in the South Pacific.

Melville had had enough of the *Acushnet*. As he looked out across the rolling, dark-green hillsides, heard the waves whisper on the beach and the birds call to each other from tree to tree, and saw from a distance the naked *"whinhenies"* (native girls) flashing through the water, he made his decision. Beside him on deck stood a young shipmate named Richard Tobias Greene, "Toby" to the *Acushnet's* crew. Together with Toby, Melville studied the marvelously smooth surface of the water, the tiny canoes shooting out of caverns festooned with multicolored foliage. To Toby it seemed like magic, after the months they had spent meandering about the always-rolling, endless Pacific. The two foremast hands promptly planned their escape.

Exactly how they got away is not known, but evidently it was not difficult. There was a reason for this. Most ship captains did not expect desertions at Nukahiva, because the interior of the island was supposed to be inhabited by two of the bloodiest cannibal tribes in the Pacific.

There were always a few seamen, though, who got to the point where they were willing to take their chances with cannibals rather than endure any more of the life at sea. Melville and Greene, knowing that the semicivilized natives along the harbor shores made a practice of catching deserters and selling them back to the ship, slipped ashore and cut for the hills as fast as they could scramble through the underbrush. The *Acushnet's* searching parties never found them. Two weeks after the ship had come into the harbor, her anchor swung out of the water again and she dropped down the tide and out onto the Pacific. Melville and Greene were not aboard.

Back in the interior of the island a strange thing was happening, something that has never been fully explained. Far from attacking the two deserters, the Taipi tribe seemed to welcome them. When the two weary white men, exhausted from their climb over one of Nukahiva's mountain ranges, stumbled into the Taipi village, the natives were at first curious, then hospitable, then possessive. Melville had developed an infection in his leg, and burned with fever. The Taipis did their best to cure him and, no doubt despite their attempts, he recovered. Native guardians were appointed to wait on the visitors—within understandable limitations. Instead of regarding the newcomers as a tasty dish, the Taipis appeared to consider them as honored guests.

Thus began the most exotic period of Herman Melville's life. He lived in a bamboo house, reclining on a mat and granting an audience to group after group of natives who came to ogle, giggle, and depart. He ate unknown, cloying foods from a calabash, washing them down with the sweet, watery milk of a hacked-open coconut. Naked girls danced for him and wove plaits of colored flowers for his bushy black hair. Young warriors with tossing head plumes volunteered to escort him on tours of the Taipi domain, even though they were carefully restricted tours. One husky native even carried Melville on his back to visit the sacred groves that bore evidences of the religious rites of cannibalism.

There were sparkling mornings beside a Taipi valley stream, when Melville lay on the bank and watched the young girls swim like porpoises in a clear pool. There were tribal feasts at which he tasted dishes of bizarre foods he had never dreamed of before and would never hear of again. And there were gatherings of men after the big meal, so like a nineteenth-century New York men's club, with the chiefs sprawled in a circle, smoking, saying little or nothing until the soporific influence of the meal and the smoke and the hum of life outside the hut finally lulled every man to sleep.

This was indeed an idyllic existence after life on the heaving, oil-slicked decks of the *Acushnet*. But always in the back of Melville's thoughts was the suspicion, the fear, that disaster could come suddenly. Simple and direct in their kindness and hospitality, the Pacific island natives could be, and had many times been, as simple and direct in their barbarity. Meanwhile both of the deserters began to realize that they could not break with the pattern that their lives had been following for so many years. As a vacation it was paradise. As a way of life it began to pall more quickly than Melville had thought possible. Within less than a month the combination of fear and boredom led the two men to start making their plans for escape.

It turned out to be more difficult than they had realized. The Taipis, they found, considered their visitors as more than guests; they had become attractive possessions, curiosities to exhibit to natives who flocked in from the nearby villages. In a sense Melville's position was the reverse of the later phenomenon of the "Wild Man of Borneo," on exhibit in America in a cage. The suggestion by Melville that he was thinking of returning to his civilization was immediately met with open objection. His still-lame leg made matters worse. It was easier for Toby; he made his way down to one of the island's beaches and there came upon a colorful character who had long since become a fixture of the island. He was a heavily tattooed renegade Irishman named Jimmy Fitch, whose business was supplying men for the whaleship crews. With Jimmy Fitch's help Toby shipped aboard an American whaler and got away; he later claimed that Jimmy Fitch reneged on his promise to bring Melville to the same ship. It was about a week later before Melville too made his escape from his embarrassingly hospitable hosts. Exactly how he accomplished it is not known. But by now nearly everyone on the island had heard about the white man living with the Taipis. And when the Australian whaler *Lucy Ann* came into the bay, her skipper was desperate for men. Either Jimmy Fitch or a native was paid to rescue Melville and bring him aboard.

The *Lucy Ann* was worse than the *Acushnet*. And Melville, who had deserted from the *Acushnet,* now became a mutineer. It was more or less a comic-opera mutiny, though. When Captain Henry Ventom became too sick to leave his cabin, he instructed First Mate James German to assume command. German apparently did with a will; because when the *Lucy Ann* dropped her hook in the harbor at Tahiti a month and a half later, Melville and most of the others in her forecastle refused to put out to sea again. Melville relied on a quibbling legal technicality: he had signed on for a short whaling cruise under Henry Ventom, not under James German. Nevertheless, with ten others who still held out, he wound up in the local prison. There he stayed until the *Lucy Ann* unfurled her stained sails and creaked out to sea again, without him. When she was gone it was apparently no difficult task to talk the local officials into letting him "escape" from the prison. Now Melville was on the beach.

He became an "omoo," as he called himself, a solitary wanderer. He wore a tapa skirt, lived in a reed hut, subsisted on the exotic foods of the South Pacific again, picking his way along the shimmering strands of coral beach while the rolling combers of the Pacific crashed, hissed, and sucked at his feet. At length he shipped on another whaler, the Nantucket ship *Charles and Henry*, but only long enough to transport him to the Sandwich Islands.

The Honolulu of a hundred and ten years ago was apparently as much the delight of the whaleman on the loose as it was the horror of the missionary. "The floodgates of licentiousness have been opened," one preacher wrote home at the time. Brothels were everywhere. The girls, lured down to the city from the other islands by the easy money, transacted their business in broad daylight. Boatloads of them floated gaily out to meet every incoming ship. In this atmosphere Melville spent three months. He roamed the waterfront. He got a job as a clerk for a local merchant. For a while he was apparently a pin boy in a bowling alley. He must have spent a nervous day when his old ship, the *Acushnet*, put into the harbor; but evidently he was not discovered before she set sail again.

Then came a stirring sight. Just before sunset on August 3 crowds gathered along the shore to watch the big frigate *United States* come gliding into the harbor. In the golden Hawaiian dusk, she rounded to, all flags flying, tucked in her great white wings, and pulled back on her anchor amid the cheers of the audience on shore.

Whether it was because of this scene, so impressive to any American far away from home, or whether Melville was simply bored with being a lonely wanderer, the general-muster roll of the frigate *United States* listed a new ordinary seaman, shipped on August 17: "Oahu. Herman Melville. O.S."

Out across the Pacific he went again, back to Tahiti. And then the *United States* set her course for the South American coast and home. Riding the trades eastward, the frigate crossed the course that had been taken twenty-three years before by the starving survivors of the whaleship *Essex*.

Cape Horn was as rough as ever, the *United States* half burying herself at every plunge. But the rest of the voyage was smooth and gentle, and every day brought Melville closer to the home he had left four years ago. On a cold October morning he was eating fresh fish provided by the little schooners spoken off Cape Cod. The next day Herman Melville was home from the Pacific.

The Melville family was used to the yarns spun by returning seamen; Herman was not the only sailor in the family. But apparently he told his tales better than any of the others, because everyone urged him to write a book about his experiences. He had not been home more than a couple months before he was at work on it.

He called it *Typee*, and he had finished it by spring. Off it went to the august publishing house of Messrs. Harper & Bros. But although one Harper editor thought it as good as *Robinson Crusoe*, the editorial decision was to turn it down, because "it was impossible that it could be true and therefore was without real value." Through his brother who was going to England, however, Melville got the book read by a publisher in London, and it was brought out there immediately. It was a big success, was snapped up by another New York publisher and quickly became a best seller in the U.S. Somewhat embarrassed by the success of the book they had turned down, Messrs. Harper & Bros. were upset even more when Richard Tobias Greene, Melville's fellow fugitive among the Taipis, popped up in Buffalo, New York, and swore to the authenticity of the account. Melville tried to capitalize on the first by writing another book about his experiences among the South Pacific natives. This one he titled *Omoo* (the solitary wanderer), and this one he took personally to Harper's. Frederick Saunders, the editor who had liked *Typee*, did not even have a chance to read *Omoo*. Mr. Harper was leaving for Europe at the moment when Melville appeared with his manuscript.[1]

[1]Saunders did not say which of the Harper brothers it was, but it was probably Joseph Wesley Harper, who usually made the decisions to accept or reject a manuscript.

Saunders ran down the steps and caught the boss just as he was getting into his carriage.

"What is it?" demanded Mr. Harper.

"Another manuscript from Herman Melville," said Saunders. "He is offering it to us. What do you say?"

"Take it at once," said Mr. Harper as he clambered into his carriage and rattled off.

Omoo did as well as *Typee*. Then came *Mardi,* another book about the "cannibals," *Redburn,* based on his first voyage on the Liverpool packet, and *White-Jacket,* describing life aboard a frigate like the *United States.* All of them did well. They did not make him a fortune, but they provided him with a comfortable income. And they made him famous. A proof of his fame was that in the summer of 1847 an early gossip column gleefully reported Melville's impending marriage to a daughter of Lemuel Shaw, the family friend and Chief Justice of Massachusetts who had granted that divorce to Owen Chase. The young author bought a farm in Pittsfield, Massachusetts. Longfellow liked Melville's books, and Walt Whitman reviewed them favorably for the literary journals of the day. Richard Henry Dana, famous for his own *Two Years Before the Mast,* was much taken with the black-haired, bristling-bearded young man who wrote about his life among the cannibals. Even halfway across the world Melville's fame had apparently touched the islands where he had so recently been an unnoticed beachcomber. A naval officer reported that at Nukahiva the local girls were adopting the name of Fayaway, the heroine of *Typee.* Most pleasant of all Melville's rewards was the friendship of his neighbor Nathaniel Hawthorne. On long summer afternoons the two men sat on a bench in Melville's woodshed and discussed philosophy. Once Melville, Hawthorne, and Oliver Wendell Holmes climbed nearby Monument Mountain, drinking champagne from a silver mug in a cave, and cheering as Melville teetered on a rock over the void, hauling at imaginary halyards to prove his seaman's sure-footedness.

But something was missing, and Melville realized it more and more. He had not written the book he wanted to write. All these best sellers he regarded as preliminaries. They were written, he told his father-in-law, as *"jobs,* which I have done for money—being forced to it, as other men are to sawing wood . . . My only desire for their 'success' (as it is called) springs from my pocket and not from my heart." To his friend Hawthorne he wrote: "What 'reputation' HM has is horrible. Think of it! To go down to posterity . . . as a 'man who lived among the cannibals'!" Had he known it, he would have been upset at the fact that Mrs. Hawthorne referred to him as Mr. "Omoo." In sardonic moments he called himself the author of *"Typee, Fiddle-De-De* and *Pog-Dog."* As his success mounted, he only brooded the more over the story he knew he must someday write. He knew that it might not have the popularity of the others. In another note to Hawthorne he predicted that the story was "short-lived as a modern book."

But write the story he must. He made his preparations. On March 4, 1851, thirty years after the sinking of the *Essex,* Thomas Macy at Nantucket located a copy of Owen Chase's little book and sent it to Lemuel Shaw; the judge had requested it for Melville.

All through the summer of 1851, through the fall and winter, through the spring of 1852, and into the summer Melville labored at his big new task. His usual writing practice had been to close himself up in his garret study until a prearranged knock at the door by one of his family signaled the end of the working day. Now the repeated knocks at the study door went unanswered. He sat at the desk all day, not eating until four or five o'clock in the afternoon. His money began to dwindle. He asked Harper & Bros. for an advance, but it was refused; he was already $700 in debt to them. He borrowed $2050 in Pittsfield and plunged ahead on his huge project. So great were the struggles going on in the locked garret that they seemed to be sensed all over the valley. Hawthorne wrote, "On the hither side of Pittsfield sits Herman Melville, shaping out the gigantic conception of his white whale, while the gigantic shape of Greylock looms upon him from his study window." As Melville read and reread Chase's account, making his careful notes in the margin, the great theme began to take its shape: the mad Captain Ahab, the climactic attack by whale against whaleship. To Hawthorne, Melville confessed that his novel, *Moby Dick*, was the supreme effort. It was, he said, broiled in "hell fire."

And it failed.

Today the story Herman Melville made out of the wreck of the *Essex* is generally referred to as America's greatest novel. But in 1852 the critics climbed all over it. Hawthorne saw what Melville had put into it—"much greater power than his preceding ones." Longfellow could hardly put it down—"Very wild, strange and interesting," he wrote in his journal. There were a few favorable reviews. But the run-of-the-magazine critics who had wallowed in Melville's tales about cannibals were appalled by *Moby Dick*. ". . . the worst school of bedlam literature," said one. Another: ". . . rhapsody run mad." The unkindest cut of all came from the critic who bluntly wrote: "The truth is, Mr. Melville has survived his reputation."

The truth was, for the rest of his life he had.

He was thirty-three years old. He was to live thirty-nine more years, to write more than a score of short stories, poetry, and more novels, including the now-famous *Billy Budd*. Yet those thirty-nine years became a succession of ironies. Though the most interesting experience in his life had been among the South Pacific islanders, they did not make his best book; a chance encounter in a forecastle did that. Though *Moby Dick* was his masterpiece, he was not recognized for it in his time; he was known just as he had promised he would not be—as "the man who lived among the cannibals." Though his early, inferior books made him famous, his greatest achievement, *Moby Dick*, marked the beginning of his decline. Though he was once a lion of the literary scene, his death, in 1891, went all but unnoticed; one of the few obituaries in the press misspelled his name. And the newspapers recalled not that he had written *Moby Dick* or *Billy Budd*, but that in his earlier days he had "gained some fame" from stories about his life among the cannibals. Add to it all the ironic fact that Melville had never been sure those natives even *were* cannibals; he thought they might once have been, but he never saw conclusive proof that they still were. And another irony: for a few years before his death one of his chief pleasures was to hoist his small granddaughter onto his knee and spin yarns for her about those days among the natives in the jungles of the Pacific islands. The fact was that, like his granddaughter in her way, the critics and the reading public were in their way paying him a tribute he had not asked for: before Conrad, before Stevenson, Herman Melville, the forecastle hand from the *Acushnet,* was the literary discoverer of the South Seas.

And there is one small irony to complete the succession. Two years after the publication of *Moby Dick,* Melville's father-in-law, Justice Shaw, found he had to hold court at Nantucket. It was summertime, and Shaw invited his son-in-law along for a pleasant vacation trip. Melville accepted, because, despite a moving description of Nantucket in his novel, he had never set foot on the island.

So it was that on a dark, foggy July night, Herman Melville and an islander were walking down Petticoat Lane to the author's hotel. Before them a door opened, and the yellow light of a whale-oil lamp silhouetted the features of a stooped, bushy-bearded man. Melville stopped in his tracks, peering through the fog that swirled around the old man as he clumped down the steps and up the lane.

"Who," said the creator of Captain Ahab, "is that man? I have never seen such a tragic face in all my life."

"Didn't you know?" said the Nantucketer. "That's George Pollard. He was the captain of the *Essex.*"

3. The rogue whale

While the sinking of the *Essex* was the genesis of *Moby Dick*, there was another element quite as important; and that was the rogue whale.

When Herman Melville was a whaleman, the relationship between hunter and hunted was a curious one. Chasing after the mountainous beast with only a harpoon and a lance was routine. Yet at the same time the quarry itself was the object of superstitious awe. There are many kinds of whales, some of them nearly as small as a dolphin; but the one that brought the whaleboats swinging out and down was the huge, oil-rich sperm whale. And a perfectly ordinary sperm whale was a weird and wondrous animal.

It weighed as much as fifteen African bull elephants. Its fantail was nearly as long as a whaleboat, and during the summer mating season the caressing whacks of these tails could sometimes be heard far off over the horizon. The jagged, underslung jaw was an awesome thing, too, so large that when one was taken home for a trophy, it made a picturesque frame for a barn door. And how explain an animal that lived like a fish, a creature that dived and swam and never went ashore, yet had to breathe air and keep the water out of its lungs like any beast of the plains? It had to breathe. Yet it could stay under water for an hour at a time. It could plunge to the bottom, deep down where the pressure ought to mash it like an eggshell. Yet it could come plummeting to the surface with such speed that nearly all its great body rose into the air, thrashing like a salmon, and the pressure changes that should have killed it outright seemed to have no effect whatsoever. It seemed to spout water. Yet it actually spouted air that turned to water. When it surfaced and exhaled in a mighty whoosh, the warm gust condensed, sometimes making a geyser twenty feet high. It had two tiny ears that closed tight when under water, and two little eyes protected by glands that made it weep big, greasy tears. Yet whalemen who tried to sneak up unnoticed, with even the thole pins wound with cord to muffle the oars, they found themselves fooled by the "glip," an oily slick that shimmered across the water; the minute the whaleboat touched this smooth area, the whale inexplicably took off.

The mysterious beast conceived and bore its young like any land animal. Yet its "babies" were as long as twenty feet at birth. The mother whale nursed her young. Yet she carried her milk supply under water, and the baby whale did not suck; the mother rolled on her side, exposing teats which had been concealed behind waterproof flaps, and special muscles pumped jets of milk into the baby's open mouth. The whale calf weighed nearly thirty tons. Yet its nursing took only a few minutes; whale's milk was three times as rich as cow's milk. When the whaleboats closed in, the mother whale refused to leave her young. Yet she would only swim off a ways and wait; she almost never fought to protect her calf.

The whale became even more an object of wonder when the chase was on. Large as a floating derelict, it could be wary as a barracuda. From the masthead the lookout could watch a whale "sound," laboriously lifting its great head, emitting an enormous spout, humping its broad back, throwing its flukes high in the air and slipping below the surface with scarcely a ripple on the water. Then, after the long row, as the beast rose, the whaleboat made its approach and the harpooner aimed his iron, the big hulk would suddenly "settle," its body sinking like lead—so fast that in the time it took the harpoon to fly through the air the target disappeared completely. A "gallied" (scared) whale would go off straight across the sea without twisting or changing its course. But it could go so fast and keep it up so long that sometimes the whaleship could come running down in a spanking breeze, pick up her boats on the run, set off after the whale with every sail pulling strong and never close the distance. Some whalemen reported pursuing the animal all day, then keeping on the same point of the compass all night; at the first light of dawn there the whale would be, still going straight and strong but by now gaining on the ship as the morning wind began to die.

If the whale were not so lucky, if the harpoon were tossed a second sooner and landed before the whale knew danger was anywhere near, the big, barbed harpoon point sank into layers of protective blubber, only stinging the animal into diving or racing off across the water, taking the whaleboat after it in a fifteen-mile-an-hour "Nantucket sleighride." But despite the almost impenetrable thickness of the whale's hide, there was a spot just behind the head where the protection was thin; that was the whale's one vital spot, where miles of arteries were jammed around the lungs. One deep, gouging thrust of the lance into this area and the blood from the arteries flooded into the lungs, "setting his chimney afire" as the scalding gore gushed into the air through the spout hole; suffocated in its own blood, the whale died in a few minutes.

If it had been a fat, healthy specimen, its oil was worth about $5000. Yet a blubbery-looking giant might turn out, only after the hours of flensing, cutting, and boiling, to be a "dry skin," with practically no oil at all. And it was just another part of the great mystery of the whale that if the animal were sickly and scrawny, it might be the prize catch of the cruise. The hardened matter that sometimes clogged a whale's intestines and made it sick was called ambergris; it was used in the making of perfume, and it was so valuable that the ambergris found in one whale could be worth as much as $40,000.

This was the kind of awe and mystery surrounding the ordinary sperm whale. It is no wonder then that the men in the forecastles heard with an apprehensive shudder the rumors that a gigantic, malevolent—and *white*—monster was roaming the Pacific.

The stories about this whale were many and varied. Some said he was pure white, as white as new snow, the strange, vivid, eerie whiteness that Herman Melville was to regard as both symbolic and shocking. Others said the whale was off-white, others that he was gray with a white patch on his head. Someone gave him the nickname "Mocha Dick," because he was reportedly first seen near the island of Mocha, off the coast of Chile. Both his nickname and reputation quickly spread into the forecastle of every whaler; because whatever the disagreements about his color, all accounts agreed that he was fantastically ferocious.

One of the mysteries of the sperm whale was that such a great bruiser was virtually harmless until attacked. Nearly always the beast was content to slop along, minding its own business, until chased and attacked by man. Then its first impulse was to get away. And even when struck by the harpoon, the animal usually stove boats and killed men only in its struggle for life. Not Mocha Dick. This ferocious whale appeared to have reversed the ordinary procedure; apparently he was cruising the Pacific looking for whaleboats to attack.

His chronicle began, simply enough, as an isolated incident, a vicious beast taking the offensive and wreaking havoc among the whaleboats—only a chance encounter with a rare whale, a yarn that traveled across the Pacific from ship to ship. Such was the wreck of the *Essex*—a mad whale, one of those disasters that are explainable only in being unprecedented. But then, more than a decade after the *Essex* had gone down, there came a period in which stories like this sprang up from everywhere. The single incident, regarded as a rarity, was followed by another, and another. The same pattern was repeated. The fame—and fear—of Mocha Dick spread across the ocean. He was the main subject of the desultory conversations around the foremast as whalers gammed in mid-ocean on a hot tropical day. His score of boats stove and whalemen killed rose month by month, year by year. This ship had raised him here, that ship there, and always he had smashed boats, killed or wounded men, and escaped. By the 1830s, when a whaling skipper spoke another in the Pacific, he would bellow not, "How many barrels?" but, instead, "Have ye seen Mocha Dick?"

The legend spread through New England as soon as the first whalemen brought it home; in 1834 Emerson wrote in his journal about a stagecoach ride during which a seaman regaled his fellow passengers with "the story of an old sperm-whale which he called a white whale . . . who rushed upon the boats which attacked him & crushed the boats to small chips with his jaws . . ." Probably all of the reported incidents did happen, and many more as well. But it is almost certain that one whale was not responsible for them all. Nevertheless Mocha Dick became just as much the white monster of the sea as he was the evil villain of *Moby Dick*. His infamy swelled with each harrowing tale told by men who had survived.

Such tales as these:

July 1840: Aboard the English whaling brig *Desmond*, cruising the Pacific 215 miles off the coast of Valparaiso, the cry from the masthead brought all hands into the rigging. He was a lone whale, the biggest anyone aboard had ever seen, and he breached nearly his full length, about two miles off. Two boats lowered and started spider-legging across the water toward him. But then he suddenly swung around and started for *them*. As he came on, they noticed that he was more gray than black, and had an eight-foot pure white scar across his broad head. While the boats tried to scurry out of his way, he caught the leading one, plunged straight for it and struck it head-on. The boat, its men flying like peas slapped out of a pod, up-ended and dived under stern-first.

The whale sloshed around, rolled over on his side, grabbed the wrecked boat, and chewed it up. Then he sounded.

He was down fifteen minutes, while the second boat scurried about picking up the men from the first. Then Mocha Dick was back; he came streaking up from the bottom, right under the second boat. There was a crackling crash; the pieces of the boat went spinning into the air and the screams of the men drowned out as they splashed into the sea. Mocha Dick surveyed the wreckage and swam away. Behind him the *Desmond* came lumbering down to pick up her men. Two of them were gone.

August 1840: Five hundred miles south of where the *Desmond* had been, the Russian bark *Serepta* lowered two boats for a lone whale, slipped alongside, got in a harpoon, and finally finished the animal off. By this time they were three miles from the ship. As they started the row back, towing the big carcass astern, Mocha Dick appeared again.

He shot up between the vessel and the boats with such force and speed that he very nearly left the water completely. When the enormous body fell back, the noise could be heard for miles. Then he made for the boats.

The first one he caught head-on, and smashed it to matchwood. He did not wait to chew it up, but went after the second boat. With great presence of mind the mate took this boat behind the carcass of the whale they had caught, foiling Mocha Dick for the moment. He sloshed off, turned, and lay watching while the men rowed, faster than they ever had before, to the ship. The *Serepta* circled around her catch, her men still hoping to retrieve it. But Mocha Dick stayed there, guarding the dead whale until the men gave up and the *Serepta* sailed away. A Nantucket ship found the carcass two days later, alone and unguarded, with the *Serepta's* line still trailing after it.

May 1841: The skipper of the whaleship *John Day*, out of Bristol, had the instincts of a British Captain Ahab. Something about the stories of this rogue whale made him vow that if he ever raised the monster he would kill him, or lose every boat and man in the attempt. The *John Day* was in the South Atlantic, near Cape Horn and east of the Falkland Islands, her trypots blackening the sky with the oily smoke of a whale her men had just taken, when Mocha Dick made his appearance. He broke the surface only three hundred feet away, again shooting nearly his full length out of the water. When his gigantic body thundered back into the sea, the waves made the *John Day's* masts sweep in great rocking circles.

The captain had three boats lowered, while Mocha Dick lashed off to windward and waited for them. The pattern began to repeat itself again; but this time, as the animal streaked straight for him, the first mate of the *John Day* maneuvered out of the line of attack and, with the precision of a matador, sent the harpoon whinging into him.

This was apparently the first time Mocha Dick had ever felt the iron. With an exploding spout he sounded, the harpoon line singing out of the tub and the men dashing water onto it to keep it from burning through the loggerhead. There was a jolt that almost sent every man flying, and the boat took off. Planing across the water, slicing through the crests and almost leaving the surface in the troughs of the waves, the whaleboat went racing along at the end of the harpoon line. For three miles Mocha Dick pulled the whaleboat after him. Then, before the mate could prepare for it, he was headed back at them. With the mate yelling, "STERN ALL!!" the boat swung about; but Mocha Dick hit them broadside. He went right on over the boat, pushing it under the water and flogging it to pieces with his flukes. When the spray had settled, only splinters and the heads of the men were bobbing in the wash. Two of the crew were gone, either drowned or killed outright; and Mocha Dick lay a little way off, waiting.

But the *John Day's* skipper was still game. Bringing the other two boats down onto the scene, he prepared to carry on the battle. In the second boat the men caught hold of the harpoon line, which still trailed across the water. Mocha Dick felt the sting again, and dived again. Rushing to the surface right under the third boat, he bashed the bottom out of it and sent it whipping, end over end, into the air. Miraculously no one was killed in this attack. But now the captain had had enough. The line was cast loose, the survivors crawled into the one remaining whaleboat and the men crept back to the ship. As they looked back, Mocha Dick lay there, snorting and thrashing his tail. But the wet, shaken men climbed aboard and hauled up their boat. Mocha Dick was still there, still waiting, when the *John Day* sailed away.

October 1842: Now came Mocha Dick's greatest battle, all the way across the Pacific, off the east coast of Japan. This time he started it by attacking a coastwise schooner. The schooner, carrying a cargo of lumber, had been blown out to sea by a gale and was making her way back when Mocha Dick spotted her. He breached two miles away, sounded, and, only fifteen minutes later, appeared in the wake of the schooner. Coming straight on, full speed, he struck the little craft with such force that her stern instantly crumpled. Chomping pieces of the wreckage in his jaws, he swam slowly off to port. While the schooner settled, the crew made a large raft from the lumber. They were about to put off from the foundering ship when they realized that the cargo was keeping her afloat, her decks awash. And just then they saw a sight that must have seemed God-delivered—three whaleships cruising in company: the *Crieff*, out of Glasgow, the *Dudley*, from England, and the *Yankee*, New Bedford.

As far as the skippers of the three whalers were concerned, this was their big chance. They held a council of war before their battle, anxious not to muff this perfect opportunity to get rid of Mocha Dick once and for all. After smashing the lumber schooner he had disappeared. But they decided to separate and hunt for him, keeping each other's mastheads in view so that the first to sight him could send a signal aloft and bring the others down to the kill.

They did not have to. As they talked, Mocha Dick hove onto the scene again, with his familiar, crashing breach. He was a mile to windward, but no one could have missed him. He surfaced with such momentum that in the distance he seemed for a moment to be standing on his tail. He toppled onto his side with the splash of a building falling into the water. Then he sounded. Immediately the captains' boats went skittering back across the water to their ships, and within minutes six whaleboats, two from each whaler, were racing toward the spot where the big animal had gone down.

There they sat, rocking in the seas stirred up by the whale, for twenty minutes. Then Mocha Dick struck again.

This time, though, the whalemen were wise to his ways. As the mountain of flesh and bone came roaring up from the bottom, one of the whalemen spotted him under the boat just in time to sing out, and the well-trained crew frantically backed off. Mocha Dick missed, thrashed into the air and crashed down again, drenching everyone. One of the *Yankee's* boats quickly plunged in over the surf he had stirred up and slid up near him. The harpoon pitch-poled over the water and landed true, quivering in his whitish hide. Mocha Dick let go a big spout and humped up. Then he lay sogging in his suds, his flukes waving feebly. Five minutes later there was not a wiggle in him, just the huge form rolling in the water. The other boats closed in, each officer warily ready with his lance, to make sure they had finally got him.

Mocha Dick quit playing dead. In one rush he ran over one of the Scottish boats, pounding it with his tail. Almost in the same attack—so fast did he turn—he made for one of the British boats. The crew managed to get out of his path, while the *Yankee* whaleboat, still fast to the harpoon, danced crazily after him. The whale spun around again, almost in his own shadow, and this time caught the same British boat before the crew could pull out of the way. As everyone watched in horror, he rolled over, snapped up the boat in his jaws and, lifting his head in the air, shook it like a terrier worrying a rat. Pieces of splintered wood rained from his mouth, and two whalemen who had not jumped quickly enough were gnashed to pulp.

While shrieking men turned the water red from their wounds, the other boats gave up the chase, picking their way among the wreckage and scooping up the survivors. Mocha Dick ran back to the lumber schooner, now a deserted hulk, and batted it about with his head. Then he sounded again and was gone.

Aboard the Scottish whaler the skipper was beginning to attend to his wounded, when Mocha Dick came back again. Rushing up under the ship, he barely missed her. His sweeping breach grazed the bow, ripped away her jib boom and bowsprit. He swam off to windward, turned, and lay watching as the three ships and their ninety men put on all sail and got away as fast as the wind would take them.

Could this white or off-white whale be the same one in each encounter—striking first in mid-Pacific, then in the South Atlantic, then off the coast of Japan? Probably not. But forecastle legend maintained that it was. A further piece of evidence is the fact that after this period of two decades, there were apparently no more such attacks by a *white* whale.

And how did Mocha Dick finally meet his end? There are a number of versions. Some said a special fleet was organized to go after him, that the fleet found him in the Pacific, that he fought weakly without even attacking the boats, and that as soon as the lance hit his lungs he expired with scarcely a shudder. On Martha's Vineyard Island, as much a whaling center as Nantucket and New Bedford, there is still living a harpooner named Amos Smalley, who darted his iron into a white whale off the coast of Africa when he was a young man. But this was in 1902, and although experts cannot agree on the age span of the whale, it is doubtful that Amos Smalley's quarry was the original Mocha Dick. Another story has it that in 1859 a Swedish whaler caught up with Mocha Dick, lowered for him, and got a harpoon into him with no trouble at all. He was old and worn out from his countless battles, and he was beyond struggling when the lance finally gouged into his lungs. Not counting the reports that were lost to history, the old white devil's record was fourteen whaleboats smashed, thirty men killed, and victory in more than a hundred watery battles. When the Swedes got his carcass alongside, they found he was blind in his right eye and had nineteen harpoon points corroding in his leathery hide.

But there were others. As whaling went on, as more ships scoured the Pacific, more incidents were reported, battles with rogue whales that reminded the old hands of Mocha Dick. Now the antagonists were as black as any normal whale, though they were every bit as ferocious.

In 1850 the bark *Parker Cook,* out of Provincetown, Massachusetts, raised a whale in mid-Atlantic, lowered for him, and drove a harpoon home. Thereupon the whale breached half out of water and capsized the boat. The whirring line looped around the boat steerer's leg and immediately chewed through to the bone. The man was able to get his knife loose and cut through the line just before his leg was sliced off. Fainting from loss of blood, he was rowed back to the ship, and the whale, trailing the cut line after him, disappeared.

The men had barely returned to the ship when the whale appeared again, plowing straight for the bow. He hit, glanced off, whirled around, and came back for a second attack. But apparently the harpoon had done more damage than they estimated; this time he hit the ship without much strength. He did not give up, though. He returned for a third run; but now the captain was prepared for him. He had lowered his boat and was waiting with one of the deadly new bomb lances. The whale slewed off and made for the captain's boat, rolling on his side and opening his jaws for the kill. Down his gaping gullet went the bomb lance, which exploded inside him. Yet the whale attacked twice more. It took three bomb lances to kill him. The captain took the time to have him cut in, and the *Parker Cook* was 103 barrels richer when she hoisted all sail and set her course for Fayal, to make repairs and get a doctor for the boat steerer.

A few months later the ship *Pocahontas,* from Holmes's Hole (now Vineyard Haven), Massachusetts, was running south southwest for Cape Horn to start her Pacific cruise. She was off the coast of Argentina when, in the faint light of dawn, the lookout spotted a whole herd of whales. Within an hour two boats were creeping up on them, and in a flashing, whistling parabola a harpoon hit home. The whale went down, the line disappearing into the water after him. There was a short run to windward, and then the whale rose to the surface and lay still, ripe for the lance. Slowly the mate directed the boat to come up, holding the lance ready and poised. Then, as he was bracing himself for the lunge and muttering to his crew to "lay me on him; there; alongside him, now," the whale burst into action again. Milling about in an instant, he rolled jaw-up and made a grab at the boat. He got it, and in one crunch bit it in two. The men, two of them badly hurt, fought through the foam to keep away from the jaw and crashing flukes, and the other boat came rushing in to pick them up. But the whale kept after the remains of the boat, whirling around and around it, so the captain had all he could do to sneak into the melee and rescue his drowning men.

He got them back to the ship and dressed their wounds. It took two hours, and during all this time the whale stayed out there, circling the smashed boat, breaking up the mast, even the oars, anything large enough for him to get hold of with his big jaw. Meanwhile the rest of the whales hung around him, almost like an appreciative audience.

The *Pocahontas'* skipper was Joseph Dias, Jr., only 28, nick-named "the boy captain." Young Dias could not bring himself to sail off while all those whales sported around the ship, almost taunting him. Despite two hours soaking in the blood of his wounded men and hearing their moans, sharp cries, and whis-pered prayers, Captain Dias had to have one more swipe at that murderous whale. He decided to run down on the animal in the ship. That was a mistake.

The *Pocahontas* plowed after the whale, nearly every man stationed in the bow and armed with something sharp to toss into the whale's back. The beast nimbly dodged the ship on the first pass, though one of the irons pricked him. Coming back on the other tack, Captain Dias made one more try. This time the whale lay still, only nudging some of the wreckage of the boat with his head. Then, just as the ship closed on him, he whirled about and made for her. Captain Dias estimated that the *Pocahontas* was making about two knots in the light breeze, but the whale had got up to almost four when he smashed into her. He struck her just below the water line, and with a jolting, groaning crunch, the plank and three timbers heaved inboard.

Captain Dias scrambled down to the forecastle, where he found the water slowly leaking into her, with only the copper sheathing between him and the sea. He set the men to work at the pumps, and found she was leaking at 250 strokes per hour.

The whales had run off over the horizon. But by now the *Pocahontas* and her young captain were in real trouble.

The nearest port where a complete repair job could be had was Rio de Janeiro, 750 miles away. So Captain Dias had the leak patched as best he could, and started north again. It was a suspenseful voyage, with rain squalls, followed by winds that blew right in their teeth when they tried to hold their course. Then came a still, frustrating calm, while the ship leaked more and more and "the boy captain" began to wonder seriously if this were his last voyage. But the *Pocahontas* finally made it, in fifteen days—more than two weeks with the water trying to force a hole in the bow and the men laboring at the pumps until they cried from the constant exertion. It was the happiest day in Captain Dias' young life when the *Pocahontas* at last rounded to in Rio's outer harbor and her anchor hit bottom in six fathoms.

Two weeks later, repaired and shipshape, the *Pocahontas* was off for the Pacific again. She rounded the Horn, made her slow way up the west coast of South America and, off Más Afuera, spoke the New Bedford whaler *Ann Alexander*. They cruised in company for a while, the *Pocahontas* having bad luck while her sailing companion prospered. But the *Ann Alexander's* fortunes were about to take a turn.

On the twentieth of August, 1851, while the crew of the *Pocahontas* was idly gathering turtles in the Galápagos, the *Ann Alexander* was 800 miles away, cruising the popular "Offshore Grounds." It was nine in the morning when the call came from the masthead, and two boats were lowered. The captain, John S. Deblois, had the starboard boat, and the first mate the larboard. It was the first mate who sank the iron. Off went the whale, and off went the boat after him. Then he turned, and with one sweeping roll had the boat in his jaws. The men all managed to jump to safety, but the boat was chomped to bits. Captain Deblois brought his boat down and picked up the swimming men. Aboard the ship, six miles away, the man at the masthead had seen the attack, so the waist boat was sent to help. The men were divided equally, three survivors in each boat, whereupon Captain Deblois decided not to give up so easily. The whale lay off a bit, rolling about and enticing them on. With the captain in charge of one boat and the first mate heading the other they closed in on the animal again. He waited for them until the mate's boat got within range, and then he charged. In another rolling swoop he caught the boat in his jaws and crunched it to bits. Again every man was able to leap clear. Captain Deblois rounded them all up; now, with eighteen men in one whaleboat, the chase was out of the question.

But the whale was not through with them. As the whaleboat with its heavy load made its slow way back to the *Ann Alexander,* the men felt their flesh creep as they saw the beast come swinging into their wake, sloshing his big tail and rolling over to make the same openmouthed assault. There were too many men in the boat to try to maneuver out of the way, so everyone prepared to jump. The whale came on, slowly, as if gauging the distance carefully, then made his lunge. But instead of leaping on the boat, he inexplicably dived beneath it. The men who had almost jumped into the sea could look over the gunwale and watch him streak under them. He did not come up for the next few minutes; but they never knew when he would be upon them again, so the oars bent into the water as never before while the whaleboat skimmed for the ship.

By the time they made it the whale had surfaced again. He lay off some distance from the ship. The sight of him sporting about out there was too much for Captain Deblois. He sent out a boat to collect the oars, buckets, harpoons, and lances strewing the ocean around the ship. Then he drove the *Ann Alexander* into what was to be her last chase.

As the ship bore down on the whale, the big animal raised his head and waited for the attack. Before the whaler got alongside, a lance arched out over the water and struck him. Stung and infuriated, the whale lunged at the ship. Captain Deblois was prepared. At the quick command to haul on the wind, the helmsman neatly sent the *Ann Alexander* sloshing behind the whale before he could stop his charge and turn around.

So he lay and waited. Captain Deblois looked at him floating astern and considered another attempt. The battle had started at nine in the morning; it was now nearly sundown. No one had had time to eat. All his men were alive, but all were worn out from the struggle and some were still shaken by their narrow escape. The sight of the big beast, though, was just too much. There was enough sun left above the horizon for one more pass at him. Captain Deblois decided to try it.

Bringing the ship about, he set her on course for the whale again. This time he got out on the knightheads, his sharpest lance carefully balanced in his hand. The whale made no move to go off, while the ship closed the gap—seventy rods; sixty; fifty-five; fifty—then, suddenly, the animal settled, sinking like a stone before Captain Deblois could let fly his lance. The captain searched the darkening horizon, but the whale was gone. Now the sun was all but down. The all-day battle was over. He started to climb back on deck.

That was when he heard the splashing, rushing noise. Off the starboard bow, only two boat lengths away, the whale was coming for the ship. Captain Deblois said later that the animal must have been traveling at a speed of fifteen knots. There was not even time to think, much less wear off from the attack. The blow came just abreast the foremast and about two feet from the keel. It felt as if they had run full speed onto a reef. Every timber shivered.

A quick dash into the forecastle and one glance at the seas pouring in through the gap was enough to convince the captain that there was no hope for the Ann Alexander. The whale had finally gone off; but that one blow had been enough. By the time the captain had run aft to his cabin, it was already three feet deep in water. He was able to grab his chronometer, a quadrant, and a chart; but when he dumped them on deck and tried to get back into the cabin, it had filled. Everywhere on board men were grabbing the first thing they could lay hands on, with no design or reason. In the time it took Captain Deblois to scramble down the companionway, find his cabin was full of water, and race back onto deck, the boats had been shoved off and he was alone. He jumped into the water and swam to the nearest one. As they all rowed out of danger, the Ann Alexander pitched over on her side.

She did not sink yet, however; and after the captain and his crew had spent a miserable night in their boats, they found her next morning still wallowing on her beam ends. The memory of the tales they had heard of the *Essex* must now have haunted them all as they rowed cautiously back to the floating wreck. They were not far from where the *Essex* had gone down. But unlike the crew of the *Essex*, they had no food at all in their whaleboats; and the laborious job of cutting through the *Ann Alexander's* timbers produced only five gallons of vinegar and twenty pounds of useless, water-soaked bread.

But what they forgot in those first hours of bowel-griping panic was that this was 1851, not 1820, and the Offshore Grounds now virtually swarmed with whalers. That is what saved them. Their desperate voyage lasted only one day; on the second someone sighted a sail. Their signals were answered. The badly frightened but still healthy men of the *Ann Alexander* were soon swinging up the sides of the whaler *Nantucket,* which promptly took them to Paita, Peru.

The whale? Five months later he was finally caught by the New Bedford whaler *Rebecca Simms*. He was diseased, emaciated, and still carried splinters from the hunks of wood in his head. In his hide were the ends of two harpoons; both bore the initials of the *Ann Alexander*.

Back in the U.S. in November of 1851, *Moby Dick* had just been published when the news of the *Ann Alexander* arrived. A friend wrote the author about the remarkable coincidence. Herman Melville replied: "I make no doubt it *is* Moby Dick himself . . . Ye Gods! what a Commentator is this *Ann Alexander* whale."

Then he added a typically Melvillean afterthought: "I wonder," he wrote, "if my evil art has raised the monster."

4. "The cannibals"

The whaleman's great quarry and adversary was indeed a creature of fearsome wonder. Whales could and did sink ships—the *Essex* and the *Ann Alexander*. But there was another creature quite as fascinating to the whaleman, and sometimes quite as fearsome; it was the Pacific island native.

Naked and ornately decorated, kind and cruel, friendly and suspicious, sentimental and bloodthirsty, the native of the Pacific was the subject of fully as many forecastle tales as was the whale. "The cannibals," whalemen invariably called them, whether they were actually cannibals or not. And what the men recalled most clearly, of course, were the chilling stories of near death aboard ship or on the beach from these bizarre, frightening people. The island natives, the whalemen said, stuck pieces of bone through their noses, killed their babies, suckled puppies, and, yes, ate other people. By the time the tales of these dark-skinned creatures had gone the rounds from fireside to inn to stagecoach, the natives were the fiercest cannibals in the history of the world.

Since the 1840s a great many anthropologists have studied the Pacific islanders and have clarified and explained most of their customs and traditions. In their time and place these customs and traditions made sense, and many of our own practices certainly would have astonished the islanders. The native of the Pacific was no more exotic than those of Africa, and a good deal less than the Asians of the nineteenth century. For purposes of not very scientific simplification the islanders were divided into three main groups: light-colored, husky Polynesians in the southeast; darker, slighter Micronesians in the northeast; and black, stocky Melanesians in the southwest. Generally they were all simple and direct in their emotions, their reasoning and their reactions to foreign stimuli. And rarely were they cannibals. Through history the practice of cannibalism has been an unusual religious manifestation, seldom a casual practice of a tribe. But at the time the whalemen came home with their stories and Herman Melville wrote his novels, the South Seas native was regarded as a fierce and fascinating fellow and usually a cannibal as well. To the whalemen, who were the first observers on a large scale, the antics of the natives were outlandish and inexplicable.

In their meanderings the whaleships of the early nineteenth century touched at countless Pacific islands, many of which had never been visited by white men before. The whaler was away from home three or four years; and every month or so the fresh water gave out, the wood for the galley was consumed, scurvy began to plague the foremast hands, who had eaten only maggoty meat for weeks. So these early whalemen were the first American ambassadors, the first white ambassadors, to many of the Pacific islands. But they rarely saw it in this light. The captain putting into the harbor of a strange island wanted only to load his wood and water, fruit and turtles and get out. The foremast hand wanted the feel of solid ground under his feet, the shade of a palm tree over his sun-scorched head, and a girl to help him forget the celibacy of the forecastle; and he was in a hurry.

So the men of the whalers were just as much a novelty to the natives—and usually an alarming novelty. Sometimes relations were established on the ship, the native canoes gliding out of their coves and the brown bodies slithering up the whaler's sides. Sometimes they met at the shore, the whaleboat rocking just beyond the surf line and the two groups examining each other suspiciously while a Hawaiian harpooner tried to make sense out of a Fijian dialect he had never heard before. Then came the international language: barter, glittering beads and pieces of colorful cloth in return for coconuts and yams. That usually got the whalemen on the beach. And from then on anything could happen.

There was the continued attempt at communication—the strange, bearded white men shouting louder and louder as Americans always do when trying to make themselves understood. Gradually suspicions would ease and the strangers would make themselves at home. Sooner or later the jugs of kava would appear, the "white lightning" of the islands. The spectacle of a dozen brawny, spitting, drunken whalemen whooping and taking off after every woman on the island was enough to chill the blood of even someone who had seen white creatures like these before. After a day or two of this kind of visitation even the most peaceful island chieftains had their troubles keeping the hot-blooded young warriors from correcting the situation immediately with spears and stones. Finally, if by some miracle total war had not swept the island, the staggering, hiccuping whalemen would drag their prostrate shipmates into the whaleboat and, bellowing songs the islanders were fortunate not to understand, row the length and breadth of the harbor in their attempt to reach the ship.

Even then, sometimes, the relieved natives would suddenly discover that they had been had. Many a skipper "paid with the fore-topsail," i.e., promised all manner of gifts in return for provisions, only to loose sail to the trade winds and leave the island astern, sending a round of buckshot into any canoes that threatened to overtake him. Usually the unhappiest results of such a visit were not even realized for a week or so; venereal disease was part of the unpleasant novelty of the white strangers.

The next shipload of whalemen to call at this particular island did not receive a cordial reception.

But the bloodcurdling tales brought home by the whalemen had a more complicated background than that. The peoples of the Pacific islands lived by a totally different set of values than their visitors. And the most incomprehensible of these values to the white men was their conception of life and death. For all his rough brutality the ordinary whaleman understood the meaning of murder. In a sense the Pacific islander did not. His aged and infirm were callously dispatched. Birth control was practiced *after* birth. If the local chief took a dislike to one of his subjects, the subject promptly died. Many of the islanders lived by rules of society more complex and rigidly defined than those of Nantucket or Edgartown or Sag Harbor; but the sanctity of a man's life was usually not one of these rules. So what the whalemen regarded as treachery most Pacific islanders would have defined as simple expediency.

If the strange white men wanted only food and fuel and water, and if they behaved themselves, the natives were inclined to be content with what they regarded as a profitable exchange of glittering gifts in return for surplus bananas that would have rotted in a little while anyway. But it was just as straightforward for the chief to conclude that if there were a great deal more to be gained by taking everything else aboard the ship—and if it could be accomplished without losing too many of his best warriors—why not kill the visitors? Of course he would be a fool not to. Most of the whalemen never grasped this fundamental idea, and many paid, quickly and finally, for not realizing it. The few who did understand had little trouble; the simplest method was to make it apparent from the start that while the captain wanted only to give lavish presents to the chief in return for some useless food, just the same, the first young buck who got too fresh would be pulling a cutting spade out of his bowels. The island chief who saw there was nothing to be gained by killing his visitors usually decided, with simple directness, not to kill them. And business was conducted in an orderly fashion—so long as both chief and whaling captain could keep their men in line.

The Pacific islanders had other values, traditions, and taboos which were difficult for the whalemen to understand. And these patterns of behavior varied widely throughout the islands in the vast watery area the whaleships cruised. So the ordinary foremast hand came home with a fantastically disordered collection of impressions out of which he formed his picture of the Pacific island native. A wondrously confused and colorful kaleidoscope it was.

Here, the whalemen said, were dirty, dark-skinned savages with beady eyes, mops of red- and orange-dyed hair, filed teeth, and noses that had been flattened at birth. Yet even though none of these peoples could write, many of them had their own poets, rhythmic songs, and epic tales that had been brought down through the generations of their rich cultural backgrounds. Some of the women were shaped like oil barrels, with breasts which they flipped over their shoulders to nurse babies hanging on their backs. Some of the men purposely disfigured their faces, to look as hideous as possible, and were tattooed until they looked as if they had scales instead of skin. Other women were pretty, clean-limbed, and graceful, and other men were handsomer and had more dignity than any of the shipowners back home. The young warriors of some islands had slim waists and hips and broad, muscular shoulders that impressed even the huskiest harpooner, while the warriors' chief was swathed in flopping layers of royal fat, carefully acquired by years of gorging, and walked with a sickening waddle. The islanders did not chew tobacco, but betel nut was constantly in their mouths, staining their lips beef red, their teeth black, and coloring everything around them red from their spittle. When some of them were first given a plug of tobacco to chew on, they promptly rubbed the juice in their hair to kill the lice. Others became angry when the white visitors offered remedies for the lice; they cherished the vermin, to pick out of each other's heads and crunch between their teeth as a delicacy.

They cultivated foods with flavors that were too delicate for the bruised palates of the whalemen; and with these delicacies they mixed such dishes as rotted worms and bird guts. They plowed into mountains of food that would nauseate the worst glutton, then lay back wheezing and belching and blowing their noses in the sand beside them. Even the more finicky natives expectorated freely with the rest, but they were careful to lift the edge of a mat or skirt and spit under that. They went off into the farthest bushes to relieve themselves, then drank the rain water that flowed down the hillside through the bushes and into the pools of the valley. Some of the islanders bathed thoroughly as often as twice a day, then anointed themselves with rancid fish oil and donned grass skirts that had not been cleaned in years and crawled with vermin. Others labored long to construct elaborately ornamented huts that omitted any protection against, and in fact invited, every jumping and slithering creature on the island.

A native woman who had one baby too many calmly handed it over to be buried alive; then she purchased another, older and more immediately able to work, from another tribe. If some mongrel puppy caught her fancy, she took it in and nursed it like a child. When it became a dog, she laughed with the rest at the sight of it being tortured or slit down the middle so it would scream and whine for a day or two before dying. The old and crippled natives were just as amusing to the others; after mocking and jeering at them until it became boring, some natives would summarily bash in the elders' brains. On the other side of the island might be a tribe of natives who spoiled their children from birth and carried their aged around on their backs.

Some islanders could hardly believe that anything existed beyond the horizon at the edge of the sea; they had never paddled beyond the outermost reef. Others were seen in the midst of the open Pacific, in their hundred-foot war canoes, paddling and sailing by the stars on a voyage of hundreds of miles. Some met the visiting white men at the beach, the chief of the community presiding over the occasion with a stately, eloquent, ceremonial speech which the whalemen were expected to listen to politely and attentively, even though they could not understand a word and it took as long as an hour. Others met all visitors with no more ceremony than a cloud of arrows or spears and shrieks that would shrink a man's marrow. Still others welcomed the whalemen ashore, exchanged gifts (i.e., drove a hard bargain) and then let go with the spears or arrows.

As more and more whaleships went around the Horn and out across the Pacific, some of the islands became their favorite stopping places; the native chiefs there had realized that with proper safeguards it was possible to do business with the white men. On many of these islands and atolls the whaling captain could find a replacement for a crew member killed by a whale— some beachcomber who had lived peacefully with the natives for a few months or a year but who had finally grown weary of his idle idyl. Throughout whole groups of atolls, though, it was vastly different. Among most of the Melanesians, the dread "Black Islands," few ships called. There were no beachcombers. Here the visitor "with salt water in his eyes" was absorbed into the community literally. Yet in their midst would be a sun-washed, palm-fringed atoll where dozens of whalers at a time rode at their anchors in the lagoon, where white traders had settled down to serve as middlemen, and where many a captain kept a second, native wife.

Here the contrasts that so perplexed and confused the whaleman were heightened still more. No wonder that although many of the Pacific islanders were never man-eaters, the whalemen classed them all under the generic heading of cannibals. A single experience ashore on one of these "Black Islands" was usually enough. In appearance the natives were handsome, clean, and intelligent. They seemed hospitable, friendly, generous, the most ingratiating of all the islanders of the Pacific. Sometimes their hospitality was enduring. On the next island the unwary whaleman was ushered ashore and into the village for a lavish feast, obsequious kindnesses, gifts and entertainment, and even a brown, buxom companion for the sleeping mat, only to be prepared for the kill; behind all the hospitality this time lurked what the white man called treachery and the islander knew only as expediency. Stuffed, drunk, and exhausted, the whaleman was not the formidable enemy he had been earlier in the day; now that the crew was disarmed, the entire ship was an easy prize.

The whaleman was easy meat. The wise old foremast hands liked to tell the popeyed young ones that cannibals didn't really like sailors: they were tainted with salt and tobacco. But that was generally false optimism. Because most of the cannibalism among the Pacific islanders was a religious rite, evidently a white whaleman served just as well for the occasion as a brown neighbor did.

As a religious ceremony, it was a strictly regimented performance. In the Fijis, on a tiny piece of land accessible to the main island by a causeway exposed at low tide, were huge ovens, used only for baking human bodies. They were set in a "sacred grove," where the tree trunks were notched to record the hundreds of victims cooked and eaten. One of the Fijian herbs was prized and taboo because it was supposed to make human flesh easier to digest. These feasts were not usually gluttonous banquets; women were never allowed to eat "long pig," as it was called, and the meat was considered so sacred that it could not be touched with the hands. Although eating utensils were not used for any other kind of food, special forks were required for man-meat. The most favored parts were reserved for and ceremoniously presented to the chief—the eyes, the intestines; and sometimes only the aristocracy was allowed to have any man-meat at all. But while the meat itself was sacred, and was eaten sparingly, the dinner sometimes wound up with wild singing and dancing and sexual orgies.

Although the cannibals may have eaten man-meat as a religious rite, they enjoyed it for a much simpler reason: it tasted good. There were chiefs who usually kept a young man imprisoned in the compound, castrated to fatten him up for the pot. Some warriors nerved themselves for battle by singing, "This is the time when men are fat." And the meal was supposed to taste better if the enemy were only wounded and then boiled or baked alive; the meat kept better that way. Occasionally the victims' bones were smashed and the still-living men were tied in fresh water for a few days to soak and tenderize. But long pig tasted so good to some islanders that it was a delicacy even when it had become tainted; sometimes when the body or bodies had putrified so much that they could not be lifted without falling to pieces, the islanders scraped them up and made a stew. Other natives even liked parts of the human body raw; bashing in the skull, they would sit down and eat the brains the same way they ate coconuts.

On rare occasions revenge added to the cannibals' enjoyment of man-meat. Warriors bathed themselves in the blood of enemy wounded during a battle; and an occasional native would smash the body of a dead foe until it was flat, cut a hole through what was left of the stomach, thrust his head through it and go on into the fight—wearing the dangling body like a cape and licking at the blood that splattered about his mouth. After the battle the chief had a few choice bodies cooked, cut up, and hung in his hut; for weeks he had only to reach up for a liver, a heart, or a tongue to nibble at meditatively. The privileged island aristocrat was the one who could afford to tie a couple of cooked or smoked hands on his belt, to munch whenever he felt like it.

This was cannibalism as the whalemen described it back home —part religion, part a plain liking for man-meat. It was also partly a love of torture. Here again the ways of the Pacific islander made the New England whaleman realize that he was in a totally different part of the world. The natives seemed to *like* torture. Young men cut slits in their arms, punctured their cheeks or burned off their nipples to show how brave they were. They were constantly torturing the same pet animals they had nurtured with such affection. They liked turtle, but they liked it best "in the shell"; they cooked it by rolling it over on its back when it was still alive and lighting a fire on its belly. A chief fattened up some of his subjects to use as soft, portable cushions and back rests, and would even launch his war canoe by using other subjects as rollers, mashing them to death as the heavy boat crunched over them and down the beach into the water. For apparently no other reason than cruelty one man was sometimes dumped alive into each of the pits dug for the posts of a new communal building, and buried with the posts. A favorite war weapon was wrapped with sharkskin, abrasive enough to flay a man alive. One particularly imaginative chief had a captured enemy tied to a tree, chopped off the man's arm, cooked it, and forced him to watch while he ate it. To some of the natives it was sport to tie an enemy's wrists behind his back, wrap a piece of tapa around him and under his crotch; then the tapa was set on fire, and everyone joined in the game of keeping the yelling man from running into the water. There was even the whaleman who claimed to have witnessed this scene: a big war canoe was sailing home from a battle; in her stern sat the huddled, moaning forms of the women captives; forward of them lay the trussed-up bodies of the fattest enemy warriors; and near the bow, suspended by their heels on long rattan ropes, were the babies, gradually braining themselves against the mast as the canoe rolled back and forth in the swells of the Pacific.

These were the sort of cannibal tales brought home by the whalemen. And then another foremast hand would return with an account of being taken in and fed and protected by cannibals until the next ship put into the harbor three or four years later; when the time for parting came, the whaleman's dark-skinned friends wept and wailed and even gouged holes in their foreheads to show their sadness at losing him. But the tales of sadism, cruelty, and man-eating only made accounts like this seem more miraculous in the eyes of the whalemen who cruised the Pacific.

In every forecastle there was some old veteran who could tell these stories by the hour. So whenever a whaler entered the latitudes of the most notorious cannibal islands, a cloud of anxiety swept the ship. Lookouts missed whales because they were so intent on the dark-bordered outline of some Black Island on the horizon off the lee bow. When the boats went out after whales, the men at the oars kept a close watch to be sure they never lost sight of the mother ship. If the skipper was one of those who led prayers on deck every Sunday, he could detect the volume of reverent mumbling by men who never prayed at other times; the volume increased the longer they stayed in these waters. The captains themselves watched the sweeping lines that indicated currents on their crude charts, studied the glass barometer more carefully than usual, and watched for the slightest sign of a calm. If the calm should come, in sight of an island and with the current making in its direction, the anxiety aboard ship turned into plain, nauseating fear.

That was what happened aboard the whaler *Charles W. Morgan* one afternoon in 1851. She was cruising down along the Line in the neighborhood of the worst Black Islands. Day by day the wind had been diminishing. Now it gave out altogether. Only out on the Pacific, and along the Line, were there calms like these—sizzling, death-still calms when the sun was like a fireball above and the sea was an unending sheet of glass, with even the swells almost imperceptible. Aloft, in the slack sails, the reef points barely moved. Silence enveloped the ship, without even the normal creak of her timbers, the rattle of blocks, the splash at her bow. Now the only sound was the trickle of water in and out of the nail holes of her copper-sheathed bottom. In the forecastle the wooden bulkhead was hot to the touch, and the men lay sweating in their bunks, neither moving nor speaking. On deck every man who could got under the shade of a mast or sail. In their pen forward the hogs shoved each other to crowd into one shady triangle, and all of them grunted happily when a thoughtful crewman doused them with a bucket of sea water. Under the direct rays of the sun the pitch oozed and bubbled from the seams of the deck. But the worst spot on the ship was at the masthead; here was actual hell, with the sun beating down from above and its reflection glaring up from the mirroring sea. The lookout's eyes burned from the brilliance of the light, and his face, hands, and arms dried and blackened in the heat.

At dusk, when the sun finally seemed to give up trying to kill them and settled into the sea, life aboard the *Morgan* was a little more bearable. Even then the ship gave the impression of being suspended in air. When the skipper looked at his compass for the seventieth time, he realized that the whaler was turning around and around; he would not have known it otherwise, everything moved so slowly. Men still baked in the stinking forecastle through the night, and in the morning the sun rose like a red ball, looking twice its ordinary size.

Then came the call from aloft: "Land, O!"

Captain John Sampson was nervously striding from rail to rail on the quarter-deck, studying the sky and horizon for any sign of a breeze. He stopped short.

"Where away?" he shouted.

"On the port beam." The skipper looked up through the tangled network of rigging to where the lookout was pointing. He walked quickly over to check its bearing against the compass. He did not have to climb the shrouds to have a look. That would be Sydenham (Nonouti, Gilberts), one of the worst of the cannibal islands. He went to the port rail, raised the glass to his eye, and searched the open sea. The island was still hull down.

Everyone on deck watched to see what his next move would be —what they should do, what they could do. These were the times when a ship's captain in name became the captain in fact, and when all the men felt it in their insides. Whatever their feelings about the food and treatment he had been giving them, the only important thing now would be his command decisions. It was at times like this that the men realized the meaning of such words as discipline, obedience, authority. Everyone aboard knew which way the current was running—straight down onto the island the lookout had sighted from the masthead. And the wind seemed to have left this part of the world. In their minds' eyes they could already see the war canoes, filled with black men and bristling with spears, shooting across the water toward them. Their only hope now rested on the stooped shoulders of the skipper, "The Old Man." How he armed them, how he stationed them along the sides of the ship, how he foresaw each move of each war canoe before it was made—on these decisions of his, made in haste and in the heat of the moment, depended their lives. This, most of the men knew, was the reason for the unquestioned orders, the marlinspike across the shoulders, the flogging for the slightest insubordination, the harsh penalty for mutiny. This was why the captain's word was absolute law. Whether the crew of the *Morgan* would be alive when the sun rose again depended upon her captain. Only one of two foolhardy men would want the skipper's job right now.

Captain Sampson felt this all the more keenly as he swept the horizon with his telescope. He had seen the men react to the shout from the masthead; they had looked immediately at him. The strategy he now devised to make a couple dozen men the equal of hundreds of savages, his own brains—and luck—were all that counted. He needed time to think out his plan of battle. He snapped the telescope shut, turned, and, muttering to himself, went below for his breakfast. There he would ponder his preparations.

The ocean current kept steadily on its course. The *Morgan's* sails still hung slack. The red had gone from the sun; now it was copper-colored, climbing slowly above them and focusing all its seething fire on the ship and the oily water around her. The pitch oozed from the deck seams again. The hogs started complaining again, snuffling about in the tiny patch of shade the mainsail cast across a corner of their pen. The masthead relief swung slowly up the rigging and the off-watch men clambered down, dipped buckets of warm sea water over their heads, and sat gasping in the shade of the foremast.

But the silence that pervaded the ship was a different kind from that of the day before. Now it was heavier, a tense, expectant stillness; everyone jumped whenever it was broken. Each man had drawn in upon himself. On deck they were strung along the port rail. One looked out across the glassy ocean, unseeing while his mind went back to Edgartown Harbor, with a Christmas snowfall spinning across the water and the wind throwing waves at the wharves. Next to him a man was seeing a fireplace, the storm whooshing over the chimney top and the rain sissing as it spattered down on the crane and the pots. Another was trying to visualize a little girl who had been a toddler when he left and was now in school. And another in the line watched cows amble along the lane into the barn, while he wondered what it was that had made him leave the Vermont mountains for a whaler. This was the period when the men did little more than worry and think of home and wonder when the command would come that would tell them just how they would defend themselves. This was when they mentally totted up their chances, considered how many stories they had heard of men who had escaped, how many in which only a charred bit of wreckage was evidence of what had happened. And this was still the time when the men, most of them, decided that their chances were pretty good.

Then the island came into sight. Aside from a muffled "There it is" and low, profane muttering, the silence remained unbroken. But men began to shift uneasily at the rail, and to look aft to see if The Old Man had reappeared yet, as if they would not have heard him. The tobacco chewers spat over the side more often now, and others stretched and yawned and scratched themselves elaborately, and others began to wonder if there had been something worse than usual in the breakfast. If only the skipper would come on deck and get things started, they were sure they would feel better. Meanwhile each man hunched nervously at the rail and waited, alone unto himself.

At the masthead the lookout was joined by the second mate. The iron hoops were scorching to the touch, but they leaned out across the royal yard and studied the island. From up there it seemed to creep toward them faster. Below them the current still rippled along, taking the ship with it. The mate had a glass with him. He lifted it, studied the island, and grunted. Neither spoke of the island or its inhabitants for a moment. The lookout broke the silence by saying the only thing he could think of; he complained once again about the heat. The mate's answer broke the subject into the open.

"There is something worse than being inconvenienced by a little heat."

The island, he pointed out, was small; but coral reefs projected out from it on all sides. Without wind to help them steer clear, the ship would probably drift onto one of these reefs. And the savages would be waiting in their canoes. It would be impossible to put out boats to pull the ship away from the reef; each boat would immediately be set on by a dozen canoes.

Did it mean sure death?

Not sure death, no. There had been cases where the natives had taken a ship's crew captive and had treated the men well enough, then ransomed them off to the next whaler for a few boxes of tobacco. But even then the trouble was that not many native chiefs could stand having all that man-meat around without having a few killed for a feast.

Had any other ships run into trouble on this island?

It was hard to tell. All the islands in this area were bad. Sometimes one or two men had escaped to tell about the slaughter of the rest of the crew. But they were never quite sure exactly which island it was; they only knew the general area. And of course the usual evidence was the blackened pieces of wood found floating in these waters. They always burned the ship when they took her—stripped her of everything they wanted, ran her on a reef, and set fire to her. The surf beating on the reef broke up her remains, so within a week or two there was nothing in sight on the beach to warn away the next captain if he didn't know his islands well enough.

The mate had been attacked by these devil's babies before. His ship had managed to keep them off and get away. But he was an old veteran, and he had known some who had not been so lucky.

They usually followed pretty much the same pattern, he explained. When the ship was under control and her skipper was looking over the island, with the idea of sending a boat in for water and provisions, the natives were friendly as could be. They came out in their canoes, bringing along their women. They invited the whole crew ashore and turned the island over to them. Then they struck.

If the ship had no wind—like now—they might still pretend to be friendly. But they might not bother with that if they thought there was no need for it. If they figured they could fight their way aboard, or if the ship were obviously going to break up on the reefs, well . . .

The two men looked out across the water again. The island had begun to take on shape, a dark fringe of green with a sloping white beach in front of it. And in front of that—the reef, with its creamy curl of surf where the Pacific beat against it.

What made these islands especially bad was when some white man started helping the natives. Every once in a while one of the convicts from the British penal colonies off Australia would escape and steal a boat big enough to work his way up to these waters. Somehow the cannibals seemed to know a fellow like that would be helpful, and instead of killing and eating him, they would make him a kind of local general.

That happened, the mate went on, at one of these islands. The mate knew about it because a good friend of his had barely escaped with his life from a band of savages led by a white man, somewhere in these waters. The friend's ship was the *Triton*, of New Bedford, and she was his first command. He had been cruising down along New Zealand, and he stood north for the Japan Grounds. That took him in among these islands. Whether it was Sydenham or not the mate didn't know. But anyway, his friend was not aware of the bad reputation of this area—it was many years ago. He took his own boat ashore. The natives gave him and his boat's crew a royal welcome. Anything they wanted was provided. It looked too good to be true. It was.

After nearly a full day of collecting provisions and water and letting his men have their fun, the skipper told his boat steerer to prepare to return. As soon as the crew had gathered about the boat, the natives jumped them, beat them up, bound them, and tossed them in a hut on the beach. That was the first time the strange white man made his appearance. He took the whaleboat and a group of natives and set out for the *Triton*. He timed everything carefully, so he arrived alongside the ship just after dark. Behind him came dozens of canoes with other savages, all armed.

It was a bloody night aboard the *Triton*. Before the first mate and the rest of the crew realized what had happened, the cannibals had control of the ship. Some of the *Triton's* men were bleeding to death on the deck, some were knocked out with the handles of scrub brooms, some were run through with harpoons and lances; and others were overboard, food for the sharks.

But the cannibals and their white leader didn't know that three or four of the men had managed to slip away and hide among the oil casks in the hold; and the third mate had hidden in one of the boats hanging on the davits. The third mate loosed one of the lances from the boat, slipped back on deck under the cover of the darkness, and stole up on the white leader of the mob. In one lunge he managed to drive the lance through the man, sticking him to the deck like a butterfly on a board. With their leader screaming and clawing at the lance but unable to get off his back, the terrified savages scampered behind the tryworks. The rest of the survivors came out of their hiding places and finished them off. It took two men to pull out the lance holding the white man to the deck. Then they chopped him up and fed the sharks with him.

And what happened to the captives ashore?

One of them was the mate's friend, the *Triton's* skipper. The men who had retaken the ship from the savages didn't dare return to the island for the captain and his boat's crew; they figured the natives had long since killed them anyway. But the islanders treated the captives perfectly well and sold them a few weeks later for some boxes of tobacco to another whaler that came by.

The mate of the *Morgan* snapped his head forward and raised the glass to his eye.

"Damn them," he said. "Here they come!"

Across the shimmering distance they looked like nothing more than specks dancing on the surface of the sea. But through the glass they were plainly canoes, slipping from the camouflage of the island and fanning out toward the ship like wasps leaving their nest. The two men at the masthead hung over the yardarm and watched them come. There were so many of them, apparently moving in and out of some formation, that it was impossible to count them. Either they were too far away to be heard yet, or they were completely silent, bent on their mission. Standing there on the platform high over the sea, watching the current carry the whaler toward the island and the black water bugs sweep toward them, the two men began to feel the frustration and panic that was soon to sweep the rest of the ship.

After a moment of paralyzed silence they shouted the warning to the deck. At once the rest of the crew erupted into action, swarming up the rigging for a look at the spectacle that was still out of sight on deck. At the sound of the commotion Captain Sampson appeared. Again all eyes were on him, all hands anxious to be busy at the preparations for defense. And now he was ready.

The two men at the lookout had only a few more minutes before their watch was finished. But by the time they were relieved and took a last look before climbing back down, the little formless shapes coming toward them had changed into miniature but clearly definable canoes.

The skipper was giving his swift commands; and the deck was a bustling mass of men, each one making himself as busy as possible, each one performing his task meticulously and elaborately. The steward and cabin boy were running up and down the companionway to the captain's cabin, bringing on deck every gun that could be found. As each weapon was dumped in the pile, more men grabbed them up, loaded them, and stacked them against the mizzenmast. Along both sides of the ship other men were swinging into the boats and unlashing harpoons, hatchets, knives, and lances. Impatiently waiting men took these and carried them to the tryworks amidships. There the harpoons and lances were stacked in line, handles projecting so they could be grasped in a hurry. On overhead racks that held the two spare boats were the cutting spades, made to slice away the toughest blubber and sharp enough to shave with. These were taken down and laid along the deck where they would be most handy, but out of the path of a man running the length of the deck; to stumble over one might mean shearing off every toe. More men were swinging out over the rail, hauling in every line and rope and chain that could help a monkeylike native scurry up the *Morgan's* sides. All over the deck, all through the lower rigging, men jostled each other, tripped over pieces of equipment being dragged across their paths, pinked each other with the ends of harpoons and lances, tangled in lines, clattered tubs, buckets, and barrels together to get them out of the way. Some yelled at each other. Some cursed softly as they worked. Occasionally one made a joke and laughed a little too loudly. Most were silent, working intently, their jaw muscles moving constantly. And now and then a man paused to look over the rail in the direction of the island.

From the deck the tree border and the white beach were in full view now. The ship seemed to be approaching the island with more speed than before. And the canoes were close enough so that the *Morgan's* men could make out the crouching outlines of the natives.

There was still plenty to do. At the captain's command, the mate called aloft for the men at the mastheads; there would be no use watching for whales during the next few hours. The boats were hauled up close to their davit heads; the defenders would have to reach down under the boats while twenty or more savages tried to clamber up the chain plates at the same time. The captain was everywhere at once, checking to see that the lances and cutting spades were placed most efficiently, peering over the bow to make sure some loose line had not been overlooked, directing the mate to get two more men to work on the waist boat, even lending a hand here and there himself.

The canoes had come close enough so that the attackers could be seen clearly. There were about two dozen canoes in the lead, the sun glinting off their paddles as they rose and fell rhythmically, swiftly, and silently. A few of the boats carried women, but most of them held five or six men each. The natives wore strings of beads and shells around their necks and waist, and nothing else. The color of their skin was an inky, evil blue-black. Behind the lead canoes was an armada that seemed to stretch all the way back to the island, six or seven miles away.

But now the *Morgan* was ready for them. The captain stationed the men along the bulwarks, working distance apart, each man armed with a lance or cutting spade. The ship was divided into fighting units; the second and third mates amidships with three boat steerers and a handful of men, the first mate at the bow with one boat steerer and a few less men. The captain took the quarterdeck with the fourth mate. The orders were passed forward: when the first blue-belly touched the ship's side, jab at him with a lance or spade. If he didn't push away, chop off his hand. But there should be no attempt to kill anyone, and no guns would be used—yet. Each man planted his legs firmly, leaned his waist against the rail, took a good grip on the handle of his weapon, and waited.

A hush fell over the ship. Still the savages made no outcry. In the silence the waiting men could hear the water washing alongside the ship, the regular dip-trickle of the paddles as they drove the canoes nearer and nearer to the whaler. But as the tension mounted aboard the *Morgan,* the men began to mutter to themselves and each other. A mate had to croak a low warning to some foremast hand obviously ready to shout an obscenity at the oncoming natives. Each man held his place, his eyes narrowed, his throat working as he swallowed, his hand white as he held onto his weapon. Raw fear was now upon the men of the *Morgan.*

More and more they swore to themselves, wiped the sweat from their eyes, spat over the side. One man shifted nervously, then urinated in the scuppers, followed by another, and another. A mate started to shout, "Belay that!" then thought better of it. The canoes were close enough so that the men could look down into them; and the word quickly passed down the line: "No guns." "No arrows." A few of the defenders sighed audibly.

With no sound but that incessant trickle-dip-trickle of the paddles, the few canoes in the lead swung alongside. Long, blue-black arms reached out toward chain plates, broken edges of copper sheating, anything that would provide a handhold. Flat faces, marked by grotesque whorls of tattooing and topped by close-cropped mats of frizzy black hair, looked up at the men ranged along the rail. The faces were expressionless, emotionless, leathery masks. Still not a sound came from their raw-red, full lips.

In unison, at no spoken command, the long, thin lances and cutting spades swung over the rail, their polished edges flashing in the hot sun. With a staccato, rolling rattle they sent splinters flying from the *Morgan's* side. Not a black hand was touched. But there was a rushing, splashing melee as the canoes shoved off. The natives' eyes bugged out. And as if it had been a signal, the air shivered with their ululating shrieks. The cry was taken up in the other canoes, now bearing down on the ship; and within a minute a hundred savage voices were screaming at the *Morgan.*

This was a battle cry long used and refined by the savages. It was intended to do more than vent rage at the enemy; it was supposed to make his flesh crawl, send tremors down his spine, frighten him as close as possible to momentary immobility. The war cry of the Pacific island savage was one of his weapons; many a warrior struck such paralying fear into his enemy with that shrill, bloodthirsty yell that his adversary was demoralized and, for an instant, was an open target for the spear or knife.

The Sydenham Islanders' battle cry could not serve its purpose against the men of the *Morgan;* there was no way to follow up the effect of the shrieking chorus. But the effect was there. While the defenders were too safe behind their stout bulwarks to be routed by the yell alone, they were momentarily terrorized by it. The din was all around the ship, but not on it. Aboard the *Morgan* no one spoke; no one shouted back at the caterwauling men in the canoes. The ship was an island of silence in a sea of bedlam.

The war cries gradually rose toward a crescendo as canoe after canoe joined the armada. It went on like this for two hours, while still more savages arrived, yelling louder and pressing in closer to the ship. When the last canoe joined the attacking force, the natives maneuvered into their battle formation.

A close-packed group gathered on each side of the ship. Both groups stretched twice the length of the ship, jammed five or six deep. There were at least five hundred attackers out there, screaming and waggling war clubs and spears. They had another weapon, one which made the men of the *Morgan* shudder at the thought of close combat. On a strip of coconut bark the natives had lashed a row of shark's teeth, sharpened so that one swipe across a man's face would saw through his nose and jaw and gouge out his eyes. As they sliced the air with these swords and yelled and formed and re-formed their groups, the men along the rails of the whaler still waited, silently, for the attack.

They did not have to wait long. But the first move of the natives was a surprise: a canoeload of women, with only enough men to handle the paddles, approached the ship in a belated and crude attempt to board the whaler by ruse. The defenders let them come alongside, then swung the cutting spades in long, whistling arcs, chopping slivers from the side of the canoe. The shrieking chorus swelled as the canoe was quickly paddled back into the line-up.

Then came attempts at intimidation, apparently designed to frighten the defenders and add to the effect of the war cries. In twos and threes canoes darted out of formation, headed for the ship and swung parallel to her but out of reach of the spades and lances. One or two men in each canoe stood up and swung a spear or shark's tooth sword around his head. Then others made the sign of decapitation, laughed grotesquely, and pointed to the island and its reefs.

The ship was now less than a mile from the island, the current carrying her along ponderously and inevitably toward it. The whalemen were close enough to make out the coconut trees, the grass houses, the white coral sand of the beach, and the crowd of men, women, and children gathered at the water's edge to watch the gruesome spectacle. And out from the sides of the island stretched the waiting arms of the reefs, the sea toppling in great breakers over the jagged coral.

It was at this point that the captain noticed a puzzling phenomenon. For the last hour the optical illusion had been one of a moving island, a mass of land and the outstretched arms of the reefs creeping down on an anchored ship. Now the island appeared to be moving in a slightly different direction—not quite so much toward them, a little more past them. The current that swept toward the island apparently swerved to go around it, either because of the backwater from the reefs or because its course was twisted by the shallows.

The men's ears had become accustomed to the pandemonium on the water around them and, at the same time, the tense silence aboard the whaler. So a few men jumped when the captain shouted the length of the deck to the mate.

"There's a good chance of getting clear after all!"

The mate studied the island for a moment, then answered, "Yes, we seem to draw by now faster than we drift on the land."

It was as if the savages could understand what was said. More war clubs waved in the air. The battle cries rang louder. A sound like thunder came across the water; they were thumping their paddles against the sides of their canoes. Then they attacked.

The skipper saw it first and yelled, "Look out for those fellows, there!" Half a dozen canoes had broken away from the formation and were coming for the whaler, the brawny, blue-black arms making the paddles flash and dig, flash and dig. At the same moment half a dozen more streaked out from the group on the other side and headed for the ship too.

The captain fitted a musket to his shoulder. "Don't let them stop alongside," he said. He was not shouting now. He spoke only loud enough to be heard over the screaming of the savages. Along the rails the men got into position, each one watching the canoes as they came on.

"Don't kill any," the captain reminded them again, "—if you can help it."

It took less than a minute. There was a crashing, bumping confusion along the water line on both sides of the *Morgan*, the grunting and heaving of the defenders as they swung their lances and spades, the yowl of a native pricked by a lance, the parabola of a spear soaring over the ship and hissing into the water on the other side, then the splash of the canoes as they shoved off. The attack had failed.

But the men along the bulwarks had hardly relaxed and rubbed their sweating arm across their sweating faces when they realized that it had only been a sparring, a preparation for the bigger assault. Now eight or ten canoes left the group on each side and came together a few boat's lengths away from the ship. This time they maneuvered slowly, taking their time to get into position. They gathered into two little knots on each side of the ship, the natives jabbering at each other.

The skipper had barely uttered his warning, "Look out, now!" when they raced for the ship.

Some made for the bow, some for the waist, some for the stern. Simultaneously the group on the other side followed the same pattern. With perfect timing, nearly a hundred savages hit the sides of the whaler at the same moment. As their shrieking reached its climax, half of the attackers dropped their paddles, grabbed at the chain plates and started to swarm up the sides. Over them, two dozen white men swung and cut and jabbed with their lances and spades as they never had at the body of a whale.

This time it was a bloody melee—no time now to make a warning swipe at the canoe or close to a native's head. With a scrambling mass of blue-black arms and shoulders swinging up against them, the whalemen could only try to chop them down. One after the other the writhing bodies plunged back into the canoes and the water, some with fingers and hands suddenly gone, a few with their arms amputated as neatly as on a surgeon's table. This second attack lasted two or three minutes. But when it was over, the departing canoes carried unconscious forms sprawled over the gunwales, blood pulsing in jets into the water. The sides of the *Morgan* dripped gore that made little colored pools in the clear blue sea.

Still the men of the *Morgan* did not shout or curse or laugh at the retreating enemy. A few looked sick, others leaned weakly against the rail. But the only sound was the diminishing war cry of the natives as they returned to their floating battle formation.

Would they try again? The defenders braced themselves for it and waited. But they did not.

Then the mate, leaning over the bow and studying the water below, explained why.

"A patch of coral!" he sang out. "Right across our bows and just under water. She'll never get over it!"

"How far are we from it?" yelled the captain.

"Only about three ship's lengths."

No wonder the natives were not regrouping for another attack. Either they knew about this strip of coral, lying like a trap just beneath the surface and nearly half a mile from the island and its reefs, or they had spotted it a minute or two before the mate. They were not attempting to attack; but their shouts were increasing again, and they were gleefully tossing their paddles in the air and catching them. The ship was close enough to the shore so the men could hear the natives on the beach, raising their voices in triumphant, jeering shrieks. Some of them broke into what looked like a victory dance.

So slow was the actual speed of the current carrying the *Morgan* that it would be fifteen minutes before she reached the submerged reef. All they could do was stand at their stations, sweat, and wait.

At his post on the quarter-deck the skipper paced from rail to rail, cradling a musket in his arms, watching the island, looking around the horizon for any last, God-sent breath of wind, and glancing warily at the crowing savages. As he looked at one of the flotillas, a single canoe slid across the water toward the ship and rounded to. A portly, gray-haired, dignified-looking figure rose, delivered himself of a jabbering oration, then turned his back and bowed low. His appreciative audience hooted even louder at this obscene insult. For an encore the stately savage repeated his oration, turned again, placed both hands on his hips, and bowed with a sweeping flourish.

This, finally, was too much for Captain Sampson. His musket was loaded with bird shot. As the broad, black, bare target glistened in the sun, he took careful aim and let go both barrels.

Just as slowly and gracefully as he had swept his insulting bow, the portly native arched over the side of the canoe and into the water. He did not come up. For an instant every shout stopped as if cut off; then the yelling redoubled.

But the natives kept their distance. And the *Morgan* eased steadily down on the submerged reef. Ten minutes were gone. During the next five every man aboard the whaler silently braced himself for the blow, a few closing their eyes and moving their lips soundlessly. A clump of coral seemed to move sluggishly by to starboard, then another, bigger one to port. Another appeared under the ship, just deep enough so that its highest branches snapped off against the keel. The ship drifted on. From as far aft as the waist the men could see the long, twisted mass of coral lying dead ahead, the water sucking over it in little eddies and whirlpools.

And then, less than a ship's length from the reef, the *Morgan's* bow began to swing. As they watched, eyes bulging and breath caught in their throats, the men at the starboard rail saw the red-brown obstruction slowly ease across the bow. The same coral reef that had seemed to draw them on like a magnet was now pushing them away. Like the current moving against the island, this one apparently drifted against the wall of coral and washed back from it; the ship, caught in the backwash, was being carried safely past the reef. And the same breathless calm that had almost destroyed the whaler was now saving her; had a breeze sprung up at this moment, blowing onto the reef, the *Morgan* would have piled up on the slashing coral before she had had time to wear off. Now the bottom dipped to ten feet, to fifteen feet. In less than ten minutes it dropped out of sight.

As suddenly as the battle had reversed, so did the scene. The savages, their prize gone, stopped their shrieking as if they had turned it off. A moment of peace and quiet fell on the sea—and then the three-hour-long, silent tension aboard the whaler finally burst. Shouting and laughing and jeering, waving their lances and whooping and shooting off their guns, the whalemen jumped all over the deck.

The Sydenham Island savages must have been mystified to hear the strange sounds of three rousing "Hip, Hip, Hoorays!" as they sat, silent and sullen in their canoes, and watched the *Charles W. Morgan* drift away from them, out into the open Pacific.

5. Trial by ice

There were other times when the *Charles W. Morgan* came nearly as close to tragedy as in the battle with Sydenham Island's cannibals—in fact, on the same voyage. Once a herd of whales was sighted in the midst of a storm so strong that Captain Sampson did not dare let his men lower for them. But the herd looked big, the whales rich and fat, and the mates of the *Morgan* pleaded with the captain until he finally let them go. Out across the house-high whitecaps they went; but the skipper had been right. It was such a long, hard chase that by nightfall three of the boats were still missing. Through the anxious night the *Morgan*, like the proverbial, worried mother hen, sought her lost chickens. Next morning, under a full gale, she found them. The boats were still fast to two big whales.

There were worse storms on this voyage, when chasing whales was out of the question and indeed the only question was survival. The seas ran high as the masthead and the big ship rode like a whale herself, more in the water than on top of it. The only thing to do was furl all sail, keep her running before the gale, and pray for sea room. The Pacific was not well charted even in the early 1850s, and what the captain thought was open water might well be a patch of tiny atolls and reefs. That was what happened when the *Morgan* got off the Friendly Islands in mid-Pacific below the equator. It was a full hurricane, with the wind making the rigging screech and threatening to blow a man right off the deck, lines parting with a sound like a pistol, deckloads of sea water roaring about the men's waists and a greenish-white phosphorescent wake heaving far astern. The wheel plunged against the lashings that bound it; two men could not hold it against the force of the storm, and its spinning spokes threatened to break their arms. It blew like this for more than twenty-four hours, each towering sea seeming about to overwhelm them before the *Morgan* inched forward just in time. Through the long, crashing night Captain Sampson stayed on his quarter-deck, pacing from side to side, his troubled frown periodically glowing in the darkness as he peered into the lighted binnacle. When the wind died, she finally rounded to, and the men crawled like wet rats out of their holes. The captain could not understand why the seas had gone smooth so suddenly; but the parting mist explained it. The *Morgan* had run blindly between two rock-edged islands, and now lay in the lee of one. A mile or two either way, and she would have struck one of them. Charging wildly before the hurricane as she had been, she would have crashed full speed onto a reef. There would probably not have been enough wreckage left for anyone to have known what became of the *Morgan*.

She not only survived such near tragedies, she brought home 1121 barrels of sperm oil that voyage, enough of a fortune for Captain John Sampson to retire. The *Morgan* didn't. She went out on thirty-seven voyages in all. She chased whales for seventy-five years. And when she tied up against a New Bedford dock for the last time, she had earned her various owners well over $2,000,000. Other whalers did as well. Other whalers had close calls, with whales, with storms, with cannibals. But the *Charles*

W. Morgan had the richest, fullest life of them all. She became the most famous ship in the history of American whaling.

You can see the *Charles W. Morgan* today. The only whaler still alive, she is moored alongside a dock at the Marine Historical Association in Mystic, Connecticut, and she is the biggest tourist attraction in the state of Connecticut. You can go aboard the *Morgan*. You can climb down into her dark forecastle, where the narrow bunks form a semicircle right at the bow of the ship and the boards are worn into hollows by the feet of the countless whalemen who tumbled out at the bellowed command from the deck. You can stoop over and waddle through the hold of the ship, where the smell of sperm oil still lingers, from row on row of casks that were stored there in the last century; that smell, long since absorbed into her timbers, will never leave her. You can poke into the after cabin, where the mates and captain lived in comparative splendor —all in a space that would not make a double stateroom in a modern liner. And then you can mount the companionway to the deck. There you can stand under the seemingly tangled mass of rigging that climbs up and up the three masts above you, swinging over spar after spar and reaching high in the sky where, even in this quiet harbor, sea birds wheel and float against the scudding clouds. And you can, for a fleeting moment, close your eyes, shut out the tourists around you, and perhaps hear, miles and years away, the flesh-crawling cry from the masthead: "Bloooows! Bloooooows! There she BLOOOOOOOOOOOOOOOOOOOWS!"

The *Morgan,* her sails stowed away, her barrel-bottom forever held tight in the sand, lies at her last mooring, the sole survivor of one of America's greatest eras. And she alone deserves to be the monument to that era. Whenever an old salt starts telling you that his father or grandfather sailed in the greatest whaler of them all, ask him about the *Morgan.* If he wasn't talking about the *Morgan* in the first place, he is a liar.

She had the skippers to match her—Sampson, Thomas Norton, Tristram Ripley, John Tinkham, George Smith, Thomas Sculliun, J. A. M. Earle—men who could take her crashing through the gales of Cape Horn, wear her off the becalmed atolls along the Line, send her frail boats driving after the huge, battling whales.

Yet one of the strangest ironies of her long, strange history was that her most famous skipper commanded her quarter-deck when her hull was fast aground. And this captain was famous for a feat he performed when he wasn't even aboard the *Morgan*.

His name was George Fred Tilton, "Captain Fred," a captain by right rather than by chauvinistic New England courtesy. When, at the end of the *Morgan's* long career, she was rescued from a ship's graveyard, imbedded in concrete at Fairhaven, Massachusetts, and made a whaling shrine, Captain Fred was her guardian. It was some years later when she was towed to her present resting place at Mystic; but while she was at Fairhaven, Captain Fred welcomed visitors aboard and explained the history and the workings of the ship. Captain Fred was a born storyteller, and he had spent most of his long life collecting the kind of experiences that were perfectly fitted to his talent. He had a piercing eye, a warm, subdued wit, and he knew with the exact timing of the master yarn spinner when to pause, light his pipe, and literally disappear behind a cloud of smoke just as he got to the important part of his story. So it was that many a visitor who came to see the *Morgan* stayed to hear Captain Fred. And so it was that another amazing chapter was added to the history of whaling, a chapter that, though told on the warm, worn deck of the *Morgan*, had nothing to do with the *Morgan* at all.

It happened to be one of the most extraordinary adventures in maritime history. As Captain Fred explained it, his eyebrows arching up as he lit his match and let it flare up over his pipe, it was the only time he knew of when a fellow *walked* back from the whaling grounds.

It was in 1887. George Fred Tilton was not a captain then. He was a young man serving aboard the whaleship *Belvedere*, hunting right whales near Point Barrow, far up in Alaskan waters 300 miles north of the Arctic Circle. The *Belvedere* was a 400-ton bark with steam auxiliary, five boats and a crew of forty-eight men. These ever-frigid waters were at the time the best grounds for the right whale, provider of inferior oil but excellent whale-bone, which was still being employed in hundreds of products besides corsets. For the whaleship owners and the more business-minded skippers the Arctic waters had one big advantage and one big disadvantage. The advantage was that during most of the summer season the sun hardly set, which meant that the lookout could do his job and the boats could be manned at any time, twenty-four hours of the day. The disadvantage was that only during the summer season could the whaleships cruise in these waters at all. The ships were usually fitted out in San Francisco, to get a head start; they set sail in late May or early June, went onto the grounds in late July, hunted the right whales through August, then got out fast before the freeze-up started in September.

The summer season of 1897 looked dangerously cold to Fred Tilton, with ice starting to form in some places even in August. But this was only his second voyage to the Arctic waters, so he could be wrong in estimating an early freeze-up. As it turned out, he was right.

Nearly all the little fleet of American whalers had gathered at Point Lay, about 200 miles north of the Arctic Circle, just a week or so before the season was due to end. Tilton's skipper was beginning to worry too, now; the ice was starting to choke the harbor entrances, the wind was blustering more than usual, and there was a wintry feeling in the air. He decided that the *Belvedere* had better start south.

He decided too late. In one direction the sea was already frozen solid. In another there were stretches of open water, but the winter gales were whirling down from the north, bringing with them enormous ice floes, so many of them that a ship could not get through them without being smashed. A few days earlier the ship might have made it; some of the fleet had. But the *Belvedere* and seven other whalers now had to sit in the harbor while, swiftly, the ice froze about them and the ships' timbers groaned in its grip. The crews climbed down onto the ice, lugged some lumber ashore, built houses, and prepared for a tough winter. Only a few men at a time stayed aboard the whalers as shipkeepers. That way not all of the crew would be lost if the pressure of the ice became too great and the ship collapsed like an eggshell.

Ashore, as soon as they had dug in and built their huts, the captains of the eight whalers held a council. There were nearly four hundred men to feed. They had provisions only for the two months it would have taken them to return to San Francisco. Now they had no hope of getting free until the next July, almost a full year. They estimated that by limiting everyone to two small meals a day, and by hunting deer, seal, and bear, they could keep alive. But it was obvious that many would die before summer came again. Scurvy, for one thing, was a certainty. And any communicable disease could decimate the fleet in a month. Even when summer came, they would be more than a month away from civilization and food. An American named Charles D. Brower kept a weather station near Point Barrow, but he did not have nearly enough food to help. When the ships failed to show up in San Francisco, their owners or the U. S. Government would undoubtedly plan to send a rescue expedition. But they might not. And even if they did, a late spring could delay the rescue ships until the whalemen were starving or dying of scurvy or some disease they were unable to treat. If many of them were to survive the winter, an overland expedition had to be sent up from the south.

Maybe just such an expedition would be forming up as soon as the whaleships were overdue. Probably the owners would realize the plight of their captains and crews and would start provisions, medicine, and perhaps even a doctor on the way overland. But to the men huddled in their huts on the shore of what had been the Arctic Ocean and was now ice as far as the eye could see, to the already jittery young foremast hands beginning to go sick with hunger and panic as they felt the wind try to whip their shelter away, to the tough old veterans already beginning to feud among themselves while they listened to the millions of tons of ice thundering out across the horizon, there was still the all-important question: how could they know? How could they be sure that such an expedition really would start out to save them?

The skippers realized there would be no getting through the winter if all they could do was sit and starve and wait for they knew not what. They were well aware that the only alternative was to send someone for help. But they knew that this was only part of the answer. The other part, the vital part, was—who?

That was when George Fred Tilton volunteered. He knew the danger; he knew that he had a lot less than a 50–50 chance; he knew how far it was, what Alaska was like at this time of year; he knew that even the Eskimos stayed close to their villages in this season. But he figured that anything was better than sitting up at the top of the world, starving, freezing, and going mad with the helpless waiting. So he offered to go south, 1700 miles overland across Alaska and British Columbia, for help.

One or two equally courageous—or foolhardy—whalemen offered to go with him. But Tilton politely refused their company. If the attempt failed, he explained with practical simplicity, one dead whaleman was enough. He did finally accept the proffered services of two Eskimos. They were from Siberia, and had shipped aboard one of the whalers, which had sunk under them. They had had experience in these latitudes, and they too preferred doing something to waiting helplessly.

Tilton equipped himself as best he could. The local Eskimos would gladly have traded their best dog team for a single barrel of flour; but that was the one commodity the whalemen could not spare. So they bought the dog team, paying about $300 per animal. The natives were somewhat baffled by the sled after Tilton had finished remodeling it. More a sloop on runners than a sled, she carried a single mast, complete with sail. They could hoist sail, Tilton figured, to slow their speed when going downhill into the wind. And when the wind was from astern on a smooth surface, they could all climb aboard, dogs included, and ride along until becalmed. At the little ice sloop's masthead flew the American Flag.

The party set off, to the cheers of the assembled fleet, on the morning of October 26. The sail was furled, but the flag whipped in the breeze. They had enough provisions for fifteen days, the length of time Tilton estimated it would take to reach Point Hope, 100 miles southwest on the coast. There he knew he would find a tiny settlement. He would buy or beg more provisions, push on to the next village, get what he could there, and so, step by step, work his way down the coast.

For two days the going was fine, with the sled running well, sometimes before the wind, the dogs pulling strong and all spirits high. But for two days only. On the night of the twenty-eighth they were at Icy Cape, when the first storm hit them, suffocating them in clouds of snow, covering the sled and nearly tearing the tent out of their grasp. All the next day they were weathered in, watching the intermittent storms and leaden skies, digging out after each snow flurry and hanging onto the tent as it danced in the howling wind. The thirtieth dawned clear; they got under way again.

They struck the Utukok River, and Tilton cautiously worked his way out onto the ice, testing it with his axe to make sure the swift current had not left a skim patch that would break under the sled. He found a way across, but in the process he lost the axe through the ice. This was the first real mishap of the trip; they would be badly hampered without an axe. On November 3, however, they stumbled upon an Eskimo village. It was deserted; evidently every inhabitant was off on a deer-hunting expedition while the good weather lasted. In one of the huts Tilton found an axe. He took it and left two boxes of cartridges in exchange—a good swap for some fortunate Eskimo.

For the next five days the going was comparatively easy again; the sail proved it usefulness on the downgrades, as Tilton had hoped it would. By hoisting it into the wind and using the brake, he could keep the sled from running onto the dogs, and he did not have to wear himself out hanging onto it as the Eskimos usually did. But the force of the wind, or the size of the sail, was not enough so they could all hop in and toboggan down the slopes. This was no joy ride.

Tilton and his guides realized that with full force on November 8. Another blizzard hit them, this one so strong that they could not pitch the tent. Expecting a wild night of hurricane winds, Tilton decided to build an igloo; here was a chance to put Eskimo guides' experience to use. He was startled to discover that they knew no more about making igloos than he. They had been

brought up in wooden houses; igloos belonged to their parents'
era. So Tilton and his Eskimos scooped a cave out of a snowbank,
tucked their sleeping bags into it and spent the night there. The
dogs dug their own pits.

The next day was the fifteenth of their trek, and they were behind schedule. Tilton estimated that they were still a considerable
distance from Point Hope. Their food was running low. At
10 A.M., when the storm showed signs of blowing itself out, they
got on their way. It was their longest day since their departure;
they kept going all morning, all afternoon, through the evening,
with still no sign of a settlement ahead. Finally, at midnight, they
came upon an Eskimo village. They were back of Cape Lisburne,
nearly fifty miles from Point Hope. The Eskimos were friendly
and helpful. They did not have much food, but Tilton traded
some more cartridges for a small seal.

Between this half-starved native settlement and Point Hope
lay a forbidding mountain. To skirt it along the coast looked too
dangerous; at this time of year it was almost impossible to tell
whether the land or water lay under the ice, and if they got too
far out, a huge cake might break off, with the wind blowing them
out to sea. So Tilton determined to find a way over the mountain.

Four days later he had given up and was back in the Eskimo
settlement, half frozen and nearly starved. Despite their own
short rations the natives gave him another seal. Tilton did not
dare hand out any more of his cartridges, so he fell back on an
old custom of whalemen in the Arctic: he repaid the Eskimos
with a written order on the *Belvedere* for a much-prized barrel
of flour. It was to be nearly a year before the I.O.U. was re-
deemed.

Unable to get over the mountain, Tilton was forced to go out
around it. And here, before he even finished the first leg of his
trek, Tilton almost died.

The first day, with his two guides and the dog team, he fought
his way forward from morning to night and made only fifteen
miles. Ice cut at their faces. The wind batted them over. When
their exertions made them breathe deeply, the cold was like a
knife in the lungs. Ten times in that one day they had to unload

everything and carry it so the struggling dogs could pull the sled up over the jagged hummocks that rose across their path. That night they camped on open ice, and nearly froze to death. The next day was just as bad, and the next night. On the third day they were desperate; only a few pieces of the seal meat were left. They pushed on, then came to a stop; they were halted by a stretch of open water.

As far as they could reconnoiter, there was no way around this water barrier. So Tilton put his ice sloop to work. Loading himself, guides, dogs, sled, and equipment on a floe, he unfurled the sail, anchored the sled, and let the wind blow their ice cake across to the other side. There the little expedition bedded down for the night. But now they had no food.

They had hardly got started again the next morning when they came to another barrier of open water. This time, though, an enormous floating piece of ice jammed itself across the stream; Tilton led his guides and dogs across in a headlong dash just before the floe worked its way loose and moved on downstream. By then it was only midafternoon; but all three men were so weak from hunger that they could go no farther that day.

By next morning they had been two and a half days with nothing to eat. They spotted an open patch of water with some ducks in it. There was a crazy race out onto the ice, a flurry of shooting and shouting. All except one of the ducks got away. While struggling back to shore they came upon the carcass of a dead whale. Despite the freezing weather the carcass appeared to be inedible; but the Eskimos cut off some meat anyway before hurrying back to land. Quickly chopping some driftwood out of the ice, they built a fire to cook the duck. Years later Tilton recalled, "I never ate anything better in my life." The Eskimos preferred the strong whale meat.

With renewed strength they were able to make a few more miles before pitching camp again. That night another hurricane came shrieking down on them. In one yowling gust it tore their tent to shreds. They dug into the snow alongside the dogs, huddled in their sleeping bags, and shivered through the night, hoping they would not be buried alive.

The storm was still raging in the morning, with the snow so blinding that the dogs could not work in it. There was no sign that the gale would let up, and starvation faced them again. They would have to leave the sled and dogs behind, try to come back for them after they had reached Point Hope.

Tilton tied the two guides to a line and started working along the coast. All they could do was push ahead blindly, leaning into the gale and forcing each foot to follow the other. To make sure they were not straying out over the water, Tilton kept digging through the ice. If he chopped down to a rock or a bush he was still on course; if water appeared in the hole he had to wear off inland before it was too late. Hour after hour the hurricane battered at them. They sucked ice for its moisture, but hunger was dimming their senses. Every few feet one of them fell, dragging his weakened companions down with him. Each time they managed to get back on their feet and struggle dumbly on. Finally both of the guides gave up. They lay down, moaned that they could not make their legs hold them any longer. Tilton argued with them. They paid no attention. He cursed them. They seemed not to hear him. He ordered them to get up. They refused.

Tilton hoisted each man back onto his feet, shook him, and slapped his face. They stayed up. He started on again, pulling them after him on the line. Again one of them fell, yanking the other down. But this time both got back on their feet and kept plodding after the hunched figure dimly ahead of them in the swirling snow. For another mile they straggled along after him, until finally Tilton fell. He tried to get up. He could not.

Then he realized what he had stumbled over. It was a snow tunnel, leading to the door of a house. They were in Point Hope.

All three men slithered through the tunnel, where they bumped into a sleeping dog. Tilton's pounding and the dog's howling promptly brought a man to the door. He opened it, looked down at the three figures hulking there on hands and knees, jumped back a step, and exclaimed, "For God's sake, where did you come from?"

Weaving, but back on his nearly frozen feet, Tilton told him. The man couldn't believe it. He led Tilton to a chair and got him

some coffee and hardtack. After some argument the weary whaleman convinced him. The Eskimos had long since stretched out
just inside the door and gone fast asleep.

Tilton's host, he recalled, was a Norwegian named Anderson,
and he ran a trading post at the settlement. He nursed Tilton,
who had a frostbitten toe, and the two guides, who had frostbitten ears and feet. After a few days, with a sled, team, and two
guides loaned him by Anderson, Tilton went in search of the dogs
he had had to leave behind. They were still where he had left
them, still alive—all but one. They found its remains on the way
back; it had been blown off a seventy-five-foot cliff.

Point Hope marked less than a third of Tilton's odyssey. But it
took him nine days to recover from his frostbitten toe, repair his
damaged equipment, and prepare to push on. Here his two guides
quit; their frostbite was much more serious, and they had had
enough. Tilton was able to find two more Eskimos, a man and
wife named Tickey and Canvanar. "Tickey was a good man,"
Tilton used to say, "and his wife was twice the man that he was."

It was the twenty-ninth of November, more than a month from
the time he had first set out from the frozen-in fleet, when Tilton
and his new guides started off again.

This time the way led out across cracking ice, around ponds
and lagoons, while wet snow pelted at them almost constantly.
Warmer weather seemed to make the trek as difficult and
hazardous as the below-zero temperatures had before. Tilton and
his new companions were hardly on their way when they found
themselves on a broad, apparently immovable floe, surrounded by
water. For three frightening days they searched for a path of
escape. They could find none. With no fuel on their bare stretch
of ice, they lived on canned meat and frozen fish. And when they
did get back on land again, they had to scramble and slosh their
way through more ponds and lagoons and more rotting ice. This
jagged terrain was murderous for the dogs. Tilton had bought
and begged sixteen of them at Point Hope. One by one their
feet were cut to pieces, and those that could hobble no farther
had to be shot and fed to the others. By December thirteenth
Tilton had reached another village. Of the sixteen dogs he had

started with two weeks before only nine were left. Nevertheless, when he found he could buy another sled at this village, he got it, dividing the load and the dogs.

Then they were hit by another blizzard, a howling, freezing storm that pinned them down and almost froze them all. But it cleared. They kept on the move again, south again.

It was Christmas Day when they reached the Buckland River. Tilton took a few hours off that day, and the three travelers squatted down to a Christmas dinner they had saved for the occasion. With unaccustomed splendor they dined on pork and beans, fried fish, fried bacon, bread, and a tin of preserved California grapes. Tilton had coffee; Tickey and Canvanar preferred tea.

Along the river the going was better; they made thirty miles a day. But when they crossed over and struck across country, they met trouble again. The snow was so impassable that they had to break the trail for the dogs, and the weather was so cold that when the work exhausted them they could not ride on the sleds; the sweat inside their heavy clothing would have frozen if they had not kept moving. The food began to give out. It got so low that they barely had enough for themselves. When two of the dogs weakened, Tilton had to kill them to feed the others. But finally, near dusk on December 28, two months from the time he had left the trapped whalers, Tilton reached the farther side of Norton Sound.

He had completed nearly half of his trek.

It was an easier journey on down to Unalakleet and then to St. Michael. But at St. Michael Tilton discovered that he had lost a day in his reckoning; although he had thought it was January 6, it was January 7. And he and his Eskimos were nearly at the end of their endurance. Canvanar was sick, and Tickey was sick out of sympathy for his wife. It took twelve days for them to recover. But Tilton could not give up; he rested, nursed his two Eskimos back to health, bought another sled and team. Then he set out again.

His plan was to strike for the Yukon River and follow it up to Dawson. But when he reached the big river he found three steamers, frozen in. This meant that provisions for the winter were getting to Dawson only on sleds and men's backs; there would be nothing to spare for three hungry travelers. He changed his course and cut across country.

It was 57 degrees below zero—"no weather for haying," he used to say—when he set out to climb the towering mountains of the Alaska Range. It took him five days to fight his way to them, and four days of hunting, exploring, and backtracking before he could find a pass. The cut was twenty miles long, but it took them three days to get through. Jagged rocks and huge drifts barred their way. It was light for only four or five hours a day. By the time they reached the other side, they were so worn out that they had to pitch camp and rest for forty-eight hours.

Then they set out across the high tableland, making good time. When they struck a big lake, Tilton promptly piled everything, dogs included, aboard the sleds and hoisted sail. Hauling in and paying out the sheets before the blustery wind, they sped across the lake. There they found a tiny Eskimo settlement.

Of the twenty-nine dogs Tilton had had at St. Michael eighteen were left. So he traded one of the sleds for more food, and struck out again. His destination this time: the Gulf of Alaska and the Pacific Ocean.

It took him twenty-one days, three weeks during which blizzards battered the straggling little train every other day. Sometimes the wind came on so strong that it knocked the dogs off their feet. The storms alternated with warm spells that turned their path to ice pudding. But when they had waded hip-deep through the last tumbling river, they were at Katmai, on the south coast. Before them lay the waters of Shelikof Strait, rolling down to the Pacific.

Across the strait was Kodiak Island, and on the island, Tilton knew, were a number of villages. There he expected to find a schooner or sloop; if he could charter one, he could sail to the nearest big town on the gulf and pick up a steamer for the U.S. But how to get across the strait?

There was a small Eskimo village, but no one there knew where he could find anything big enough to take three people across the strait. Tilton poked along the deserted shore until he found an abandoned dory. It was so leaky, he recalled later, that it "wouldn't hold pumpkins. Her seams had opened so that when I looked at it I felt that a man would fall through if he wasn't too beamy."

But it would have to do. Tilton gave away his dogs among the natives and set to work patching up the dory. Tearing the sled apart, he strengthened the dory's sides with the lashings. His deerskin suit and his only set of heavy underwear, which had served him so well on his overland journey, now provided the caulking for the dory's gaping seams. At daybreak on March 17 the dory and its three sailors splashed out into Shelikof Strait.

It was thirty-seven miles across to Kodiak Island. Every whaleman knew those straits; they were to be avoided if at all possible. When the wind made against the current roaring through that passageway, the sea could run too high even for a whaleship. But luck was with Tilton; he had picked one of the rare calm days on the strait.

It was the longest row he ever had, though. He started at dawn, kept the oars digging all morning, past noon, while Canvanar spooned food and water into his mouth, and all afternoon. His shoulders quivered with the pain, his gulping breath seared his throat, and where blisters had formed and broken on his hands, smears of blood made the oars slip in his grasp. Tickey and Canvanar spelled each other at the bailer; with the sea sloshing in at nearly every dip of the dory and streams trickling through the makeshift caulking they could never relax. It was two hours before sunset when they finally nudged ground on Kodiak Island. They limped out on the beach, wrestled the dory above the high-water line and set up camp. At dusk Tilton stood studying the expanse of water he had just crossed. He had made it with not much time to spare. Now the powerful tide was racing out, a wind had sprung up against it, and the boiling, angry sea was a frightening sight.

For the next four days Tilton and his two guides rowed along the coast of Kodiak Island, poking into each sheltered bay, looking for a town. Every hour or so they pulled onshore to dump out the water that had begun to fill the dory despite their constant bailing. Tilton was back in his element. But this ceaseless rowing and fighting to keep the leaky old boat from sinking under them was beginning to wear him down. Tickey and Canvanar, who had been stolidly uncomplaining no matter what the hardship or danger, finally began to mutter to each other. But Tilton kept the oars creaking steadily. He knew that sooner or later they would find an inhabited town, and transportation to the States.

He found his town on March 22, 1898. He had traveled 1200 miles, by foot, sled, and ice floe; he had been on his way five months. Now he came into St. Pauls Harbor, Kodiak Island, where there was a whaling station of the Alaska Commercial Co. More important, a schooner rode at anchor in the harbor.

Tilton found the schooner's owner. His name was Herron, as Tilton remembered it, and he ran the whaling station. Yes, Herron was sure that only 200 miles across the gulf, in Prince William Sound, Tilton could make contact with one of the many steamers running prospectors up to Anchorage and the gold fields of the Yukon. Herron would charter his schooner, with captain, to Tilton so he could get across the Gulf. But the price would be $7000.

Tilton argued a bit, but it was obvious that the owner of the schooner knew he had the whaleman where he wanted him. Tilton thought back over his long trek, of the white traders who had given him provisions, equipment, and dogs, of the Eskimos who had dipped into their dwindling supplies to give him food. "I hadn't realized until then," he used to tell the tourists on the *Morgan*, "that I had reached civilization."

With no alternative he chartered the schooner and signed a contract that pledged the owner of the *Belvedere* to pay the $7000, knowing full well that Mr. Herron would have his well-deserved troubles trying to collect. Tickey and Canvanar did not look with favor on the prospect of an open-water voyage after that trip across the strait; but they stuck by Tilton and reluctantly climbed aboard.

Tilton had thought that this last leg of his journey would be a simple one. But he was mistaken. They were not six hours out when the schooner rocked over under a northwest gale. It was strong enough to "blow the hair off a dog," he used to say, and they could not carry sail in it. They ran before it until it blew itself out. But then the schooner's captain turned out to be no navigator. They were out of sight of land, and the captain had no idea where they were. Tilton took over and, by following the stars and dead reckoning, got them back on course for Prince William Sound. Their first landfall was barely in sight when the next gale hit them. Tilton had had enough; refusing to turn and run before it again, he reefed the schooner down and fought through the deck-smashing seas to the nearest sheltered harbor.

Here his good luck returned. The gasoline schooner *Albion* had put in to the same harbor for shelter and had gone aground. But the next tide floated her. And she was bound for Portland, Oregon.

Still followed by faithful Tickey and Canvanar, Tilton shipped south aboard the *Albion*. When the gasoline schooner chugged into Portland, none of his equipment was left. His provisions, his sleds, his dogs were gone. All he had now were the Eskimo couple and fifty cents in his pocket. Behind him lay 1700 miles of blizzards, rotting ice, starvation, frostbite, and gales at sea. It had taken him five and one-half months. But he had made it.

Yet his odyssey had been in vain.

There had been no way he could have forseen it, but the U. S. Revenue Cutter Service had gone to the rescue of the trapped whalers. While Tilton was fighting his way south, three men of the Revenue Cutter Service were going north, also overland. Their plan was to push up the coast to Cape Prince of Wales, just below the Arctic Circle. There they would round up some of the Cape's famous reindeer herds, then drive them the rest of the way up the coast to Point Lay to provide the needed extra rations. The plan succeeded, and since one of the men on the rescue expedition was a doctor, the sick and scurvy-ridden were treated as well. The stranded whalemen were helped too by the loyal Eskimos who worked for Charles Brower at his weather station. Despite the winter storms they went off into the frozen wilderness and returned with enough reindeer to keep the whalemen fairly well provided for until the rescue expedition arrived. It turned out to be one of the best reindeer-hunting seasons in years. By midsummer the last whaler was free from the ice and headed south.

But meanwhile there was George Fred Tilton in Portland, Oregon, broke, unknown, and with two homesick Eskimos on his hands. He wired the *Belvedere's* owner in Boston, William J. Lewis, to announce his arrival, tell the plight of the whalemen, and ask for money. Back came a telegram to the effect that this man must be an impostor. No one could have made such a trek. If indeed this was Tilton, Lewis wired, he had obviously deserted the *Belvedere* before she went north a year ago.

Tilton was not stumped yet. Years before, he had left the sum of $450 with a ship chandler in San Francisco, as a "little sheet anchor to windward." Now he wired for the money, got it, and boarded the next steamer for San Francisco. The *Belvedere's* owner had agents there; Tilton was sure he could convince them and get a relief expedition headed north, even though help could not reach Point Lay now until the end of June.

Tilton was beginning to have his troubles with Tickey and Canvanar. They had never seen anything remotely like Portland, and they were popeyed from morning to night. By the time the three boarded the steamer, Tilton was so tired of answering questions that he had to lock himself in his stateroom, "to keep from being talked to death."

He did not know it until later, but on April 17, 1898, the same day his fantastic journey finally came to an end in San Francisco, the Revenue Cutter Service expedition was beating its way into Point Lay, with fresh reindeer and medicines and new hope for the whalemen who had sat out the long winter night north of the Arctic Circle.

Tilton found the agents for the *Belvedere's* owner easier to convince. It was obviously Tilton who stomped into their office; he showed the effects of his long trek; and he had the Eskimos to prove his story. The agents immediately equipped a merchant ship with supplies and sent it racing north. Then they wired William Lewis. The answer was delayed a bit, but when it came,

Mr. Lewis authorized the agents to give Tilton $100, in exchange for an I.O.U. "Pretty generous, wasn't he?" Tilton used to say. With the $100 he sent his faithful Eskimo guides back home by ship. The spectacle of San Francisco had more than surprised them; it had scared the daylights out of them. They were glad to be on their way back to the little trading post at Point Hope.

Years later, as shipkeeper and skipper of the grounded *Charles W. Morgan*, Captain Fred used to give his account of this spectacular odyssey, pause, light a match to his pipe, and then recall one more little thing. He had, he said, received a letter from Mr. Lewis. The owner asked him to go back north and rejoin his ship that spring.

Tilton puffed at his pipe, disappeared behind the cloud of smoke, and flicked out the match. "He didn't say how I was to get there," he remarked. "So I wrote and asked him if he wanted me to walk back."

Another cloud of smoke, as he leaned back against the *Morgan's* mainmast. "But," he said, "I didn't get any answer."

6. Tyrants, marooners, and kindly old souls

George Fred Tilton did go back. And nine years later, still making annual cruises north of the Arctic Circle, he was Captain Tilton. His ship was the *Bowhead*. Like the *Belvedere* of his younger days, she fitted out every spring, sailed and steamed up into Alaskan waters to hunt right whales for their bone, then got out just before the ice formed in September.

Captain Fred was known in forecastles all through the fleet. The story of Tilton's walk home from the Arctic Circle had been told, in gam after gam, wherever whaleships met. Everyone knew that Captain Fred was as tough as whale hide. He ran a taut ship. He was fair; he asked no more than he could perform himself. Of course that was a lot more than normal. But everyone knew that life aboard the *Bowhead*, rigorous enough for the man who pulled his oar, could be pretty rough for the slacker or troublemaker. Everyone knew it, that is, except landlubbers.

That was the trouble with the fellow who shipped aboard the *Bowhead* one spring day in 1907, while she lay at her dock fitting out for her next cruise north. The man had been serving a fifteen-year stretch in San Quentin prison. But he figured he was too smart for that, so he broke out and made a run for it. He worked his way to San Francisco without getting caught, whereupon he discovered the fleet of whalers. Here, he realized, was a real opportunity to escape pursuit. So long as he used a new name and kept his real identity secret, he was safe. And not only would he be out of reach of the law for the summer, but he was told that these whalers sometimes got in close enough to the coast of Russia or Alaska so that he could steal a whaleboat and slip ashore. Even from the Russian coast he figured he could find passage on some ship that would take him down past the Kurils to Japan and the exotic Far East. Congratulating himself on his wisdom and good fortune, he picked out the likeliest-looking whaler and offered his services. His mistake was that he chose the *Bowhead.*

These were the days when good whalemen were hard to come by, and the skippers were forced to take nearly anyone they could get. So some pretty ornery beachcombers got aboard the *Bowhead* every season; but Captain Fred had long since learned how to handle them. As it developed, he knew how to handle this one too. It took the *Bowhead's* new hand only a short time to discover that he was not going to have any vacation cruise. But he was imprisoned aboard the whaler just as surely as if he were still back at San Quentin. So he temporarily made the best of his bad bargain, meanwhile plotting his escape for the first time any promising shore appeared on the horizon. He found that one man alone in a whaleboat was virtually helpless, and that he would need at least two companions for the long row to land. Proceeding with great care, he found his men, three of them. Cautiously, secretly, they worked out their plot. There was no chance of sneaking any guns or ammunition out of the main cabin; Captain Fred was too smart for that. But the *Bowhead* carried blasting powder, for breaking out of ice blocks. The four men managed to purloin some of the powder, which they rolled in newspapers and fitted with fuses to make crude bombs. They selected their whaleboat, got their gear ready, argued over the details of the break until all four were agreed and each man knew his job. Then they waited.

They had a long wait. It was two months from the time they left San Francisco before the *Bowhead* came in sight of land that looked right to the convict. But even this chance presented a dilemma. Captain Fred knew nothing of the plans for the break; but he knew his beachcombers. The *Bowhead's* course was set so that although she was cruising near the Russian coast at daylight, she gradually left it astern during the day; by nightfall land would be below the horizon. The convict knew that the opportunity might not present itself again for weeks. So he decided to take his chance while he had it. That was another mistake.

He and his fellow conspirators waited only until Captain Fred was below for dinner. Then they slung their ready-packed sea bags over their shoulders and went swiftly to the whaleboat. It took only a minute for them to clamber in, loose the lines, and drop the boat to the water.

But they had moved a little too fast. The whaleboat's bottom had a plug, which was pulled out while it hung on the davits so the water would drain out. In their haste the escapees had forgotten to replace it. Now one man had to shove his thumb in the hole while the others scrambled about looking for the plug. By the time they found it and got it in place, they had wasted only another minute. But that was all the time Captain Fred needed.

The moment the boat's bottom had touched water his keen ears had heard it. He was on deck in three bounds, and he sized up the situation even before he reached the *Bowhead's* rail. While everyone else aboard stood and stared in surprise, Captain Fred went into action.

He took one vaulting leap, clearing the waist-high bulwarks of the ship and landing catlike in the whaleboat amid the startled deserters. Before they could duck out of reach, he had grabbed

up the nearest weapon handy; it was one of the wadded newspapers, and in one swinging swat he broke it over the head of the
closest man. When black powder sprayed out of the mashed
newspaper, Captain Fred got angry. Bounding to the stern of the
whaleboat, he seized the long, heavy steering oar and waggled it
over his head like a club; it whistled through the air over them
as the deserters cowered in the boat. Paddle alongside the ship,
Captain Fred warned them, or he would brain all hands. They
paddled.

Back aboard the *Bowhead*, with the whaleboat once more
swinging on its davits—plug out and draining—Captain Fred
lined up his four recalcitrant seamen and asked a few questions.
Singling out the ringleader, he dismissed the other three and
confronted the rebellious convict. Captain Fred would, he explained, give the man three alternatives: (1) He could be put
in irons for the rest of the cruise, on bread and water twice a day.
(2) He could turn to, get his three meals a day as long as he
worked the ship, and be put in irons every night. (3) Or he could
fight it out with the captain in the waist of the ship. If he won,
he could have a whaleboat to go wherever he liked; if he lost, he
would turn to and try no more tricks.

The convict was a broad-shouldered, burly brute, hardened by
his years at San Quentin and two months of pulling an oar in the
Bowhead's boats. So, out of a misguided self-assurance, he chose
the third course.

With the first mate as referee the two men removed their shirts
and squared off. It took only a few minutes. Captain Fred mashed
the man to a pulp. The loser had to be carried to his bunk, and he
failed to live up to his part of the bargain only because it was a
week before he could stumble on deck again. Captain Fred had
no more trouble with him.

A month after the abortive escape the *Bowhead* dropped
anchor off Cape Nome. There two police officers, who had
tracked the convict to the *Bowhead* and figured she would put
in at this harbor, were waiting for their man. Captain Fred had
not known until now that he had an escaped prisoner aboard; but

he assembled the crew, let the officers pick out the man, and take him ashore.

It was one of the few cases in San Quentin's history in which an escaped convict was glad to get back.

The man from San Quentin probably did not appreciate it, but he had been taught an important fact about the skippers of the whaleships: they were different. They were brave and they were tough, some brutal and some just. But so were the captains of the packets, the clippers, and the frigates. What the whaling skippers seemed to have besides these qualities was a kind of immediate resourcefulness, an ability to be equal to almost any situation, to handle the emergency promptly, with a minimum of fuss, and move on to the next problem. They got this way through a process of selection, mostly. It took only a few cruises to separate those who had the talent from those who did not. One or two turns at the steering oar of a whaleboat were some-times enough by themselves—with the bow nudging up against a rolling mountain of flesh and a split-second decision meaning the difference between another catch and death for half the boat's crew. A multitude of near disasters continually tested each skipper —cannibals swarming around the becalmed ship, as they did around the *Morgan;* two whaleboats being smashed simultane-ously by whales, with not enough wind for the ship to work her way down in time to save the men; a line, made fast to a whale, looping around a man's leg and whipping him beneath the sur-face before he even had time to cry out; a spark from the try-works almost sending a flash fire the length of the oil-washed deck; and the rarer, extreme challenge, like the sinking of the *Essex* more than 3000 miles from land or the ice trapping a whole fleet north of the Arctic Circle. The men who could meet these tests and without hesitation make the right decision went on to become whaling skippers; the rest stayed ashore, if they got ashore.

There were enough of these challenges in the nature of their occupation alone. But there were others as well, especially when the U.S. was at war or on the brink of war. Here too the whaling skippers proved their ingenious and contrary resourcefulness. In the few years before the War of 1812 the captains of all kinds of American ships were constantly in trouble with British skippers, who were forever trying to abduct U.S. sailors on the pretext that they were British subjects. So whenever British and American captains met in a neutral port, the atmosphere was understandably tense. Sometimes sarcasm led to insult and insult led to actual fisticuffs. This was especially true with the independent, ornery whalemen. All along the coasts of South America, British and American whalers dropped anchor alongside each other; and rarely was the town big enough for both the skippers, not to mention the brawling crews.

Which is where the whaling skippers' resourcefulness came in. Sometimes a particularly violent argument between a British and an American captain was settled promptly in the nearest alley or right at the bar. This was not always the case, since even whaling captains who were also Britons felt it beneath their dignity to engage in brawls. Their customary procedure was the challenge to a duel, complete with seconds, choice of weapons, and the meeting at dawn on the field of honor. But although this was a time when many Americans still regarded the duel as honorable and its punctilious rules as sacred, most U.S. whaling skippers viewed all the attendant protocol with amusement.

Accordingly one New England captain, after insulting a particular British captain to the best of his ability, which was considerable, accepted the challenge with studied decorum. He delegated his second, promised satisfaction, and accepted the chosen location. But his challenger was not a whaleman. And the American, as the challenged party, had the choice of weapons. He chose harpoons. One look at the whaleman poised on the dueling ground, the polished point of his harpoon flashing in the early sun, and the challenger changed his mind.

Another American whaling skipper found himself in a little more difficult situation. He had chosen to insult a Briton who was also a whaling captain. He was equal to the occasion, however. He chose pistols, proposed a dueling ground which he knew and his opponent did not, and insisted on twice the usual number of paces. When the two met, the Briton found himself on the crest of a hill; and when they had paced off the distance, neither could see the other, much less hit him. To the sputtering protests of the Briton the American argued, still with a straight face, that the challenger had agreed to the rules. They had been followed to the letter. Surely it was not proper to change them in the middle of the duel. Satisfaction, he concluded, had now been given. With unaccustomed dignity he stalked off.

There were, of course, times when no amount of ingenuity could overcome a situation that had been impossible from the start. Even then, however, the whaling skipper did his best. The story of Captain Thomas G. Young is a tragic one, because he never had a chance and he knew it. There are many versions of the story, but as best it can be pieced together it is a tale of bravery on the high seas, stubborn and praiseworthy resistance against impossible odds, and courage that, for the moment, stopped the conquering enemy in his tracks.

Captain Young never had a chance because he had sail and the enemy had steam, because he had an unarmed whaler and the enemy had a warship. It was during the Civil War, when the leaders of the Confederacy had decided to try to cut off the fuel supply of the north. In the 1860s that meant whale oil. So the Confederate cruiser *Shenandoah*, Captain James Waddell, steamed down around the Horn and into the Pacific, searching out every Yankee whaler she could find. The procedure was cruelly routine; when a slow-moving whaler was discovered, the *Shenandoah* steamed smartly alongside, boats were sent over for captain and crew, and the whaleship was touched off. The highly inflammable whale oil did the rest. One by one Captain Waddell caught up with the whalers of the Yankee fleet and burned them, while thousands of barrels of painfully collected whale oil went up in clouds of greasy, black smoke. It was so simple it was almost boring.

The greatest catch of the cruise was an entire fleet of whalers crowded together in a harbor in Bering Strait. Swooping down on the huddled ships, Captain Waddell quickly captured eight of them. But then he tried to take the ninth.

She was the *Favorite*, out of Fairhaven, Massachusetts, and her master was Captain Young. She looked to be as easy a prize as all the others when the *Shenandoah's* boat went over the side. The oarsmen took their positions. A young officer seated himself in the stern sheets. The boat shoved off and the oars swung down. The boat crawled across the harbor to the *Favorite*, hauled alongside, and the oars were peaked. The officer looked up at the whaler's quarter-deck and got the surprise of his young life.

At the rail stood Captain Young. His legs were wide-spread; his face was grim; and his arms cradled a whaling gun. Its sharp, barbed lance was aimed straight at the Confederate officer.

With accustomed Southern gallantry the officer called politely: "We came to inform you, sir, that your vessel is a prize of the Confederate steamer *Shenandoah*."

With accustomed Yankee cussedness Captain Young replied: "I'll be damned if she is."

There was a moment's silence, broken by Captain Young. "And now," he said, "keep off, or I'll fire into you." He waved the vicious-looking gun for emphasis.

The young Southerner from the *Shenandoah* did not know what his next move should be. One thing he did know: clearly, there was no precedent for this. He ordered the boat about and was rowed back to the *Shenandoah*. He reported to Captain Waddell, who ordered the *Shenandoah* to steam up alongside the whaler, her guns ready.

Captain Young was still leaning against the rail, still waving his whaling gun. Waddell called across the water.

"You will kindly haul down your flag."

"Haul it down yourself, God damn you," was the reply. The gun leveled on Captain Waddell.

The Confederate captain knew his rights; after all, who was capturing whom? His voice grew properly harsh and authoritarian.

"If you don't haul it down, we'll blow you out of the water!"

The answer from Captain Young, had it not been for the utter hopelessness of his situation, might have been one of the remembered war cries of U.S. history. It was, simply:

"Blow away, my buck."

But nobody blew away. The *Shenandoah's* sailors rowed over and swarmed aboard the whaler. Soon Captain Young's arms were pinned behind his back. To some unknown but more discreet members of the *Favorite's* crew they owed their lives—Captain Young's whaling gun, obviously unbeknownst to him, had been disabled. Still, they had to truss up the captain and lower him over the side of his ship with a block and tackle before they could row him across to the *Shenandoah*.

There Captain Waddell stepped up to greet him and discovered the cause of the entire incident, the mundane explanation for the seemingly indomitable act of courage.

Captain Young's gun may not have been loaded; but he was.

The courage, direct action, and stubborn tenacity of Captain Young did not pay off. Indeed, it apparently did not even win the respect of his captors—he claimed that while he was a prisoner aboard the *Shenandoah* somebody stole his watch. And a further, bitter irony of his story was that, although neither he nor Captain Waddell knew it at the time, the Civil War had been over for more than a month. Nevertheless it was usually the creed of the whaling skipper to keep fighting, down to the last possible moment, even if he had nothing to fortify himself with but a whaling gun and a bottle of rum. Captain Young lost his ship, as he had figured he would. But nobody could say he hadn't tried. Some thirty years later another whaling skipper found himself in just as impossible a situation. He too kept fighting to the end, in his own way. He probably figured he would lose, just as Captain Young had. But nobody was going to say he hadn't tried. He tried for ten years.

He was Captain Thomas Scullun, master of the *Cape Horn Pigeon,* and he was in the Okhotsk Sea hunting right whales, in the summer of 1892. At 3:30 A.M., on September 10, a Russian naval craft suddenly hailed the *Cape Horn Pigeon,* a naval officer came aboard and brusquely demanded that the captain be roused. Still wiping sleep from his eyes, Captain Scullun listened as his visitor informed him that foreigners had no right in these waters.

Captain Scullun did not say so right away, but he knew better. He had been cruising this area for three seasons; and he knew that seventeen years before the Russian Government had admitted to a British captain that Russia's jurisdiction did not extend beyond the three-mile limit. Captain Scullun was a lot more than three miles offshore.

After listening for a while he imparted this information to the Russian officer, and discovered that it made no difference whatever. He and the *Cape Horn Pigeon* would have to put into Vladivostok Harbor; there they would argue the case. Captain Scullun was about to argue the case, with force if need be, right there on deck. But then he had a better idea.

He followed the Russian ship to Vladivostok. There, while firm, he was formal and polite. Calmly he let the Russians haggle and argue and remonstrate with him about defiling their territorial waters with his whaleship. This went on until September 19, nine days after the *Cape Horn Pigeon* had been boarded by the naval officer. At that point the admiral in charge of the area put in a belated appearance; he promptly announced that Captain Scullun was free to go now.

There Scullun had him. The Russians, who had been so punctilious about foreigners entering their waters, were now letting him go without punishment. Therefore, he pointed out, they now realized that he had *not* been inside the three-mile limit. Captain Scullun made it clear that he did indeed respect the Russians' position; had he not shown his good faith by bringing his ship to Vladivostok? So naturally, he said, he knew that the Russians would respect his rights too. Accordingly he would submit a bill for the expense he had incurred by staying in the harbor while the Russians considered the case.

The admiral, doubtless feeling he had nothing to lose, replied that if the American captain would present an itemized bill, he would be glad to submit it to his government.

That was all Scullun wanted for the moment. Returning to his cabin, he made out his bill. The actual expense amounted to little. But what made it a large bill was the reason Captain Scullun had had for bringing the matter up in the first place. The delay in

Vladivostok meant that he was unable to go north and complete
the season's cruise. Whether he would have made a good catch
or not he had no way of knowing; but to discuss such a matter
would needlessly clutter up what was supposed to be a simple
bill. He merely listed the value of what would have been a very
good catch, and added it to the other expenses. "Total," he wrote
at the bottom, "United States Gold, $49,500." Then he submitted
his bill, hoisted anchor, and sailed home.

The Russian Government naturally filed the bill away and
forgot it. But they had not reckoned with Captain Scullun. He
had known when to use his wits instead of his fists or guns. And
he knew when to be just plain stubborn.

Through the owners of his ship he referred the matter of the
unpaid bill to the U.S. Minister to Russia. The Russians promptly
started procrastinating. That was fine, because they had now admitted they should pay it sometime; and Captain Scullun was in
no hurry.

He waited a year, then asked the minister to call it to their
attention again. This time the Russians announced that a committee had been appointed to look into the matter. Silence, so
Captain Scullun and his owners needled them again. The answer
was that the committee had just finished its investigation. There
had been a misunderstanding; the *Cape Horn Pigeon* was officially
released. Fine, thank you, was the reply. And now, about the
bill . . .

There was another delay. Captain Scullun let it be known again
that he was in no great hurry, but he made it plain that he would
never quit reminding them. The Russians replied that $2500
seemed to them a more realistic figure than $49,500. Captain
Scullun and the owners answered calmly that they had submitted
a bill, not a bargaining figure. Please remit.

The Russians delayed some more, and Captain Scullun and
the owners waited patiently, meanwhile reminding them periodically. It was two years from the time of the incident when the
Russians came up with a request for expense vouchers. Captain
Scullun answered that it was too late now, adding the implication
that the admiral who had not asked for them at the time must

not have known his business very well. The Russians retreated again.

Four more years went by, while the Russians tried to be more stubborn than Captain Scullun. They might have succeeded, if they had been as truculent under the Czar as they are today, and if Scullun had not kept the U.S. Minister hounding them politely, patiently, but unceasingly. It was now eight years since the incident, and the matter had obviously become a test of endurance, a measure of who could be more stubborn, the Russians or the Yankee whaling skipper.

The last desperate stratagem of the Russians amounted to a confession that they had lost the battle. Finally, wearily, they agreed to arbitration of what they still tried to call "the claim." The arbitration hearing was set in the Netherlands, which meant that counsel and witnesses would have to be sent from New England. The Russians should have known better by now. Counsel and witnesses were sent.

In November of 1902, more than ten years after the Russian naval officer had boarded the *Cape Horn Pigeon,* the arbitrator decided that the Russians must pay the bill in full. But what must have galled them more than anything else was the amount the arbitrator decreed that they would have to pay—$56,675.63. This was $7175.63 more than the bill Captain Scullun had handed in that day in Vladivostok Harbor. And it explained why the captain had been so patient for ten years. He could afford to, since he was charging interest on the money for all that time.

Where the whaling skippers' ingenuity reached its perfection was in their methods for handling recalcitrant members of the crew. Some of these methods had the kind of justice administered by Captain George Fred Tilton. Others did not. There were skippers who singled out rebellious hands and abused them particularly, keeping it up until the men were frantic for a chance to desert, then putting into a harbor where there was known to be a supply of good *Kanaka* (native) men willing to ship for a short cruise; the deserters thus forfeited any shares of the voyage they had earned since shipping aboard. There were skippers who

had a simple and efficient solution for the problem of low supplies of fresh water; if the crew used it up too fast despite orders
not to, the dipper for the drinking barrel was hung from a peg
high in the crosstrees, and it had to be replaced after each use.
There were skippers who kept the best sperm oil for themselves,
cheated on rations, and made money on the slop chest where
crew members were forced to buy new gear when theirs wore
out. Indeed, according to legend, there was one who carried this
petty graft too far. On one cruise a harpooner sharpening the
tools of his trade in his bunk happened to gouge a chunk out of
the beam overhead. It was not enough to damage the beam, but
it was enough to suggest to the skipper a means for making a
little bit more profit for himself and the owners. When the harpooner was discharged, he found that the price of a new beam
had been deducted from his pay. For once, though, the harpooner
was too smart; he demanded a receipt. Then, a month or two later,
an hour before the whaler was to cast off for her next cruise, the
harpooner came aboard with his receipt. He had paid for the
beam, he pointed out. The captain would kindly hand it over.
After a few minutes of choice profanity that was wasted on the
harpooner, the captain paid him in full. The legend does not say,
but it is a dead certainty that that harpooner went on to be a
whaling captain.

There was one ingenious disciplinary device of the whaling
skipper, though, that was calculated to strike respectful fear into
the hearts of the most hardened sea dogs, and it usually did. That
was marooning. If the boys get too sassy, pick out the ringleaders,
have them row you ashore on a tiny, barren atoll, and come back
alone, leaving them to starve to death. In the nineteenth century
many a little rock outcropping in the Pacific was decorated with
the whitened bones of whalemen who had got too sassy.

To the rest of the crew and anyone ashore the captain always
maintained that these castaways were deserters. Admitting anything else would amount to pleading guilty to murder. And despite pretty clear evidence of marooning, the U.S. consul in some
far-flung place like Honolulu or Lima or Callao could rarely
make the charge stick. One reason was that as soon as marooning

became prevalent, every deserter immediately claimed he had been dumped ashore by a murderous skipper. In the resultant welter of confusion it was impossible to know who was doing what to whom.

That was the dilemma that faced the U.S. consul in Callao in the fall of 1833, when five men presented their grievances before him. There had been a "row," as they put it, between themselves and Thomas Brown, master of the Warren, Rhode Island, whaling brig *Magnet,* off the Peruvian coast. Result: the men were "taken ashore and over the surf with our arms tied behind us and left on the shore . . . without anything more than what we stood in." But they managed to flag a passing vessel, were picked up, and landed at Callao. Now they wanted the consul to arrange their passage home.

What made it a delicate dilemma was the arrival only a few days later of Captain Brown himself. No sooner had the *Magnet* swung to her anchor than word reached him that his missing men were in this port. The captain promptly requested that the consul hand them over. They were, he announced unequivocally, deserters.

Here was the all too frequent problem, the whaleman versus his captain, the seaman entreating protection from what he swore was tyranny, the skipper righteously demanding that the "deserter" be turned over to him. The consul was quite aware that many an honest-appearing foremast hand was actually a liar and a deserter; and many a kindly-appearing captain was actually a bloodthirsty brute. Which one in this case told the truth? The spokesman for the five sailors seemed convincing enough; his description of their experience had the ring of honesty and authenticity to it. Yet Captain Brown seemed convincing too.

Had the captain mistreated the men so brutally that they finally could stand it no longer, had defied some impossible order, and had thereupon been dumped on the island to starve to death? Or had they planned desertion? Had they, knowing how difficult it was to escape the efficient dragnet of the well-bribed Callao police, skipped ashore on an island, taking the chance that one of the many whalers running up the coast would sight their signal and rescue them?

Look at it another way. Suppose the consul decided that the men had been marooned. The New England whaleship owners had powerful connections in Washington, and would be howling for the consul's scalp if he proved to be wrong. An arbitrary decision, based only on a hunch, could not only be unfair to Captain Brown; it could also be illegal. And it could mean the end of the consul's diplomatic career. But suppose he decided in the captain's favor. Suppose he handed the men over to him. And suppose they had been telling the truth. The consul could see in his mind's eye the grisly scene on the waist deck of the *Magnet,* once the Peruvian coast had dropped below the horizon—the ten arms triced to the rigging, the whistling lash, the dripping blood, the groaning, cursing, praying men. And then the lurching ride once again through the surf, this time to an island too far off the beaten track for the men to be sighted before they died. Clearly the consul's decision might be a death sentence for five innocent men.

What to decide? It was the word of a captain against five of his men. And one of the two parties was lying. But which one?

Then the answer came, clear and simple, in a note from Captain Brown. The consul read the note, reread it to make sure, then made his decision. The men would not be sent back aboard the *Magnet.* He so informed Captain Brown, and thereupon set about arranging passage home for the castaways.

The letter from the captain was polite, if slightly illiterate. He was anxious to be on his way, and he wanted his men back. "I should be happy," he wrote, "if you will have the goodness to git the men down as soon as convenient." And at the bottom of the letter, the explanatory note which had resolved the consul's dilemma: "I have no one," Captain Brown added, "I can trust out of my ship or I would send someone up."

There was only one group of American ship captains who belonged in the same class with the whalemen. The sealing skippers were the other hunters of the sea. Like the whalers, the sealers traced wandering, zigzag lines on the map of the Atlantic and

Pacific. Like the whaling skippers, the sealing captains were intent on the out-of-the-way areas, the uncharted seas where no packets, no naval ships, and, in many cases, no explorers had bothered to go before. Like the whalemen, the seal hunters lived by a kind of calculated daring, skirting reefs, slipping in and out of unknown coves, and living for years in the waters other captains only used as a highway. There were some canny skippers and owners who had their ships fitted out for both whaling and sealing, thereby promising an earlier return voyage with a full hold. But the usual sealer was equipped for her business alone, unencumbered by rows of whaleboats and cutting stage and try-works. Finding and killing seals was enough to keep most of these skippers well occupied.

The whaleship, big and heavy enough to withstand the weight of a whale carcass hauled up on her windlass, was not well adapted to sealing. Whales lived in the deeps. Seals were found on rocky shores. So the best sealing craft was only big enough to ride out the storms of the Atlantic and Pacific, with the emphasis on maneuverability and shallow draft. The sealer went from island to island, poking along the shore, as close in as possible, on the lookout for the herds that could sometimes blend perfectly into the brownish-black landscape. Once a herd was spotted, the boats went riding the surf onto whatever stretch of smooth beach there might be. But the sealing captain had to wear in close enough to sight the animals first.

Once on shore, the crew rounded up the slow-moving seals and sea elephants, clubbed them to death, and skinned them. The pelts were then salted down in the ship's hold. Usually these pelts were brought back to the home port, Stonington or New London, Boston or Salem, New Bedford or Nantucket, where they were prepared to be shipped out aboard the merchant ships. Across the Atlantic and Pacific they went again, this time to China, where they brought as much as $15,000 per shipload. The money was invested in tea, spices, silks, and other rarities of the Orient, which brought even better prices back in Salem and Boston and New York. It was a profitable enterprise.

Which is why it led to the indiscriminate slaughter of seals.

One by one the better-known islands and stretches of coast were swept bare of the animals. And year by year more sealing skippers were forced to become explorers as well. In the Atlantic they crept farther and farther south, until they were nearly to the then unknown continent of Antarctica. In the Pacific they sailed off the ends of every known chart, hunting for islands that were unvisited since Cook or, even better, that no one had seen at all.

Their relentless, unceasing, greedy search for new seal rookeries, together with the whaling cruises, probably constituted the greatest period of ocean exploration the world has ever known. But a great deal of what was discovered will never be recorded in history. For the essence of sealing was secrecy. A skipper who was fortunate enough to find an island swarming with the beasts was smart enough to keep his good fortune to himself; on his next cruise he planned to call there again, and he did not want to find the place already cleaned out because he had been unwise enough to mention his discovey. The sealers kept their secrets well. The log of a whaler was usually laconic, but it was complete; sometimes the pages were proudly embellished with the black outline of a sperm whale for every one caught. Not the sealing logs. The general course of the voyage was revealed, the number of seals taken and the location if it had already been known to other sealers. But invariably if the sealing captain claimed credit in his log for the discovery of an island it was a cinch that there were no seal rookeries on it. In the sealing business modesty was literally a rewarding virtue.

Even so, these skippers made some finds that became milestones of history and, because no seals were involved, recorded them for posterity. It was in January of 1808, for example, when the Nantucket sealing captain Mayhew Folger gave up a frustrating search of the waters below New Zealand and headed north, toward the equator and warmer latitudes. For almost a year he had been sailing his ship, the *Topaz*, across trackless expanses of the South Atlantic and South Pacific, looking for new islands, knowing that if he could find only one that harbored seals and had never been seen by man before, he could fill the *Topaz's* hold in a few days. But he had found nothing. Now he set his course east northeast, in a wide arc; and for almost a month the *Topaz* plowed through the wide wastes of the Pacific, with not a spit of land in sight.

On February 6, 1808, he swung south, about to trace the lower arc of a great circle across a fourth of the Pacific. It was a little after noon when he saw an island.

It lay off the starboard bow, looking like one black rock rising out of the sea. From the distance Captain Folger could not see the shore; but a volcanic island like this usually meant a rocky beach. And rocks meant seals. The *Topaz's* helm went over and she pointed for the dark peak.

By 2 A.M. of the seventh the island was only two leagues off. Captain Folger had the *Topaz* tack back and forth along the shore while he waited for daylight. By 6 A.M., with dawn just breaking, the captain and some of his crew were in two boats heading for shore, to hunt for seals.

Then they noticed the smoke.

It came as quite a surprise to Folger. He thought he knew which island this was supposed to be. It had been discovered forty-one years before by Captain Carteret of *H.M.S. Swallow*. This was a good many miles west of where Captain Carteret's discovery had been placed on the charts, but Folger had allowed for some error. However, his island was supposed to be uninhabited. So what did this tall, straight column of smoke mean? Had he found a hitherto unknown piece of land? Who were the inhabitants? Were they of the friendly tribes to the northwest? Or from the cannibal kingdoms to the west? Or were these shipwrecked seamen? Was the smoke a signal of distress? Or could it be the ceremonial cooking fire of a cannibal tribe, already sending its smoke into the sky while the savages waited for them, hidden behind the island's tall trees and bushes? Captain Folger surveyed the island again, then suddenly called both boats to a halt. He had just seen a canoe, slipping around a promontory and coming out to meet them.

The men of the *Topaz* rested on their oars and watched the canoe come on. As it drew nearer, Folger could see that there were three men in it. They looked like savages. He glanced toward the *Topaz;* it would be a long row back to the safety of her bulwarks. Then he studied the shore of the island again, and decided not to backtrack, yet. His force greatly outnumbered the three men in the canoe, and he could see no more boats putting out toward them.

When the canoe was almost within hailing distance he became puzzled at the features of the three men. They were nearly naked and brown like the natives of the other islands. But their faces, as well as he could make them out, looked strangely different. There were a few more minutes of expectant silence while the *Topaz's* boats rolled on the sea, their oars dripping softly. The canoe rapidly closed the distance, the three men staring at them intently but making no move except to raise and dip their paddles. Then the canoe was nearly alongside, and one of the three men spoke.

It was in pure, clear English, with a British accent.

"What ship is that? Where do you come from?"

Captain Folger relaxed against the gunwale. "It is the ship *Topaz* of the United States of America," he said. "I am Mayhew Folger, her master, an American."

"You are an American?" the man asked. "You come from America?" He seemed puzzled. "Where is America?" he asked. "Is it in Ireland?"

Captain Folger had assumed that he had come upon ship-wrecked British sailors. Now he began to wonder again.

"Who are you?"

"We are Englishmen."

Still, there was something strange about British sailors who had never heard of America in 1808.

"Where were you born?" Captain Folger asked.

"On that island, which you see."

"How then," Folger wanted to know, "are you Englishmen if you were born on that island?"

"We are Englishmen because our father was an Englishman."

The realization of his discovery had not yet dawned on Captain Folger. He asked: "Who is your father?"

The answer: "Aleck." The man added nothing. It seemed to him perfectly obvious that anyone would know who Aleck was.

He showed his surprise when Folger replied with, "Who is Aleck?"

"Don't you know Aleck?" he asked. He paused.

And then he said: "Well, then, do you know Captain Bligh of. the *Bounty?*"

With a gasp Captain Folger realized what he had found. Like nearly every other sailing man he knew the story of the mutiny aboard the *Bounty*. Led by the mutineers' mastermind, Fletcher Christian, they had set Captain Bligh adrift in the longboat and had sailed off in the ship. For nearly twenty years the British Navy had scoured the Pacific for them with no success. The few who had elected to go ashore at Tahiti had been caught; but to what corner of the seas had Christian and his remaining followers gone? They had disappeared just as completely as if they had sailed off the edge of the world. To every ship captain, as well as the British Navy, it was one of the most intriguing mysteries of the sea.

And now here was the solution. It was, as Folger had reckoned, Pitcairn Island, discovered by Captain Carteret and named after the midshipman who had first sighted it. It had been uninhabited when visited by *H.M.S. Swallow,* and it still had been uninhabited when Fletcher Christian, his fellow mutineers, their Tahitian wives and manservants ran the *Bounty* onto the rocks and set her afire. Since then this jagged, precipitous mountain peak and its lush-growing plateau had been their hideout—and their prison.

Captain Folger lost no time in going ashore. There he met "Aleck," Alexander Smith, the last survivor of the original mutineers, who later changed his name to John Adams. Long since aged by the experience, Smith was the patriarch of the little community of thirty-five Tahitians and half whites living in their absolute isolation. The others? They had either died or been killed by the servants they had brought with them from Tahiti.

Captain Folger stayed on Pitcairn Island all that day and most of the next, while the old mutineer tearfully chattered away about the *Bounty,* the life on the island, and the bloody night when the Tahitians murdered all the white men save him. Then Folger gave his host a résumé of world history for the past twenty years, while the white-haired man listened hungrily and interrupted with countless questions. Glossing over the American Revolution as diplomatically as he could, Folger dwelled on the naval victories of the British. The mutineer listened, his chest swelled and he half shouted, half sobbed, "Old England forever!"

Late in the afternoon of the second day Folger got back into one of the *Topaz's* boats, climbed and plunged over the surf of Bounty Bay, and headed out to his sealer. He had found not a seal. But he had closed an important chapter in maritime history.

And it remained closed. Although Pitcairn Island was visited many times after Captain Folger's discovery of the mutineers' refuge, the British Government allowed Alexander Smith to finish the rest of his days in self-exile on his towering green plateau. As for Captain Folger, he went back to his search for seals. But he always remembered his last look back at the shelf atop Pitcairn's plunging cliff—the little group of exiles waving to him, the white surf smashing its spray up toward them, the palm fronds behind them bending to the steady trade wind, and Alexander Smith, looking out across the Pacific, thinking, as Fletcher Christian had too, of that one impulsive moment so long ago that had meant self-imprisonment for life on this rock, halfway around the globe from home.

It was only a few years after Captain Folger's discovery in mid-Pacific when a fellow sealing skipper found himself on the verge of a far more important one in the South Atlantic. In fact, during the same year that Folger was sweating under the tropical sun as he climbed the steep path to Pitcairn's plateau, many other sealing captains were nearly freezing in the raw winds and fogs south of Cape Horn, while they hunted for seals on Deception Island and Ragged Island, in Yankee Harbor and Sheriff's Cove. They were looking for seals, but they were looking for unknown islands too, just as Folger had been searching the Pacific. For years they had heard of an apparently mythical string of islands called the Lost Auroras, about which many a weird and wonderful forecastle tale had been told. The "Ororors," it was said, had been seen only by gale-driven skippers, blown off course while running before the storms off Cape Horn and going where the wild wind took them. No one had ever been able to take a bearing on these islands, and it was doubtful that they existed at all. But the sealing skippers reasoned that if there were still some undiscovered islands below the Horn, they ought to be swarming with seals. So the hunt for the Lost Auroras went on. The islands were never found; but the search for them led the sealing skippers to the South Shetlands, even farther south than the Falklands, and into a large, curved anchorage that became known as Yankee Harbor, the gathering place of all the sealers.

From here some of the more daring and resourceful sealing captains sailed even farther south. Among them was a young skipper from Stonington, Connecticut, named Nathaniel Palmer, sealing in his thirty-eight-foot sloop *Hero*. Beating his way south through a violent blizzard, he came upon Deception Island, where he found a circular harbor fashioned by a volcano that had been breached by the sea. For Palmer's purposes it was a perfect anchorage. Because of the volcano's steep sides the *Hero* could sail right up to the shore. Jets of steam curled out over the water along the bank, and the combination of warm water and frigid air kept a bank of fog swirling about the island virtually all the time. It was loaded with seals. More important, it was hidden from other sealers by its almost perpetual bank of fog.

Making a careful chart of the island's position, Palmer set out to reconnoiter a little farther south. He had not gone far when he barely clawed away from a swift channel, packed with huge ice cakes and roiling southwest currents. As he made his way north, away from the channel, he looked astern. There, rising out of the ice, was a line of black, towering peaks. He noted this discovery in his log and set his course north again.

Thus Nathaniel Palmer is credited with the discovery of Antarctica. The claim, however, was not made until 1940, in an attempt to settle a century-long controversy. While some historians had credited Antarctica's discovery to the American naval lieutenant Charles Wilkes, others had maintained that the credit really belonged to Admiral Dumont D'Urville of the French

Navy; by a startling coincidence both sighted the continent in January of 1840. The evidence in Nathaniel Palmer's log seemed to prove that he had made the discovery fully twenty years ahead of them. Geographers and historians joined in belated tribute to the venturesome sealing skipper. The long arm that stretches north from the continent was named Palmer Peninsula, in honor of the American who had been first to sight Antarctica.

But had he? The claim has not been accepted by everyone; the British, for example, call the same arm of the continent Graham Land. The reasonable doubt is raised by the same piece of evidence, the notation in the log of his sloop *Hero*. For Palmer remarks on seeing the black cliffs *after* he had turned and headed north, away from the ice-packed channel that we now know leads past the continent. And his course was set to the north side of two islands lying off the continent. These islands, unlike many others in the area, have steep, black cliffs. So what apparently happened was that although Palmer got very close to seeing Antarctica itself, he had to shy away too soon. He then turned back and passed the black-hilled islands lying off the mainland. And as a clincher, the anti-Palmer faction points out that if Palmer had indeed spotted what he thought to be a continent, why didn't he say so? What his log says is: "Bore away to the Northerd & saw 2 small islands and the shore every where Perpendicular." No mention of any suspicion that he had seen the coast line of a continent at all.

So the controversy still goes on. But now, only recently, there has come a new claimant—a hitherto unknown man, and a sealing skipper. The historian who puts forward the new sealing skipper's claim is Edouard A. Stackpole, formerly president of the Nantucket Historical Association and now curator of the Marine Historical Association in Mystic, Connecticut, home of the *Charles W. Morgan*. While at Nantucket, Mr. Stackpole collected all the logbooks there were available, then started on ancient scrapbooks. He knew that many times a log, considered useless once the voyage was completed, had been converted into a scrapbook and had been so covered with old advertisements, Godey prints and news clippings that a few generations later its inheritors did not even realize they had a ship's log. Sure enough, one day a woman showed up with a particularly venerable scrapbook she had found in her Nantucket attic. It was, she pointed out, filled with pretty pictures, and she thought Mr. Stackpole would be interested in it. Mr. Stackpole was indeed. As he thought, it turned out to be a very old log. But this one contained a surprise. It had been kept by a Captain Christopher Burdick, master of the Nantucket schooner *Huntress,* bound down to the South Shetland Islands for seals. And it proved that Captain Burdick had a stronger claim to the discovery of Antarctica than any of the other explorers and sealing skippers thus far advanced.

Captain Burdick and his crew "hove anchor" in Nantucket Harbor on August 4, 1820, the same year that Nathaniel Palmer left Stonington for the same South Shetlands. It was four full months before he had made his landfall, and after feeling his way through a huge fog bank, he glided into Yankee Harbor. "Went into the harbor," he scrawled in his log, "came two at 6 a.m. in 16 fathoms. Found five Stonington vessels here."

Although Nathaniel Palmer was cruising all through this area at the same time, neither he nor Burdick makes any mention of a meeting between the two. But after spending a few weeks working the nearby islands for seals, Captain Burdick was off on his own, off on the kind of lone search that had uncovered the hideout of the *Bounty's* mutineers. Like Captain Folger, Captain Burdick was looking only for seals, for the hidden island still unknown to anyone else and covered with seals. In his log he had just noted: "Captain Johnson came in in shallop from a cruise of 22 days . . . whether he had found any seal he did not inform . . ." This was all Burdick had needed. If Captain Johnson would not say whether there were any seals farther south, there must be thousands of them. So out of the harbor went the *Huntress,* sloshing southward into unknown waters. During the next month her skipper made a good catch. He also made history.

On February 15, 1821, he wrote in his log that he was favored with "pleasant wether," so pleasant, in fact, that he could clearly make out a small low island six miles to the southwest. It looked like a good seal island, and he sent the *Huntress* bearing toward it. Then he noticed something far more impressive. To the south southeast a long, black coast line rose sheer out of the water, capped by ice and snow.

It was the continent of Antarctica.

Behind the steep cliffs a mountain plateau stretched away for miles toward the horizon. Around the shore the water sparkled under the sun. Pack ice slowly drifted by the banks. But there were no big hilly islands to block his view. Here was Antarctica, the last undiscovered continent of the world. And he was the first man in history to see it.

The pack ice kept him from approaching any closer to the shore line. But he immediately took his exact bearings, something the sealers did only on important occasions. Here are his observations: ". . . at meridien latitude by obs. 63° 17' south. President Island bearing north, 3 leagues. Mount Pisco southwest by west, distance 7 leagues. The Peak of Frezeland northeast ½ west, 11 leagues. Deception Island northeast by north, 8 leagues; and a small low island south southwest 6 leagues, to which I am bound; and land from south to east which I suppose to be a continent."

By these bearings Captain Burdick's position can still be plotted. He had sailed the *Huntress* to a position off Hoseason Island where there was nothing between him and the great looming continent of Antarctica. And unlike Captain Palmer, he had realized what he had discovered. Yet more important to him at the moment was the sight of seals flapping about on Hoseason Island. He made for the spot and sent a boat ashore. His log laconically records the day's practical achievement: "They returned with 22 seal."

Burdick spent two days here, just across the channel from Antarctica. Then he headed north again. Two months later he was back home in Nantucket. About his discovery of Antarctica he said nothing. To do so might mean revealing that across the channel from it was an island swarming with seals. So his log was put away, as far as possible from prying eyes. A few generations later it was used as a scrapbook until every square inch of paper was covered by some industrious child. Then it was thrown in back of the dress forms and parrot cages, where it sat and yellowed until it was rescued by historian Stackpole. So it was that after more than a century recognition finally came to the practical Nantucket sealing skipper, who regarded fame as a lot less important than a seal-covered island all his own.

Calculating and gambling, businesslike and adventurous, the sealers and the whalemen ran their ships into the remotest corners of the globe, despite grinding ice packs and murderous coral reefs—but always for a single, simple reason: more seals or whales. That was the main motivation for their courage, their perseverance, and their resourcefulness. Captain Burdick went dodging among the ice floes of the South Atlantic, right up against the continent of Antarctica, because it meant more seals. Captain Scullun and the owners of the *Cape Horn Pigeon* kept up their incessant badgering of the Russian Government for ten years because they had been done out of a season's catch of whales; besides, it was an unpaid bill, wasn't it? Despite the blood-chilling stories of what Mocha Dick had done to other whaleboats and their crews, the next skipper to sight the white monster lowered for him; he was big, therefore he would fill a lot of barrels. And there were the unpleasant instances of skippers whose practicality turned to greed, manifesting itself in cheating and brutality. Here was free enterprise operating at its best and at its worst.

Of course it was not always as simple as that. Part of the paradox of the sealer and whaleman was that he chose this manner of making his living. With the same combination of talents, with the same sharp eye for profits, he could have amassed a comfortable fortune without going near the water, without leaving home and wife and children for three or four years at a time, without confining himself to the little floating world of a whaler, without spending decades literally up to his hips in stinking whale grease, without taking his life in his hands every time he guided a whaleboat up onto the back of a thrashing bull whale. Yet it was not simply the lure of the sea or a love of adventure or any such romantic nonsense. When a sealing skipper or whaleman made enough money to retire comfortably, he invariably quit, even though in many cases he was not past his forties. And anyone who asked a husky, forty-five-year-old retired whaling captain if he missed the excitement of the chase was answered with a sardonic laugh, if not with a look of utter bafflement.

The answer usually lay in a combination of factors. In a town dominated by the whaling industry there was not a great variety of other occupations. And the town was much more of a self-contained, insular community than it is now. Many a Nantucket whaling captain had been a dozen times around the world, but had never been up to Boston. In a whaling town there was a certain prestige attached to the calling; it sometimes went so far that a young girl refused to marry her fiancé until he had harpooned his first whale. There was the ameliorating fact that long absence from home was not so bad when so many other husbands were off on the Pacific too; indeed, the petticoat aristocracy that emerged at such places as Edgartown, Sag Harbor, and Nantucket was probably enough in itself to send many a young man off to sea.

Added to these factors was the strong feeling of family tradition. Whaling had been a part of a boy's life from his earliest days. He could recall the first time a bushy-bearded man clumped into his bedroom at night, picked him up, and hugged him—the boy was four years old and this was his first meeting with his father. The boy was brought up amid the clutter of whaling gear, with the smells of whale oil always in his nostrils, to the sounds of drays loaded with full barrels, rumbling over the cobblestones as they were hauled up the street to the candle factories. A part of this tradition is the tale about the small boy playing in the sitting room, seizing his mother's needle, and darting it at the cat. "Pay out, mother! Pay out!" he screamed. "There she sounds through the window!" By the time the boy was in his early teens he was a skilled seaman. And when his father or his uncle or just some friend of the family asked him if he would like a berth on the next voyage, the boy went.

For such reasons as these New Englanders became whalemen. It was then that the ones with abilities for the job rose to captain. By the time the man was a skipper, he was all through asking himself, while he hung onto his bunk and listened to the storm thrashing the timbers a few inches away, what in God's name he was doing out here, why he had not chosen a life ashore, why he had not gone west and gotten a soft job laying timbers for the railroad. Such questions rose only when he was a foremast hand. Now, as a captain, he was resigned to the life; he was used to it; he even liked it at times. And he made the best of it.

He did that by concentrating all his energies, courage, and resourcefulness on one goal: more whales. If he was harsh on the crew, it was so they would make an efficient team for catching more whales. If he promoted some first-voyage "greenie" to harpooner, it was because he thought the fellow had the kind of arm that would make him fast to more whales. If he deliberately sailed his ship into waters infested with cannibals, it was because he figured the area had more whales. It was not simply greed; it was an ingrained habit, an unquestioned way of life. George Fred Tilton's dangerous, humanitarian gesture of walking 1700 miles should have been enough to make him realize that there were better ways of making a living; but he lost no time in going back to sea, after more whales. The disaster of the *Essex* and the experience of three months in an open boat while shipmates slowly died beside them should have convinced the survivors that they had had enough; only five Nantucketers lived through it, but they all went back after more whales, and they all became captains.

It was this single-minded purposefulness that directed the entire course of the whaling cruise. Many of the skippers, especially the Nantucketers, were Quakers; despite the rough life and the language and behavior of the crew these skippers never used profanity (although it was said that some kept specially picked mates to swear for them). They "kept the Lord's Day," mustering the crew and reading to them from the Bible every Sunday. But it was their considered opinion that the Lord provided them with the whales they sighted and caught. Some of these religious whaling skippers observed the Sabbath by not working the ship or chasing whales. The less religious crewmen noticed, however, that when one of these captains sighted a whale on Sunday, he managed to keep it in sight until Monday. Religion was part of the lives of many of these captains; whaling was all of it.

Captain George Howland, master of the New Bedford whaler *Canton*, was one of these men. So he was not as surprised as his crew by the strange phenomena that occurred on the morning of November 28, 1890, off the Cape of Good Hope. For a week the *Canton* had been thrashing along under favorable winds, headed eastward, toward the Indian Ocean and good whaling grounds. But as the week ended the wind hauled around into the east. Beating back and forth into it, Captain Howland found he was getting nowhere. He tried an easterly course again; the wind swung into the east; he tacked ship; the wind died. When the sails filled, he tried the easterly course again; the wind hauled into the east. It was baffling, frustrating and, to the crew at least, a little eerie. It was as if the wind—or something—didn't *want* the ship to continue east.

Captain Howland studied the horizon, the sea, the clouds, the glass, and was convinced. This must be some kind of divine intervention. The Lord wanted the *Canton* to go north northwest, and had provided the wind for it. Why He wanted the ship to sail in that direction Howland couldn't guess; maybe He meant there were whales off there. Howland gave the simple order to his mate: "Alter the course, Mr. Cruz, to the north northwest," he said. "Let the wind take us as she will." The ship fell off on the new tack; the wind held true. What happened then convinced Captain Howland that although he was wrong about the whales, he was right about divine intervention.

All afternoon, all that night, all the next morning the *Canton* sailed north northwest, her canvas swelling before a steady wind. The course was almost directly away from the good whaling grounds of the Indian Ocean, but the *Canton* was not ordered about. Then a herd of whales was raised. But they were off to windward. Captain Howland kept the ship steady as she went.

It was noon of the twenty-ninth, after almost exactly twenty-four hours on the north northwest course, when one of the men at the *Canton's* masthead said to the other:

"What do you see on the horizon, over the starboard bow?"

"I don't see anything. Do you?"

"I think I do. Look again. Low down."

What the young man high on the masthead saw were two life-boats of the bark *British Monarch,* from Liverpool, bound for Calcutta. The *British Monarch* had caught fire and blown up, just after sixteen of her men had escaped in the two boats. For twenty-four hours they had been bobbing about in the Atlantic Ocean—until the American whaleship *Canton,* driven by an extraordinarily freakish wind and her skipper's belief that it was divine intervention, had come straight across the path and to the rescue.

They were religious men, like Captain Howland. They were profane, like the legendary skipper who had the fantastically bad luck to spend two years at sea without catching one whale; when he came sailing back into Nantucket harbor again, he was ready for the Quaker shipowners and their grave, anxious questioning. "We didn't get a single, goddam barrel of oil," he announced, "but we had a goddam fine sail." They were brutal, some of the skippers; one of them listened calmly to the news that a foremast hand had died from a beating, then said, "Have to lose two or three more before the voyage is a success." And some were kind-hearted, a few of them even so lax that they became easy marks for any troublemakers among the crew.

That is what happened to Captain Isaac B. Hussey, who had taken the whaleship *Planter* out of Nantucket to the Pacific in 1847. Exactly how it happened no one is certain, but one day in 1850 off Strong's Island, a diminutive, reef-girdled member of the Carolines, some of his crew decided they would rather loaf for a while. Captain Hussey mustered all hands on deck and calmly asked the rebellious ones to go back to work. Instead a sullen knot of men formed in the waist of the ship, muttering to themselves. Every skipper knew that this was the beginning of open mutiny. Captain Hussey had armed himself. He raised his pistol and ordered the men back to their stations. They refused, and the muttering grew louder. He warned them once again: disband and return to duty or he would fire into them. No one budged. Raising the pistol higher, he fired over their heads. The crew scattered. But where they had stood, one body lay on the deck.

Captain Hussey's pistol, unused for years, had kicked and he had shot one of the crew. By the time he got across the deck the man was dead.

Hussey was overcome with anguish. In the moment, taking no time for reflection, he made his hasty decision. He ordered his first mate to take over the ship. He went below, packed some belongings, then had himself rowed ashore. The *Planter* sailed on without him.

For the next two years he was a solitary figure, seen here and there as he wandered about the Pacific islands. He had a wife and child home in Nantucket, and the thought of them tortured his soul. He knew what the correct legal procedure was—he should finish the cruise, return home, and announce the death of the crewman. He should ask for a trial. His officers would then testify to the mutiny of the crew and he would be immediately exonerated. But how could he face his neighbors, his wife and child? And how could he face the parents of the boy he had killed? Maybe time would ease their tragedy. Maybe in a few years they would realize that Captain Hussey had only been doing his duty, protecting his ship. And maybe then they would be able to accept the fact that, despite the provocation, it had been an accident. But until then—only the lonely islands and the rolling seas of the Pacific.

He was a beachcomber, a trader, a plantation foreman, always a forlorn figure of self-exile. By 1852 he was master of the schooner *William Penn,* trading among the constellation of islands and atolls. His crew was made up of natives, usually unruly when not handled with firmness, always ready for treachery if it suited their purpose. And apparently Captain Hussey still had not learned how to assert his authority; for suddenly one day his native crew decided to take the ship.

Again Hussey armed himself. Again he stood his ground on the quarter-deck. "Stop where you are," he commanded, "or I'll fire." The men slowed, but one or two of them also had guns. They kept on coming. And as they converged on him, the two-year-old memory flashed before his eyes: the *Planter,* the mutinous crew, the sullen muttering, the single shot, the crumpled body on the deck. Captain Hussey held his fire. The men were almost on him when he finally raised his pistol toward the brown chest of the leader.

A single shot cracked out across the quiet bay. As it echoed back, Captain Hussey fell to the deck. This time he had held his fire until too late.

7. Yarn spinners, wharf rats, and a young gentleman

There were other self-exiles besides Captain Hussey. But few of them were skippers. Usually it was the foremast hand who could endure the dingy forecastle, the bad food, and the blister-cracking hours at the whaleboat oar only so long before he rebelled. One look at a calm, blue-green South Seas lagoon, with the sound of palm fronds sighing in the trades and the languorous murmur of the natives lying about on the beach, and the sea-weary whaleman was more than ready to go over the side. If the ship happened to be at an island where there was a good supply of willing seamen, the skipper was glad to see him go, and the Kanaka who was shipped in the deserter's place usually made a better whaleman anyway. Sometimes, too, if it were a big island community long since used to their blubber-hunter visitors, there were plenty of replacements among the whites who had deserted from other

ships and were now surfeited with indolence. If the island were
not a good recruiting port, the captain promised a sizable reward
to any native who returned the deserter; he could afford to because the amount was charged against the man's pay, usually plus
25 per cent. This could almost always be counted on to produce
the escapee, whereupon he was given a "taste of the cat," which
left scars on his back to remind him of the penalty the next time
he thought about quitting ship.

Those who did make good their escape usually became harmless beachcombers, "omoos" wandering aimlessly from island to
island like Herman Melville. Others became dangerous renegades, falling in among savage tribes and leading them in bloody
attacks on visiting ships, like the strange white man who directed
the attack on the *Triton*. But there were also a very few who
seemed born for the South Seas; it brought out the best in them.

There was one man who probably accomplished more for his
white countrymen out there than he could have if he had stayed
aboard the whalers. David Whippey was a Nantucket boy when
he shipped out in 1819. But he found that a whaleship was not
for him, and he was soon "on the beach" in the Fijis. Evidently
David Whippey was a born diplomat, because although the Fijis
were the most dangerous of all the cannibal islands, he was soon
popular among all the natives and the royal favorite of King
Kakombau. This native ruler was one of the most powerful in the
Pacific, and Whippey was apparently the only white man who
ever became his intimate friend. The Nantucketer wasted no time
preaching to his cannibal friend or trying to change the natives'
way of life. He learned how to eat birds' intestines and drink kava
without gagging. He taught himself their language. Most important, he showed them how to use muskets and fought alongside
them when other tribes made marauding expeditions on them.
He went with the king and his warriors on their own expeditions,
helping his native friend consolidate his sprawling island king-
dom. He did not remonstrate when after each battle the canoes
were loaded with women prisoners and bodies of enemy warriors
for a cannibal feast. And he whiled away long, lazy afternoons

beguiling King Kakombau with his stories of the weird customs and habits of the white men at the other end of the world.

So although most whalemen were met with a shower of spears or a volley of musket shot when they approached the Fiji Islands, David Whippey was made a chief and given an island for his own domain. On Ovalu, a few miles off the shore of the king's capital at Viti Levu, Whippey ruled a community where the natives' age-old traditions were respected and where at the same time well-planned cultivation made the island the prize exhibit of King Kakombau's empire.

There David Whippey stayed the rest of his life. He became well known throughout the Fijis. To the islanders the bearded whalemen who came ashore from the big ships were strangers who therefore had to be considered enemies. But David Whippey was their friend. Dozens of shipwrecked whalemen owed their lives to him. Whenever word reached him that a ship had gone on a reef or had been taken by the savages in the Fijis, Whippey went to their aid as quickly as he could. If he got there too late, and especially if the whalemen had made the mistake of violating some taboo or antagonizing the local chief, Whippey found only roasted bones as evidence. But if he got to a shipwrecked crew before violence had broken out, or if he found survivors of a native attack being held for ransom, his arrival meant their salvation. The islanders could understand him; they knew he understood them. And they could trust him. Besides, they were well aware that any friend of Whippey's was a friend of powerful King Kakombau. The castaways were released. Whippey took them to his island, and so long as they behaved themselves they were safe from the cannibals until the next ship arrived and rescued them. Invariably the grateful survivors asked Whippey to return to America with them; and always he explained that he had no desire to live anywhere but among the Fijis.

When Lieutenant Charles Wilkes reached these islands on an exploring expedition in 1840, David Whippey was there to act as interpreter and to guide the Navy officers among the islands. He was appointed U.S. Vice Consul in the area, and when the islands were ceded to Great Britain in 1874, Whippey acted as official interpreter at the ceremonies. He still stayed among his dark-skinned friends, and watched them gradually turn from savagery to civilization. Today hundreds of David Whippey's descendants live all through the islands, proud reminders of the days when a man from Nantucket made the white man's country across the Pacific the natives' most respected friend.

Many of these self-exiles were, like David Whippey, moved by fascination with the natives and a humanitarian urge to help their unfortunate countrymen in these watery outposts of the world. Others were romanticists, adventurers or, at worst, criminals as bloodthirsty as the most savage cannibals. But, originally at least, the majority of them were plain escapees. For although life aboard any ship was harsh in the nineteenth century, life aboard a whaler was generally the harshest.

In the 1820s and 1830s many a whaleship's forecastle hand was the son or nephew of the skipper or mate; already a seasoned sailor, he was ready and eager to learn. These would be the skippers and mates of the mid-century whalers. But by then the lure of the clippers and packets, the gold rush, and the opening of the West had precipitated a vicious circle in the forecastle. Because there were fewer good hands, the officers bore down harder on the malingerers they were now forced to take. And because the foremast hand's life was harder, more and more of the better men shied away from the "spouters," the "blubber-hunters," the "butcher shops adrift." So the situation aboard the American whalers grew worse year by year.

Recruiting moved farther and farther inland, where sailors' tales of life aboard the whaleships had not had as much effect as along the coast. The Vermont farm boy who noticed a lurid handbill on his Saturday-night trip to town and went to the traveling representative heard a description that suddenly made the Green Mountains seem drab. A spanking new ship riding at her wharf; a fatherly skipper and smiling officers lining up to welcome you aboard; a new chest of clothes waiting by your neat, warm bunk; a rousing sailor's chanty ringing up from the forecastle and off across the quiet bay; a laughing, cheering crew heaving at the anchor windlass. Off she goes, with the Stars and Stripes whipping in the wind and a white bone in her teeth as she glides down the harbor and out onto the sparkling sea. And then —tropical sunshine bathing you while you loll against the fife rail and listen to the old seamen's yarns and the big ship rocks gently across the deep blue waters of the Pacific; spice islands send their exotic smells out onto the ocean to meet you; voluptuous brown-skinned island girls swim to the ship and climb aboard, naked; you eat foods you never dreamed existed—the man who hasn't tasted fried whale's lip washed down with Galápagos turtle soup hasn't been weaned yet. And—the only time there is any work—the exciting dash across the water after the whale, the dart of the harpoon, the ship sailing down alongside with the skipper leaning over the rail and shouting, "Hurrah! Well done, my boys! Come aboard, get into dry clothes and there'll be an extra ration of rum waiting for all hands!" The time goes so fast that before you know it you are back home, bronzed, strong, rich, and the wonder of every girl in town.

So after a few days of daydreaming the typical farm boy sneaked down the lane one early morning and kept on going. In New Bedford or Nantucket or New London he found a shipping office or a whaler at the wharf and asked uneasily if there were still room for another hand. The agent or mate usually managed to mask his amazement and get the lad's signature as quickly as he could. Then the young man looked about him and started asking questions. And he found out.

The nauseating odor that he thought was coming from the fishhouses across the wharf was not fish at all; it came from the ship, from a substance the whalemen called "gurry," a combination of brackish sea water, sewage, decayed bits of whale meat, and rancid whale oil. The decks were clean of it, but the effluvia fairly danced like heat waves above the hatches. The "pocket full of money" he had heard about was actually a "lay," a share of the ship's earnings from the voyage—a poor cruise, poor pay. And even if the ship had exceptional luck, the new hand would receive very little money. His lay was generally 1/190, which meant that the ship had to take 190 barrels of oil for every one he got, and the value of each barrel had already been set considerably below the going rate. He was presented with an outfit, all right, but it was charged against his lay, plus 25 per cent interest. And if any of it wore out during the voyage, he would have to purchase new clothing from the ship's "slop chest," at an increased cost. Besides all that, he was usually docked 3 per cent for insurance (for the ship, that is; the owner kept any insurance settlement), his share of the value of the empty oil casks, a commission for selling the oil on the ship's return, another charge for fitting out the ship, another for discharging the ship, another for use of the medicine chest and 10 per cent for "leakage." The cruise, advertised to him as a two-year junket, actually was for an undetermined time, probably nearer four years. And if he decided to leave the ship at any time before the end of the voyage, there was no part payment; he lost it all. To forestall desertion, no advances were given; the only way to get a little money for a port of call was to buy something from the slop chest, at the usual high price, and sell it ashore for a tenth of what it cost him.

And then he saw the forecastle. There was no merry song welling up from it, as advertised, but there was usually a noise. It was a cacophony of groans, retching, cursing, and the screams of delerium tremens. Unlike the farm boy, most of the men had sailed on mid-century whalers before, and they had to be drugged with drink and knocked senseless by the boardinghouse and brothel crimps in order to get them into the forecastle again. Down in the twelve-foot-square room, with no ventilation and bunks for sixteen men, the air was even worse than in the hold; the stench of the gurry was complemented by that of mildewed oilskins, ancient pipes, cigar butts, rotted bits of garbage, sweat, urine, and vomit. The only light was a tiny lamp, sputtering and gasping for oxygen in a noisome cloud of stale smoke that had hung there in clouds since the first voyage twenty years and five circumnavigations ago. On bunks that looked more like shelves the heaving, slobbering bodies gave the little room the impression more of a pauper's hospital ward than the lively clubhouse afloat which the boy had heard about. Amid the welter of bodies, unwashed clothing, gear, and filth an old wharf rat would be sitting, calmly picking his nose as he sized up the newcomer and greeted him:

"Welcome aboard our luxurious whaler, greenie, you stupid son of a bitch."

As soon as the new man found the only bunk left, up against the bow and farthest from the tiny shaft of sunlight seeping down the hatch, suddenly the yards seemed to come crashing down on the deck above him. It was only the mate banging on the forecastle scuttle to rouse all hands for the anchor windlass. Somehow all those who were not still senseless managed to climb on deck and limp to the windlass. Instead of the cheerful sea chanty there was the usual slipping, sprawling, and swearing before the anchor was hauled tight and the dock lines cast loose. A few who were sober enough pulled themselves aloft and unfurled the sails, spurred on by obscene abuse from the mates. Then the big ship eased from her wharf and got under way, slowly picking up speed as her sails filled and she slid down the harbor. She was not even in the outer bay before the greenie began to feel the strange sensation. He was seasick.

So did a landsman usually become a whaleman in the mid-nineteenth century. By the time he had recovered from his seasickness and was able to lift his head from the bunk, some order had been restored to the forecastle, the men had been divided into their watches, and the whaler was beginning to look shipshape. That was when the greenie's hazing would begin.

The first time he went aloft he got sick all over again. Climbing slowly, hanging on for his life, he took half an hour to inch up to the topgallant crosstrees. When he tried to squeeze through the "lubber's hole" still above his head, he brought a scream of rage from the mate. He was forced to swing, hand by hand and with feet dangling, on the futtock shrouds to get onto the trees. Climbing back to the deck was even worse. And if he tried, while off watch, to catch a nap in the open instead of in the stinking forecastle, a playful shipmate quickly flipped a line about his foot and he found himself hauled high aloft, hanging by one ankle and shrieking with fear as he swung out over the sea with each roll of the ship. But all the hazing was only a lead-up to what happened to him when he crossed the Equator the first time. That was when he was "keelhauled," i.e., tied arm and leg to two ropes, tossed over the bow, and yanked under water the full length of the ship's keel before being hauled, more dead than alive, over the taffrail to be dropped like a sopping rag on the deck.

Homesickness was only a minor problem, and there was plenty of time to get over it. The four-year cruise was common, the two-year cruise rare. Some whalemen got so used to it that, it is claimed, when one man about to leave for a "plum pudding" (Atlantic) voyage was reminded that he had not said good-by to his wife, he answered, "Oh well, I'll only be gone a year." It is further said that when he returned, his wife spotted him from the window as he came through the gate. Meeting him at the door with a bucket in her hand, she greeted him with: "Now fill this at the pump; supper will be ready in a few minutes." During the long years while the whalemen were off on the other side of the world, babies became children and little boys and girls grew up. Sometimes a boy who was still learning to read when his father sailed had shipped out himself by the time his father was home again. In the ship's log one lonely January day in mid-Pacific a mate wrote: ". . . Let me see. Today Susie is eleven months old. Oh God bless her . . . Kiss Susie eleven times for me. Good night Sarah." For those three or four years of long loneliness the only connection between a man and his family was the occasional whaleship plowing back around the Horn for home. To make the most of this thin line of communication, the whalemen had a "Post Office" of their own in the Pacific, a mailbox nailed to a tree on Charles Island, one of the Galápagos group. Here nearly every whaler stopped on her way out, to leave letters from home and to stock up on the islands' gigantic, edible turtles. And here whalers put in again, en route home, to pick up the letters to wives, children, and sweethearts. These were properly addressed, but the ones coming out usually bore only such directions as "John Smith, Boatsteerer, Ship *Minerva*, Pacific Ocean." Little of this personal correspondence has survived. But legends tell of one exchange that, though apocryphal, does typify the whaleman's extended absence from home:

> Dear Ezra,
> Where did you put the axe?
> Love,
> Martha

The answer, received in Nantucket fourteen months later:

> Dear Martha,
> What did you want the axe for?
> Love,
> Ezra

The answer, received on the Pacific one year later:

> Dear Ezra,
> Never mind about the axe. What did you do with the hammer?
> Love,
> Martha

The absence was made even worse by the week-long, sometimes month-long periods aboard a whaleship when the only work was boring drudgery. The work was undeniably interesting when whales were about, but it was not exactly easy. As soon as the whales were sighted, the men found themselves slaving at the oars, the cutting stages, and the tryworks until they dropped from exhaustion—only to be booted to their feet again when the call came once more from the masthead. But if nothing broke the far-off surface of the sea for days and weeks, most of the whaleman's occupation was make-work.

The skipper and his mates managed to provide a good bit of that, though. The ship was hardly in the open Atlantic, running down to the Horn, when each man was assigned to his station and all whaleboats were hoisted over the side. For hours the men drilled at the oars, making her race ahead, turn in her own shadow, and reverse course within a split second of the yell "STARN ALL!" Then there were the long tricks at the wheel, heavy and tall as a man; in rough weather it sometimes took all the strength and weight of two men to hold it steady. The delicate job of keeping her on course even in mild weather was not easily learned; many a greenie felt his stomach go out from under him when the wheel pulled from his hands, the yards slatted, a sail fluttered ominously, and the mate let out his angry bellow as the ship seemed to go completely out of control. It took many days for the new hand to master the art so the wake did not look, in the seaman's phrase, "like a dog wetting the snow."

It took even longer for a greenie to get used to working aloft. Out on the fore royal, with any roll to the ship at all, there was nothing most of the time between man and water ninety feet below. From that height a fall into the sea meant that even a good swimmer might go too deep to be able to fight his way back to the surface before he blacked out. Still that chance was preferable to plummeting off the yard and head over heels onto the deck. The Cape Horn squall was the seaman's worst nightmare—slithering out on the ice-coated footropes and hauling in at frozen canvas that ripped off a man's fingernails while sleet and spray stabbed him in the face, the gale grabbed at him, and the ship bucked under him like a mad horse. If in a howler like this the mournful, heart-stopping cry of "MAN OVERBOARD!" came down from aloft, all the skipper could hope was that the telltale mess of brains and blood on a yard or the rail would show that the man had mashed his head on the way down. That way it was over quickly for him. There could be no turning back in such weather, even assuming it might be possible to spot his bobbing head.

The lofty yards could be dangerous in the best weather, especially aboard a whaleship. Once a man accustomed himself to the height, once he could look below without losing his stomach, he ran the risk of being too sure of himself. Then, on a beautiful, sun-washed, soporific day, when the ship rolled gently through the sea and the timbers creaked in soothing rhythm and the trade wind crooned through the rigging, a man who made the mistake of sitting on the yardarm, leaning back against the mast, and closing his eyes never knew when the deck hit him. The lucky ones who managed to catch a last-second hold on the rigging not

only lived to go aloft again; they also never made the same mistake again.

On deck there was plenty of make-work too—seams to be retarred where the heat had brought it oozing out; harpoon and lance points to be polished and sharpened until they would slice through the thickest blubber; casks to be wet down so they would not shrink and start leaking oil; whale line to be coiled in the tub so carefully that it took half a day per tub (one kink while it whirred out after a whale could loop around a man's neck and throttle him before he had time to drown); shark hide to be peeled off and used to sandpaper the decks; and always the pumps, because there was no whaleship built that did not leak a little, especially after the warm-water borers of the Pacific had honeycombed her hull.

Then, finally, the excitement of the actual chase. This, after all, was what they were out here for, and it was every bit as thrilling as advertised—and a lot more dangerous. From the time the first yell came from the man hanging in the iron hoops high aloft to the time when, hours later, the monstrous carcass wallowed fin out, the whaleman's heart never stopped racing. But it was shoulder-wrenching work too—lowering in "white ash weather," without a breath of wind for the whaleboat's sail; straining at the oar while the mate urged and cursed and exhorted and pleaded, until every man's hands were glued to the oar by his own sun-

dried blood; backing for their lives when the harpoon hit home; and hanging on as they raced across the tops of the waves and trying to keep wetting the line as it threatened to burn right through the loggerhead. And then, after the kill, the real work.

Rowing back to the ship while towing a seventy-barrel whale looked impossible; the oar seemed to dig into the same little whirlpool of water it had just left. The long chase was nothing compared to this. Once the whale was alongside the ship and the boats were again hanging on their davits, the men were ready to collapse on the deck. But now it was time for cutting in. While the windlass shrieked under the weight, the ship rolled nearly onto her beam ends, and every timber looked about to start from the hull, the men worked out on the oil-smeared cutting stage and on the glassy black back itself—cutting, hacking, slipping and sliding, and trying to keep out of range of a flotilla of sharks that snapped all about them. One slip and a man was crushed like a peanut shell between the rolling carcass and the side of the ship.

First the huge body was stripped, its blubber unwound like the peeling of a gigantic orange. Then the great head, one third the size of the body, was hauled aboard, or alongside if too large to be brought on deck, and was cut open for its spermaceti. Sloshing into the cavernous "case," the spermaceti-filled forehead, one man stood up to his waist in the rose-tinted, butter-thick stuff while he bailed it out and it was passed in a bucket brigade to the tubs. Meanwhile, to catch up the gobbets of flesh and smears of spermaceti that had slopped over the side, men in whaleboats circled the ship scooping up the mess amid voracious gulls swooping from above and sharks from below.

The work was still not done. The blubber had to be converted to oil, with fire spouting up from the tryworks, grease washing across the deck, grime coating the men from head to foot, all in a miasma of smoke and stink that seemed to cut right through the bulkheads and stifle all life aboard.

Now all there was left to do was the cleaning up. That could take as long as a week.

It was healthy work, which was what the whaling skippers always said when asked why there was no doctor aboard. The captain usually served as doctor, setting the splints, doling out the patent medicines from the chest in his cabin. The whaling captain became fairly expert at pulling teeth, amputating with a cutting spade and setting bones (he could always rebreak them if he made a mistake). But there was little he could do about small-pox, venereal disease, and the many cases of internal injury when an oar or a piece of stove boat drove into a man's stomach or groin. Then a patient simply sickened and died. If he were a foremast hand he was usually buried at sea; an officer was some-times preserved in a barrel of rum for shipment home, and the rum was saved for rations on the next cruise. There was one malady, though, that the whaling skipper had a sure cure for: Cape Horn Fever, i.e., malingering. A remedy employed by a Nantucket captain was a plug of tobacco steeped in a pint of blackfish oil and administered internally every half hour until the man decided he felt well enough to go back to work. Another, more universal cure was simpler: "belaying-pin hash."

Despite the propaganda there is little evidence that the whal-ing skippers were any worse as a group than those of other ships. Just the same, there were plenty of "shore saints—sea devils." There was many a whaling captain who slugged a disobedient foremast hand and inquired into the matter afterward, and many a mate who, with the skipper's tacit consent, walked the deck with a length of rope in his hand, whipping it at anyone who did not happen to move fast enough to suit him. Normal punishment was "the cat," the many-tailed, knotted whip. The victim was hung by his thumbs, so that he swung off the tips of his toes with the motion of the ship; his back was bared and he got as many lashes as the captain thought he needed. It did not take many strokes of the cat to cut a back to tatters and drench the seaman in his own blood. And if he escaped the full punishment by faint-ing, a bucket of salt water sloshed on his lacerated back usually brought him screaming to life. The first hint of mutiny was re-pulsed with firearms. This happened just as frequently in the merchant service, even more frequently in the Navy. And it is true that as more and more men felt the call of the land frontier to the west, the situation worsened on all kinds of American ships, whalers included.

Yet, although democracy was never thought possible aboard a nineteenth-century ship, look at what happened on the whaler *John Adams* in 1823. Her captain died during the cruise. Her mate was lost; he and his boat's crew were last seen heading into a school of whales. The *John Adams* came home under command of Peter Green, her second mate. Peter Green was a Negro; like a great many other New England Negroes he had proved a good whaleman and had become an officer on his own merits. This was when Negroes in the American south were legal slaves—a full forty years before the Emancipation Proclamation.

It was not so much abuse and lack of freedom that bred rebellion aboard the whalers. The prime cause was the living conditions. The food of the isolated, wandering whaleship was usually garbage. The meat was salt pork and beef that had to be steeped in a tub for a day before it could even be used in a stew. Both were "saltier than Lot's wife"; both were called by the generic term "salt horse"; and both were the subject of a dirge sung in every forecastle:

"*Old horse! Old horse! What brought you here?*"

"*From Sacarap to Portland Pier*
I've carted stone for many a year;
Till, killed by blows and sore abuse,
They salted me down for sailors' use.

"*The sailors they do me despise,*
They turn me over and damn my eyes;
Cut off my meat, and scrape my bones
And heave the rest to Davy Jones."

The skippers who had some consideration for their men or, more realistically, wanted the crews to be in good working condition, laid in a supply of vegetables and filled a few pens—forward near the forecastle—with hogs and chickens whenever these fresh provisions could be purchased cheaply. But it took only a short time for the vegetables to rot in the tropical heat and only a little longer for the hogs and chickens to be killed off and eaten. During this time the salt horse was saved and, paradoxically, the men grew so tired of a steady diet of even these items that the skipper began to hear grunts and cackles coming from the direction of the forecastle and the yards above. For a few days then the crew did not complain about going back to the stand-by of salt meat. In fact, there were some old hands who claimed that it was, after all, the best fare for a seaman. "You can talk about yer flummadiddlers and fiddlepaddles," one veteran used to say, "but when it comes down to gen-u-ine grub, there ain't nothin' like good old salt hoss that you kin eat afore you turn in and feel it all night a-layin' in yer stummick and a-nourishin' you."

The usual meal was built around, i.e., consisted of, what whalemen called "lobscouse," a stew made by taking hardtack, pork fat or grease left after boiling salt horse (which the men called "top of the pot") and boiling it with molasses and water; if there were no pork fat or "top of the pot," any sort of "slush" would do. After a few days of this, when the men were on the brink of rebellion, the cook would substitute "potato scouse," which was the same mess with potatoes in place of "slush." There were other variations of this dish, known under such names as "burgoo," "dough-boys," and "dog's body." Often, in desperation, the men would fish for their meals. Some whalemen preferred the fish's intestines; they called them "innards" and ate them broiled, boiled, or even raw. Once, in a burst of charity, an old hand offered some to a greenie; he got small thanks for it. When he sloshed the stuff about in his mug and asked his shipmate, "Have some innards?" the young man took one look, turned green, then white, and muttered: "Jesus. Whose?"

There were also old veterans who regarded whale's brains as a delicacy. The barnacles from a whale's nose were supposed to have a particularly good flavor too, as did fried whale's lip. Herman Melville was fascinated by the spectacle of a whaleman, at night after the cutting in, sitting in front of an oil lantern and eating the whale by its own light.

The banquet of the whaleship was a meal consisting of "dandy funk," a baked concoction of powdered hardtack, molasses, and water, followed by a dessert of "plum duff," a gum-mangling delicacy made of flour, lard, and yeast boiled until it was hard as a rock, and flavored with whatever dried fruit there might be aboard. And God's gift to the whalemen were the enormous turtles of the Galápagos Islands—great, lumbering beasts which could be caught with practically no trouble at all and which could live with no sustenance for months without losing weight. Old hands liked to tell the greenies that these ancient, waddling, blinking tortoises were actually reincarnated ship's officers, especially captains.

But the delicacies were rare indeed, and the usual bill of fare was sickening—puddings and stews containing bits of rope yarn, slivers of wood, and broken nails, hardtack so maggoty that it was said to move across the deck until the weevils were beaten out of it, tea that was no more than "frightened water" and coffee so strong, bitter, and black that it seemed to have been brewed in the trypots with the oil.

The whalemen liked their coffee, though, just as much as seamen do today. It was not kept hot for them, of course, so a forecastle hand sometimes stowed a covered cup of it near his bunk. Even cold, it helped get the salt taste out of the mouth after a few hours aloft. The trouble was that often, groping about in the dark forecastle at night, he would drain his cup, then gag and curse as he spat out a huge, scrambling cockroach.

This was life in the forecastle, the filthiest place in the filthy whaleship. After the first cutting in the reek of oil hung in the heavy air for the rest of the cruise. Gurry had oozed through the deck and had been tracked down the narrow steps by the men's boots. Tattered clothes swung on their pegs like pendulums to the creaking roll of the ship, spattering every inch of the forecastle deck with oil. The atmosphere never cleared, and the pipe smoke and oil stink of the first few days were there, in one of the many layers, two years later. Hundreds of insects scuttled about the dark corners, burrowing into the men's bunks and skittering away when they found the warm hollow of a greasy blanket already occupied by a huge rat.

The men smelled as bad as the forecastle. There was never

enough fresh water for washing, and sea water was not so cleansing. A cask near the bowsprit contained urine; it was supposed to be a good dirt eradicator, but it didn't improve the smell of the forecastle. When the food was sent down, spoiled by the tropical heat, crusted with congealed grease, and infested with vermin, one man held the bowl while another turned his back and called off the names of the crew. That way each man got a fair chance at an edible piece of salt horse—and took his chance at a mouthful of maggots. It was a human cesspool, where the men coughed their lungs up, had screaming nightmares, swore at each other constantly, played vile practical jokes, and occasionally fought violent, bloody brawls.

There were the exceptions, especially when the skipper and his officers made the crew police up the forecastle and when the men were not terrorized by the captain. One imaginative yarn concerns the skipper of a "happy" (as opposed to "taut") Nantucket whaleship whose name is lost in legend. The men became aware that the skipper prided himself on his ability to tell where he was on any ocean in the world simply by "tasting the bottom." It was his boast that he could send down the sounding lead with tallow attached, taste the gravel, sand, or coral that came up, and thereupon give the longitude and latitude. This was too good a thing for the men to let pass. So one evening a couple of the boys swiped some dirt from a flowerpot the captain had with him, carefully soaked it in sea water, and spread it on the tallow of the lead. With the mate in on the gag they presented themselves in the captain's cabin in the dead of night. After waking him they explained their mission. They were worried about their position, they said, because of the curious look of the bottom they had brought up. Would the skipper kindly assure them that they were where they thought they were?

The story goes that the captain took the lead, studied it, touched his tongue to it, and handed it back. With a cold, sarcastic stare he announced:

"By the taste of it I should say that there has been a dire calamity. Nantucket Island has sunk and we are sailing right over Marm Hacket's garden. Now unless you men would like the rest of the flowerpot shoved down your throats, you will return to duty and let me return to my sleep. And JUMP!"

Despite all the work the skipper and mates could provide there were always long periods when the time hung heavy on the whaleman's hands. So it was that he developed scrimshawing, the only indigenous art of the American white man. No one knows for sure where the term came from, though the colonial name for a loafer was a "scrimshander," and scrimshawing was sometimes called "scrimshanding" or "scrimshonting." No matter how harsh the discipline, it was the tradition of the whaler that the whale's teeth went to the crew. Given this rock-hard, coarse substance, the whaleman set out on a project that might take him more than a year; but he had plenty of time. A few weeks of soaking in brine softened the tooth enough to make it workable, whereupon, amid much free advice from most of the crew, the artist went to work. After months of cutting, gouging, slicing, peeling, and polishing he usually wound up with nothing more than a crude hunk of bone with the outline of a whale or a ship carved on it. But there were veterans at the job who made fantastic arrays of little sculptures—candlesticks and cribbage boards, chessmen and crochet shuttles, snuffboxes and slide rules, bird cages and bodkins. Some of these experts even carried with them what Herman Melville described as "boxes of dentistical-looking instruments" in their sea chests. But most achieved their little works of art with the simple jackknife. India ink served for the decoration, and wood ashes helped give the finished product a polish. But there was no substitute for the long and loving massage of the hand, over a period of a year or more. The most popular subjects chosen by the whalemen indicated where their thoughts lay as they sat against the forecastle scuttle whittling, whistling and idling the off-hours away. The scrimshaw most often made was the jagging wheel, to be used for crimping the edges of that delicacy rarely seen aboard a whaler, the pie. Another of the most popular items was the busk, designed for the bosom of the loved one's corset. Some of these bust supporters were lovingly decorated with such gentle scenes as the battle of the *Bonhomme*

Richard and *Serapis* or a harpooner killing a whale. Others had romantic verses. Such as:

> *Accept, dear girl, this busk from me;*
> *Carved by my humble hand.*
> *I took it from a sperm whale's jaw,*
> *One thousand miles from land!*
> *In many a gale,*
> *Has been the whale*
> *In which this bone did rest.*
> *His time is past,*
> *His bone at last*
> *Must now support thy breast.*

Few were the amusements of the whaleman besides scrimshawing. Bloodcurdling practical jokes were played constantly—keelhauling, swinging a sleeping seaman out over the water, trying to nudge the footropes from under a man's feet when he was out on the yardarm. Another idle amusement was to catch a fish, kill it, leave it on the hook, and float it astern for a gull; the gull gulped the bait down, started to fly away, and found itself caught. Then the sport was to let it fly off for a short distance and reel it in until it finally flopped exhausted on the water. Of course it had to be killed then; there was no way of getting the valuable fishhook back without cutting the gull open. Another bird that could be caught this way was the albatross; one smart rap over its head with a bung starter or belaying pin finished it off, and the albatross' legs made excellent pipestems.

Out on the broad expanse of the Pacific a whaleman got the feeling that he was walled in by the bulwarks of the ship, imprisoned for years aboard a floating slaughterhouse, with nothing beyond the rising and falling walls but an eternity of sea and sky, rolling endlessly past him. Day after day, week after week, and month after month it was the same wide sea, stretching off over the horizon in every direction, the same flat blue ceiling of sky, the same unending monotony. So it took only the slightest change in the routine to transform the whole ship; which is what happened one day in the 1880s aboard the New Bedford whale-ship *Splendid*. The *Splendid's* skipper was John M. Soule, also of New Bedford, and he was known in his forecastle as "Good Old Soule." This was partly because John M. Soule was a popular skipper; but mostly it was to distinguish him from another whaleship captain named Soule. The men in his forecastle had a nickname for that Soule too. It was a lot more picturesque, but it was unprintable.

Not that the men aboard the *Splendid* spoke only in printable language; they were as rough and dirty a crew as any of the 1880s, which is saying a lot. But it may interest those who maintain that all whalemen of the late nineteenth century were half animal to consider what happened aboard the *Splendid*.

She was cruising the South Pacific north of New Zealand when she put in for wood and water at Sunday Island, one of the Kermadec group. A crewman in the shore party happened to spot a nanny goat and take off after her. Ordinarily he would have known better; it was about as easy to catch up with an island goat on foot as it was to swim after a dolphin. But this nanny happened to be about ready to produce a kid, and her speed and maneuverability were accordingly limited. After a chase and tussle that took the best part of the day, the puffing sailor managed to make his capture and drag her aboard the whaleboat.

No doubt the experience speeded up her time. For Sunday Island was hardly below the horizon when she went into labor. The entire crew naturally attended her, and the delivery was accomplished amid a great deal of interested, ribald comment.

But then they took a close look at the kid.

He tried to stand, flopped down, tried again, and this time wavered on his spraddled little legs as the ship rolled under him and his mother leaned over him, licking him from head to tail. He looked up at the faces around him, blinked, and waggled his ears. The ribald comments stopped. Then he staggered again as the ship lurched, and sprawled on the deck, his four legs seeming to point north, south, east, and west.

The nearest man was over him immediately, cradling him gingerly and slowly lifting him to his feet. The kid promptly fell in a heap again. The men laughed, then elbowed and shoved each other out of the way as they crowded solicitously around him to stuff their jackets under his still-weak head.

Within an hour the kid had moved into the forecastle, where he stayed except for eating and sleeping time. He was the darling of every hand. Men going on watch, especially those about to climb the rigging for the long, dreary search for whales, tweaked the kid's tail for good luck. As the watch changed and the whale-men stomped below, each one paused to hold out a finger, which the kid obligingly grabbed and nibbled. And woe to the foremast hand who inadvertently stumbled over the sleeping form sprawled across the narrow space of the forecastle.

In a surprisingly short time the kid had developed his sea legs, whereupon he clattered up the companionway to the deck. The stink of the forecastle was too much for him. This confirmed every man's claim; but with whoops of laughter they herded him back below. After a few such futile escapes the kid resigned himself to the place. And when he developed the habit of waddling up and nuzzling the knees of each man who came below, the atmosphere in the forecastle became positively maudlin.

Then came the crisis. The kid's mother sickened and stopped giving her milk. The men spent hours clumsily trying to force the milk, then attempting to wean the kid. They saved their precious fresh-water ration and mixed it in a gruel. They tried watery pudding. They even offered him the carefully hoarded beer they had manufactured from pilfered potatoes and molasses. The kid refused it all. Day by day he grew weaker as the men kept watch on watch over him. Finally, in a sentimental con-ference the likes of which the *Splendid's* forecastle had never seen before, they reached their sad decision: put the little fellow out of his misery. The most unfortunate whaleman aboard ship was the one to whom the executioner's lot fell.

That night the men sat gloomily on their bunks. Hardly a word was spoken. When supper was brought down there was none of the usual argument over who would divide the food and who would turn his back and call out each man's name for his share. Silently the man nearest the companionway reached for the mess.

Then he examined it more closely and exploded. The forlorn little body they had put aside for a morning burial at sea had been stolen by the *Splendid's* black-skinned, black-hearted cook. It was now their stew.

The cook may well have wondered why the first fresh-meat meal he had provided in months came back uneaten. But he could not have missed the dark looks of the crew, though he never knew how close to death he came that night. Like the officers, however, he noticed the change that came over the ship next day. The men who had baffled Captain Soule by laughing and singing chanties as they went about their work now moved slowly, spat behind the officers' backs, and argued among themselves in language that nearly curled the sails. The slightest disagreement in the forecastle set off a fight that all but made the ship wallow in her seaway.

The kid in the forecastle was gone. And the creaky, lumbering, stinky old *Splendid* was back to normal again.

Rare was the livening episode like the kid in the *Splendid's* forecastle, though. Usually it was the same dreary succession of days and nights plodding about the Pacific, the boredom broken only occasionally, never often enough, by the cry from the lookout and the chase after the whale. Even the seemingly aimless wanderings about the huge ocean took on a month-by-month pattern. The whaling skippers did not roam haphazardly looking for whatever whales might cross their paths; they went to the "grounds" where previous experience—and other skippers' logs—indicated the animals ought to be at certain times of the year. So in a general way the ships followed much the same course through the year—north of the Sandwich Islands in June and July, across to the waters "on Japan" for the autumn, until November, when they started the "great circle" cruise back across the Pacific to the coast of California. By spring they were touching at the Galápagos Islands for more turtles and by early summer they were off across the Pacific again, this time south of the Equator and in the general direction of the Marquesas or the Society Islands. This took until February or March, by which time they stood up toward the Equator, then off west toward the Kingsmill group (Gilbert Islands), where they cruised through the summer. By August they were pointed south again, toward the Ellice and the Navigators Islands (Samoa). In the fall they were heading back east, working in the direction of the Societies, where they usually were by October. Then—after two and one-half years of crossing and recrossing the Pacific—west again, this time along the Line. By then, although the whalemen did not use the term "forecastle-happy," most of them were.

And during most of that time they were left to their scrimshaw-ing, their horseplay—and their yarns. That is why the whaleman was usually far and away a more imaginative, practiced, and accomplished man with a yarn than the crewman of any merchant or navy ship.

There were Pacific nights made for those yarns—with bright stars lighting the silken water, sea fires flashing along the hull and gilding the wake, the whaler sighing as she rose over the swells, and no other sound save the low monotone of an old whaleman saying, "There she was, a-lyin' on the coral beach in the pale moonlight, nekkid . . ."

Many of their stories were dreary old tales known even to landsmen. But some of them nearly constituted an art form of their own. Many whalemen could take the simplest story, elabo-rate on it, add other elements from other stories, and spin it out until the absolute minimum listening time was two hours. By the time the story of the *Essex* had been told and retold in floating bull sessions across the Pacific, only one member of her crew had survived, and he had subsisted the last four days by eating off three of his own fingers. The Mocha Dick of the forecastle yarns was the size of a whaleship and had sent more battered hulks to the bottom than the *Shenandoah* had in all of the Civil War. Many were the tales of men being knocked out of stove boats and riding whales' backs until they could be rescued. Accounts of narrow escapes from cannibals were especially popular, and there was even one in which the whaleman was tied to a tree where he could watch the fire being built and the kettle being hung over the fire; for an hour he sweated while he watched the pot come to a boil, whereupon the natives burst out laughing, tossed a dozen chickens into the boiling water, untied him, and invited him to the feast.

Then there were the thousands of yarns about love between the whaleman and the native girl, some romantic, some far from it. It took roughly two and one-half hours to tell correctly the story of the proper young greenie from Boston who shipped aboard a whaler and eventually found himself on a tropical island. He had been at sea eleven months, so he forgot all about being proper and made a direct approach to the first good-looking native girl he saw. He was pretty startled at her willingness; but he was a lot more startled when he found he was expected to perform before an applauding native audience.

It took even longer to do justice to the simple story of one boat that was stove by a whale. The spinner of the yarn was always a participant in this one, and he spared no detail on how the whale's flukes caught the boat's underside and sent her and all her crew flying into the air. There followed considerable description of which man was flying faster and higher than the other. After half an hour of telling, the teller finally started to recount his downward flight toward the water. As he looked below him, he found the whale lying there, its mouth open and ready for him (exact description of the whale's mouth, tooth by tooth). "You know what I thought then?" There was almost always a wide-eyed greenie who could be counted on to exclaim, "For God's sake, what!"

"I thought," said the spinner, shifting his cud, "he'd make about seventy barrels."

A comparatively short one, which averaged three hours, concerned an eighty-year-old whaleman who finally retired and built boats in a village in Maine. One day he disappeared. He didn't show up again for eight years. When he did, his friends naturally asked him where he had been.

"In jail."

Why in jail? What on earth for?

"Rape."

Good God! Rape? When he was eighty years old?

The old whaleman's answer was taciturn but to the point: "Evidence was so complimentary," he said, "I pleaded guilty."

But no matter how good a foremast hand was at spinning a yarn, he seemed to save his finest performance for the deck or forecastle of another ship. For, with the exception of a green-bordered tropical island, nothing was as welcome a sight as the royals of another whaler heaving into view. It almost always meant that the two ships would come up to each other, haul the main aback, and exchange crews for a gam. That was when the stalest anecdote suddenly became a colorful tale. Then, for weeks afterward, there were new yarns, woven about the same old framework but new just the same, to fill the idle hours aboard each whaler.

There usually was a strict etiquette to these gams. After the preliminary hail of "How many barrels?" between the two skippers, one was rowed over to visit the other. During the row across to the other ship the captain was expected to stand upright in his whaleboat, meanwhile being whapped in the small of the back by the steering oar and cracked in the knees by the backswing of the after oarsman. But the etiquette demanded that the skipper could not use his hands for holding on, no matter how rough the day, no matter how his boat pitched in the troughs of the waves. Sometimes, though, for a very short moment in dire emergency, a captain *had* been known to grab hold of the nearest oarsman's hair and, as Melville described it, "hold on there like grim death."

For as long as the skippers wished to gam, the crews could have their own session forward. Usually they exchanged true stories—well, they were based on true happenings. They had, of course, been improved with the countless tellings and retellings, and now that they were being presented to another crew they were approaching perfection.

This was the case one day in 1850 when the famous *Charles W. Morgan* crossed paths with the *Christopher Mitchell* of Nantucket, and an old salt hauled himself aboard the *Morgan* while his captain gammed with the *Morgan's* skipper. The visitor from the *Mitchell* settled himself down, leaned back against the forward fife rail, and proceeded to go through all the carefully studied delaying motions proper to the beginning of a good one. He unbuttoned his greasy shirt, scratched himself, slowly buttoned his shirt again, shifted his rump into a more comfortable position, accepted a bite off a plug of moldly tobacco offered him by one of his hosts, nodded a polite "thank ye, thank ye," swallowed some of the juice, and wiped away the tears that flooded to his eyes. Then, while the men sprawled at his feet, he told his story.

It was about a young hand on the *Mitchell*. How he had blundered aboard a whaler no one could figure out, because he was the perfect gentleman. He never cursed or smoked. He kept himself as clean as anyone can in a whaleship forecastle. Not that he was a sissy when it came to working the ship. For the first few days he was deathly seasick, but what green hand isn't, plunging down across the Gulf Stream in an old hooker? As soon as he got his sea legs under him he pitched in with the best of them, scampering up the rigging to the topgallant yards, hauling his oar in the whaleboat, clambering out onto the slippery back of a whale when they cut it in. Naturally the officers liked him fine. The men in the forecastle didn't very much at first; even after they gave up riding the other greenies they saved their choicest abuse for the young gentleman. He never took it in bad grace, though, no matter how badly they hazed him. He laughed, more politely than in amusement, at their foul stories. But the fact that he never used the whalemen's obscenities himself only urged the others on to greater excesses. For a while some of the worst language ever heard even in a forecastle was spoken as a regular course aboard the *Mitchell,* just to shock the young gentleman into being one of the boys. He never did become one of the boys; but he never seemed to mind the terrible language, either. Finally the hands became bored with it and gave up teasing him. The forecastle settled down into its usual life.

Then one day as the *Mitchell* was rounding the Horn she was hit by one of those sudden, screaming snow squalls that have dismasted so many ships down there. In one howling blast she was over on her side, while the skipper hollered to put the wheel hard up and the ship heeled farther and the seas rushed in over her lee rail. The men near the main and mizzen halyards got them loose; but with tons of water pouring over the bow and the deck nearly vertical the men forward could only jump for the weather rigging and hang on. So the fore-topsail and main were still set and drawing, and the *Mitchell* hung there, threatening to go over. But not a man dared let go of his perch in the rigging, no matter how the skipper yelled.

Then who should come scrambling up from the forecastle but the young gentleman. He saw the trouble in a glance; he crawled over the plunging tryworks and cooler, braced his feet against them, made a wild grab for the halyards, caught them and cast them off. The bucking ship rose onto a more or less even keel and fell off before the wind. She was safe. Everyone agreed that the young gentleman had turned out to be the best hand on the ship. He was no hero, but he was a little nearer to being one of the boys.

They had been eight months out and were cruising along the coast of Peru in stinking hot weather when the young gentleman took sick. For two days the fever kept him in his bunk. He was still below on the third day, when one of his shipmates climbed down into the forecastle to get his pipe. The other men off watch were asleep. It was as still there as on deck—not a word spoken, not even the thud of anyone walking about, just the slow creak of the masts, the groan of the ship's joints as she rolled from side to side, and the swish-trickle as the sea slid past. The man got his pipe and turned to go on deck again. But then he happened to look at the young gentleman's bunk.

"Well, sir," the old yarn spinner said, "the next thing we knew about it on deck, this fella was fallin' all ova himself to git back out of the fo'c'sle. He come screamin' past me so fast I decided to git up and folla him aft. Turned out I didn't haf to. He hauled up afore the first mate, who was sittin' on the rail, and he yelled loud enough so you could hear him all ova the ship. 'That young fella who's sick, the young gentaman,' he said. 'He's a girl!'"

The old man chomped his chaw quietly while he gave his listeners time to savor the full effect of the announcement.

"The mate was about to knock the man down," he went on.

"He jumped down off the rail and yelled, 'What in hell's the matta with you?' But there was nuthin' the matta with him. The mate found that out when he went below—follad by about the hull ship's compleement. He was a she, all right. Yes, sir, he sure was."

The young gentleman, the best hand on the ship, was a girl. In her feverish sleep her shirt had come undone; so had the canvas corset she had concealed for eight months.

The old yarn spinner chomped meditatively again. One man broke the silence and spoke for all the listeners aboard the *Morgan* with the obvious question. For eight months these men had thought and talked practically nothing but women. Now here was a woman right in the forecastle with them. What happened?

The old man had been waiting for the question. He got creakingly to his feet, ambled over to the lee rail, hawked and spat, then wiped the back of his hand across his mouth and on his shirt. Leaning back against the rail, he surveyed the *Morgan's* assembled crew and smiled.

"Nothin'," he said.

Talking big about women is one thing, he explained, especially after a few months at sea. Island girls are another thing, especially the ones that are dark brown and don't wear any clothes to speak of and will do anything to get a white man. But a white girl right there in the forecastle, a girl you've lived with for eight months without knowing it—well, that's quite a third thing altogether. Mind you, these men weren't the kind who only talked big about women. You only had to see them hit the beach where the brown girls were used to sailors—like shaking a beehive. But a girl right in the forecastle, lying there with her shirt off—yes, sir, that's something else; that's something else altogether.

The mate helped her aft to the cabin, where there was a spare stateroom. She stayed there until the skipper could get to Lima, which he did as fast as the *Mitchell* would sail. She told him her story, and of course it was all over the ship within minutes. She came from a little town on the Hudson River, and she had fallen for some man who had then gone off and left her. But this girl had a lot of spunk, and she took out after him. She heard that he had gone to Nantucket to ship aboard a whaler. At New Bedford somebody told her a man answering his description had signed on the *Mitchell*. So she got into boy's clothes, went over to Nantucket, and easily got a berth. By the time the last man was aboard and she realized she had the wrong ship, the *Mitchell* was leaving the harbor.

The old man had been to sea a great many years, he said, and he had seen some mighty peculiar things in his day. But he swore he had never seen anything like that parting aboard the *Mitchell* the day she dropped anchor in Lima harbor. The young girl stood there on the deck, looking pretty already, with the color back in her cheeks and a blouse without any canvas corset under it and the breeze ruffling the hair she no longer kept balled up under her cap. She thanked the captain, shook hands with the mate, and made a little speech about how nice everybody had been to her and how she would never forget them. The old man had to blink to make himself believe he was still on the deck of a whaleship. Then the girl came down the deck and shook each man by the hand. And what impressed the old man more than anything else was that, while she hung her head a little, so did every one of those tough bastards in the line.

Long after the gam had ended and the decks were cleared and the old man had returned to his ship, the men of the *Morgan* were still talking about it. And it was not until then that somebody pointed out that, with the possible exception of the captain, you could bet the old whaleman was the only soul aboard the *Mitchell* who told that yarn the way it really happened.

8. Wives, children, and a girl on the beach

In a contemporary newspaper account there is evidence that the yarn spun by the old man of the *Mitchell* was a true story. And the evidence indicates that the girl was treated just as he said she was. But, as the old man pointed out in his yarn, it was a different matter on the beach with the island girls.

It is therefore one of the mysteries of the age of whaling that so few accounts of the whalemen's bawdy escapades have come down through history. The mystery is not that they *wanted* to keep it to themselves; their reasons, especially the married ones', were obvious. What is strange about it was that their censorship was so successful.

Dozens of missionaries wrote home about the "lewdness" and "licentiousness" with which the whalemen "disported themselves" with the island women. But the missionaries' chief purpose was to impress the religious at home with the need for more funds with which to set up more missions, convert more natives, and put more clothes on them; and the faithful at home did not make the best audience for graphic accounts of misbehavior. The dark hint served better than the lurid, detailed story. So the missionaries' accounts, though titillating, did little to penetrate the whalemen's curtain of silence.

There were others who offered tempting but insubstantial tidbits of information on the subject. The forecastle braggart did not suddenly become a closemouthed gentleman of honor when he arrived home. His stories were graphic, all right. But they bore the same ring of authenticity as the tales of sea serpents, mermaids, and ghost ships. Many too were the romantic accounts of the lure of the islands—and island women—spread abroad by captains and shipping agents for the benefit of gullible farm hands; and these stories were as accurate as the promises of jolly shipmates, fatherly officers, and hot mince pie on the afterdeck.

There were plenty of bawdy island stories going the rounds of taproom and eating club in the nineteenth century; but for their own good reasons the skippers and mates kept them out of the logs and chronicles of the day. The wives sitting out their empty years at home were having it hard enough; no point in torturing them, even with the truth. So there was little verification for most of the stories in any of the official or reliable records.

Nevertheless, despite the censorship and camouflage, some of the carefully hidden activities of the forecastle hands, mates—and captains—have been pretty well established, if only by what can be called internal evidence. The spread of venereal disease is evidence enough; it was the scourge of the forecastle, and it swept every island visited by the whalers for the first time. There could be no more perfect setup in the eyes of the sex-starved whaleman than the moral code of the Pacific islands. On some of them promiscuity was an accepted part of life. When American missionaries tried to translate the Ten Commandments into Hawaiian, for example, they found there was no native word for "adultery." The best they could do was: "Thou shalt not commit mischievous sleeping"—an injunction that served only to puzzle the natives. On other islands the codes were stricter. But the novelty of a white man was usually sufficient excuse for breaking the sex taboos. And many a green foremast hand was baffled when, on hitting the beach and taking off after an island girl, she didn't run. On the rare occasions when war broke out between a whaling crew and the islanders over a woman, it usually was not because the visitor had taken advantage of her, but because the whaleman was outraged to find "his woman" in the arms of a shipmate or another islander an hour or so later.

It is true that on many a soft, starlit night the waters around a whaleship suddenly came alive with naked brown girls swimming out from the beach to climb aboard. Some were driven off; but the skippers most fondly remembered by their crews were the ones who let the girls slither up the sides and spend the night aboard. By morning the crewmen turned to their work with a will, and the girls, their new trinkets stuffed in their hair or tucked in their mouths, were happily swimming back to shore. It is true that many a native merchandiser quickly made the discovery that, while he could enrich himself in canny trading with the visiting whalemen, he could do even better if he had a girl to act as "liaison" for him. It is true that in many of the larger island communities such trading became a profession and red-light districts sprawled all across the waterfront. And it is even true that there were a few isolated islands which some whaling skippers adopted as their homes away from home—complete with native wives and children. Many of these skippers, being God-fearing men, did not commit the sin of solemnizing their island marriages by any ceremony, which was all right with most of the native women, who would have regarded actual marriage, especially a Christian one, as a sin against their beliefs too. The usual pattern of such relationships was a year or two at home in New England with the real wife and kids, then the voyage out to the island, which was used as the base of operations for the next three or four years of cruising. In both ports the happy families grew and multiplied and waited for Father's return. The New England wife and children knew nothing of the island family, of course. And

the island family either knew nothing of its New England coun-
terpart or couldn't care less.

There were excesses, and probably the worst of them were in
Honolulu. Here the earliest whalemen of the nineteenth century
found a somnolent tropic town with a beautiful and well-pro-
tected harbor. They turned it into the pesthole of the Pacific.
"Cape Horn," the whorehouse district, was so named because of
the truism that the whalemen hung their consciences on the Horn
on the voyage out and picked them up again on the way home.
The district was known all over the world for its riotous de-
bauches, and the whalemen accordingly felt called upon to go on
their wildest sprees in Honolulu. Whalemen have been praised
as the saviors of Honolulu because on one occasion they organized a bucket brigade and doused a fire that was threatening to
wipe out the whole town. But it seems only fair that they should
have—it was apparently a mob of drunken whalemen who started
the fire in the first place. When a policeman clubbed a roisterer,
the mob chased the cop into the police station, beat him senseless, and set fire to the building. Only the threat to the oil-soaked
fleet moved the whalemen to attack the fire, and while they were
fighting it many of their shipmates went rioting through the
wreckage, plundering everything in sight.

The situation along the waterfront got so bad that some whaling skippers did not dare let their men go ashore, not so much out
of sympathy for the Hawaiians as in fear that less than half the
crew would ever return to the ship. They found a way out of this
dilemma, though. A few dollars invested in the right places
helped effect an arrangement whereby *wahine* who had been
jailed for public fornication were allowed out for the night—if
they would spend that night aboard a whaleship in the harbor.
In fact, the shrewder skippers and mates made a practice of inspecting the women beforehand, visiting them in their cells for
the afternoon.

So it was no wonder that although a returning whaleman could
spend days regaling his wife and children with stories about
Pacific storms, cannibals, and the big whale that got away, he
would become reticent at the mention of island girls. Just the

same, many of the true accounts of their amorous escapades did get home as more and more whaleships went out to the Pacific. And the reaction of some wives, fitting as it might be, was almost unheard of in the nineteenth century of the double standard: they strayed themselves. Owen Chase, who survived the wreck of the *Essex* to return to sea and become a whaling captain, may have led a blameless life on the islands of the Pacific; no one knows. But when he returned from one of his voyages he divorced his wife for adultery. And Captain Robert Cathcart, master of the whaleship *Otter,* was off the South American coast when he heard that his wife had been unfaithful; he promptly took the ship into Santa Catarina, sold her, and pocketed the money, which was an ingenious form of revenge, since his wife had sinned with the owner of the *Otter.* The other reaction to these accounts was a much more practical one. The wives decided they would go along on the next cruise.

It was no fun; a number of whaling skippers' wives went out on only one voyage, then decided that home without a husband was better than life with him in the impossibly crowded, oil-smelling, isolated whaleship cabin. For one thing it meant taking the children along. And it was just as unnatural a life for them as it was for their mother. Children being the adaptable creatures they are, they usually learned to enjoy it as a four-year adventure, though many of them were horrified to discover that no school meant lessons from mother anyway. The skippers' wives suffered most— from the lack of any feminine companionship, the brutishness of whaling, the vile food, the terror of the Pacific's typhoons, the sickening fear when a child hurt himself and there was not a chance of doctor's care.

Probably the first woman to go on a whaling voyage was Mary Hayden Russell, wife of Captain Joseph Russell of Nantucket. At the time, 1823, her eldest son William was a boat steerer aboard his father's ship *Emily.* Apparently on an impulse Mrs. Russell packed up a few belongings, took her younger son Charles by the hand, and boarded a ship for London. There, as she had calculated, she found the *Emily* fitting out to cruise for her British owners. When the *Emily* set sail, the whole Russell family was aboard. And then, far out at sea, young Charles tripped in the cabin companionway, fell down the steps, and broke his arm at the wrist. There was, of course, no ship's doctor. There was no anesthesia, nor were there drugs of any kind. While Charles' mother apparently looked on and tried to soothe the boy's agonized screams, and while one of the crewmen pinned down the thrashing body, Captain Russell cracked his son's little arm back into place and bound it in splints. In her relief after it was over Mrs. Russell wrote in her diary: "The dear fellow bore the operation with courage that would have done credit to a man." Taking the family on a whaling cruise was no picnic in the nineteenth century.

Nevertheless most of the wives not only stuck it out, but also went along on the next cruise and the next and finally settled down only when their husbands retired. Mrs. Charles A. Grant of Nantucket shipped out with her husband and gave birth to her son George on a little South Pacific island. After that experience she decided to skip the next cruise. She stayed home, but not for long. Soon she and her infant son were on a ship bound out to Melbourne, Australia; from there she got passage on a schooner to the Bay of Islands, New Zealand, where, sure enough, Captain Grant's whaler *Mohawk* came gliding into the harbor on schedule. The captain was pleased, but not very surprised, to see his wife and young son come aboard halfway around the world from where he had left them. After that Mrs. Grant went on every cruise with her husband, for thirty-two years, having her babies here and there on whatever island or coral atoll (including Pitcairn Island) was nearest at her time.

Very few whalemen resented the skipper's bringing his wife along. Those who were superstitious about having a woman on board soon forgot all about it at the sight of a stack of blueberry pies, a laughing, pig-tailed girl swinging on the rigging, or even, a thousand miles from home, a woman singing in the morning sun as she hung out her wash on the spanker boom. Indeed, it was while hanging out her wash one day that Mrs. Grant earned one of the silver dollars her husband offered to anyone who sighted a whale. Evidently the lookout was asleep at the crosstrees, for Mrs. Grant glanced over her jury-rigged clothes-line, spat out her clothespins, and bellowed: "BLOWS! THERE SHE BLOOOOWS!" It was a big one, and its carcass was rolling alongside in a few hours.

The treatment was better too when the skipper's wife was aboard. At Talcahuano one day in 1868, twelve men succumbed to the lure of the tropics and deserted the whaleship *Iona*. But Captain John Norton was too smart for them. He upped anchor, set sail, and put out of the harbor. Behind a nearby island, how-ever, he hauled the main aback and waited a while, then cracked on everything and came booming back into the harbor. As he had figured, his deserters had come out of hiding as soon as the ship had disappeared. It was a simple matter to round them up and get under way again. Once safely at sea, he had the men seized up to the rigging and prepared to give them a "taste of the cat." Thereupon his wife Charity appeared on deck.

"John," she said, "what are those men in the rigging for?"

"I'm goin' to lick 'em," said Captain Norton.

"Oh no, you're not," said Charity. And he didn't.

But there was another reason why most whalemen liked to have the skipper bring his wife and kids along, a reason not many of them admitted openly. With nothing but thousands of miles of rolling seas between a man and home it was a wonderful thing to climb down from the masthead on a bright, sunny day and see a wooden horse rocking to the motion of the ship, or a doll or toy bear perched on the forecastle scuttle. And what more apprecia-tive audience is there than a wide-eyed six-year-old listening, trancelike, to the most preposterous account of superhuman bravery on the high seas?

It was the ultimate in flattery to the foremast hand to be sub-jected to the unrelenting barrage of children's questions. A whale-man knew a great deal before he had mastered his difficult job, and on a lazy day on the open Pacific it gave him considerable pleasure to impart his wisdom. What were those boats hung on the outside of the ship for? What were all those tools in the bot-toms of the boats? Why did you climb way up there to the top of the ship? Wasn't it scary up there? What would you do if you started to fall? If you fell in the water from up there, would it hurt? What did the whale do when you got the boat up close to him? Did he cry when the iron stuck him? Did whales have babies? How? Did a whale pull a boat faster than you could go on a horse? Could a whale pull the whole ship? This ship? Did a whale really spout water? Was that thing in your hand really from a whale's mouth? Were his teeth *that* big? Did he brush them at night? Why not? Any whaleman knew the answers to all these questions, and it was an enjoyable experience to be asked.

These boys and girls who went down around the Horn visited the faraway corners of the earth that landsmen never saw in their lives. By the time George Grant was two, he had already been around the world. It was nothing to hear a couple nine-year-olds in Edgartown discussing the relative merits of Truk and Upolu as harbors. These youngsters, thrown on their own devices for three or four years of confinement aboard ship, seemed to mature faster than their friends ashore. The boys learned seamanship quickly, and many of them had harpooned their first whale by the time they were in their teens. The girls learned housekeeping more readily because there was more time for it, and they learned the art of self-sufficiency and became expert at the invention of countless games that could be played by one. Undoubtedly they saw and heard things their parents would have preferred them not to. But there is no evidence that their young minds were warped by the experience.

A case in point is that of young Laura Jernegan, a perceptive little girl whose father was master of the New Bedford whaleship *Roman*. When the *Roman* set sail on October 29, 1868, bound around Cape Horn for the Pacific, Laura was six years old and her little brother Prescott was two. It took Laura practically no time at all to discover that lessons and games and incessant questioning of the crew were not enough to occupy her busy mind sufficiently. So Laura kept her own ship's log. It has been preserved, and it presents a revealing child's-eye view of life aboard a whaler. But it does more than that, as the following passages from it illustrate—it is a lively testimony that a little girl, wherever and whenever, is a little girl: proud of each day's new ac-

complishment, however imperfectly it may be accomplished;
uncompromisingly frank and honest; scornful of any younger
brother; gravely interested in the vicissitudes of animal life; and
quick to appreciate the importance of events that slower-witted
adults would regard as trivial.

Dec. 1st 1868
  *It is Sunday and a very pleasant day. I have read two story
books. This is my journal.*
                              Good Bye For To Day

Tuesday 15
  . . . We have four ducks on board of our ship.
                              Good Bye For To Day

Friday 18
  . . . We had ducks for dinner.
                              Good Bye For To Day

Monday 11 [January]
  *. . . We had corn beans for dinner. I am geting along with my
lessons nicely.*
                              Good Bye For To Day

Sataurday 16
  Prescott is on the floor looking at pictures.
                              Good Bye For To Day

Tuesday 19
  . . . Thare is a fly on my finger. He has flew of now.
                              Good Bye For To Day

Saturday 6th [February]
  *It is a warm day. I shall finish my third reader this afternoon
. . . Prescott goes to bed every morning at ten oclock.*
                              Good Bye For To Day

Sunday 14
  . . . We have six pigs on board.
                              Good Bye For To Day

Tuesday 16
  The men have killed one of the pigs. We have five now . . .
                              Good Bye For To Day

Friday 19
  I have had my lesons perfect . . .
                              Good Bye For To Day

Saturday 20
  *I have had my lessons perfect two day . . . Mama says come
up on deck.*
                              Good Bye For To Day

Friday 10th [February, 1871]
  *it is quite rough today. But is a fair wind. We have 135 barrels
of oil, 60 of hump back and 75 of sperm. We had two birds, there
is one now. One died. There names were Dick and Lulu. Dick
died. Lulu is going to . . .*
                              Good Bye For To Day

Saturday 11th
  *Lulu died last night. It is quite smooth today. It does not blow
very hard . . .*
                              Good Bye For To Day

Sunday 12th
  *it is Sunday. it rained last night. Papa made a trap and caught
5 mice, and mama has some hens that have laid 37 eggs . . .*
                              Good Bye For To Day

Thursday 16th
  *. . . I went on board the Emile Morgan and had a nice time.
Mrs. Dexter gave me some cards to play with, and a bottle of hair
oil. and she gave me a little dog but we forgot him.*
                              Good Bye For To Day

Sunday 19th
  *. . . I can't think of much to write. We had pancakes for sup-
per. they were real good. it is most night. the Longitude was
117–23. I don't know what the latitude was.*
                              Good Bye For To Day

Monday 20th 1871

it is quite pleasant to day we saw whales this morning, we lowered the boats and we got six, the men are cutting them in now. Papa said the men would get 2 cut in to night but I think we shal only get one cut in. Prescott is up on deck seeing the men cut the whale in. the first Mate got 2 and the Second Mate got 2 and the third mate got too. I cant think of much to write . . .

Good Bye For To Day

Tuesday 21th 1871

It is quite pleasant today. the men are cutting in the whales. they smel dredfully . . .

Good Bye For To Day

Wednesday 22nd

. . . I went to bed last night and got up this morning. we had baked potatoes for supeper. and biscute. would you like to hear some news well I don't know of any.

These were the families who brought a touch of home not only into the floating whaleship cabins but also into the forecastles so far from home. Out on the broad reaches of the Pacific there were no others to remind a homesick whaleman of a farmhouse kitchen, a Saturday "social," a parlor love seat, a buggy built for two. Among the scattered islands of the great ocean there were only the brown-skinned girls, and the brown-skinned girls nearly always meant a fleeting, inadequate release of tension, an experience as far from New England domesticity as the distance across the sea and continent to the wife or sweetheart left behind.

To the whaleman the Pacific island girl was a secondary, otherworldly part of his life. She belonged to that strange existence he lived when he sailed down the Atlantic, fought his way around the Horn, and put his home, his family and everything normal in his life behind him. The island girl was something he never talked about to those people at home who had not, like him, seen the strange wonders on the other side of the globe; they would no more understand her than they could the Spice Islands (Moluccas), the charming and savage cannibals, the bread that grew on trees. The native girl hardly seemed to belong to the same species as the women of New England. They made a virtue of trim plainness; she was unfettered, unclothed, and sometimes tattooed as well. They at least affected maidenly modesty; she was simple, direct, and accustomed to being as much the pursuer as the pursued. They were cool and sometimes a bit calculating; she was softly luxuriant, warm, and all-consuming in her passion.

Sometimes the island girls made a whaleman nostalgic for the cleanliness of the women at home. The native girls wore their hair long, unwashed, and piled high on their heads; a common sight on many of the islands was a pair of girls calmly picking each other's heads and eating the lice, for all the world like two contented monkeys. But a little filth could not long deter a man who had been living in the sewage of the whaleship forecastle for half a year without getting close enough to a woman to touch her. And, as everywhere, there were beauties—island girls who were lovely in their dark and sinuous way, with burnished, silk-soft skin, a walk that spelled desire and a way of dancing in the caressing firelight that made a man think he had never been a man before. On the rare and wonderful occasion that a whaleman found himself ashore among girls like this, any thought of the clean, plain, prim women at home was snuffed out like a candle in the trade wind.

But it was almost never a particular native girl; it was the prettiest one a whaleman could find on whatever island he happened to touch. He never saw her again; she never saw him again. It was not love, not even a transitory affection. The lonely, sea-weary whaleman wanted to be swallowed up by the luxuriousness of the islands, to wallow in the lushness of the tropics, to forget the lean, rough months aboard ship. The island girl wanted a white man. It was usually that and nothing more. The whaleman would return to his ship, return to his home port, return to his wife who smelled of laundry soap and the cool crispness of New England autumn, and the mellow, tropical heat of the island girl was forgotten again—until he sailed into a shimmering coral atoll harbor once more. Then it was another native girl; and the first one no longer existed. There were few lifelong love matches among the islands of the Pacific.

Yet even among the islands there were the exceptions. There were the island women who defied all tradition to cast their lot with whaling skippers, remaining more or less faithful to "husbands" who visited them only for short periods of time every year or so. This was not the custom of the islands, but the whaling captain provided well for her and her children, asking only a home and an island wife to come to when his ship put into the harbor. What these native wives got in terms of material security was well worth their constant devotion—or the semblance of it anyway.

Constancy like this was usually not in their upbringing, and most of them were puzzled at their lovers for demanding it, especially the men who had wives at home. But these island women, like many of the Pacific natives, were better at adapting to the ways of the whalemen than the whalemen were at taking to the islanders' ways. Monogamy, though, was carrying it a bit far, and the whaling skippers' island wives were the exceptions among the brown-skinned girls who willingly and casually lived with any whaleman; to be taken as mistress by a white man was an honor. After the brief affair, when the whaleship set sail again, there might be a tearful display of sadness at the parting, in the way of the islands. But in the way of the islands, the lover was soon forgotten and the next whaleman easily replaced the last.

So the story of one of these island girls is all the more remarkable. Her constancy was greater than that of most of the native wives. More than that; from the time she met her whaleman on the beach at Ponape, she began to change his whole life. Her name was Lipei Naij.

Her story is shrouded in even more mystery than the accounts of the other island girls. It is passed down only in a few letters from her whaleman, in reports and hearsay evidence from other New Englanders who visited her island and in one letter from her, written in her native language. As best it can be reconstructed from these sparse sources, it is this:

Like other Micronesians, Lipei Naij was darker than the

islanders to the east, with more delicate features, sparkling eyes, jet-black hair and eyebrows, full, soft lips, and teeth that flashed white when she had not been chewing betel nut. Taller and slimmer than the girls of Tahiti and Samoa, she wore a skirt—short because she was still young—and nothing else. Her lover never described her appearance, but those who saw her on their visits to her island said she was pretty as only a lithe, full-lipped, full-breasted island girl can be. That she was also a girl of intelligence and purpose is shown by her story.

It begins with her whaleman. Henry Worth was the son of a carpenter of Martha's Vineyard, Massachusetts. Henry was a good whaleman, good enough to be a harpooner when he was twenty-one, and at first there was every reason to believe that he would be a whaling captain someday. But something always seemed to thwart him. In 1871 he sailed to the Arctic. That year an early, disastrous freeze-up destroyed most of the whaling fleet, including Henry Worth's ship, and he was brought back south to Honolulu aboard one of the whalers that escaped. There he found another berth; but he teamed up with a sailor who led him on a wild drinking spree, and when his ship sailed he was in the local jail. He worked his passage to San Diego, California, where he found employment in offshore whaling for a time, going out in whaleboats by day and returning each night. It didn't last. He wandered to San Francisco, where he was able to sign on a whaleship for the Arctic again. He was harpooner in the second mate's boat; but, he wrote home, "the second mate did not like me from the beginning." He stayed with the ship until she returned to Honolulu, where he left her. He signed on another whaler; then, before she sailed, he gave up that berth for one that sounded more attractive: a trading voyage out among the islands. It lasted until the ship reached Ponape, a luxuriant volcanic island among the Carolines. Again Henry Worth found he could not get along with his superior officer; after a bitter argument he went ashore at Ponape.

There his career seemed to have reached an ignominious end. He was a beachcomber, nothing more. He lived in a shack, collecting *bêche-de-mer* (sea slug) and selling it to visiting traders who would peddle it to Asian gourmets. Other New Englanders came to Ponape—it was a favorite stopping place for whalers. Some were friends of Henry Worth's family. They saw him there, a ragged, solitary figure crunching along the coral beach, a forlorn remnant of the man who had sailed so confidently from Edgartown harbor eight years before. When one skipper offered to ship him aboard and give him passage home, Worth refused. All he had left was his false pride. "I do not calculate to go home foremast hand again," he wrote his parents. He assured them, in glowing terms that were unconvincing, that he was comfortable, had plenty to eat, and even thought he could make some money trading in the area. ". . . if I only had a little capital," he hinted broadly, "say about fifty dollars in calico, tobacco, etc." He may have been as comfortable as he pretended. But he was far from content. "The fact of the matter is," he wrote, "I have been back and forth around the world . . . and have nothing but hard luck."

His luck, however, had already begun to change. He had met Lipei Naij.

So little is known about her. Was she the daughter of a local chief, or just another island girl? Was Henry Worth the first white man she had known? How did they meet? No one knows. But probably it was as straightforward as the thousands of other island romances, at first—a meeting on the beach, a few walks through the twisting paths of the island jungle and along the lagoon's lapping edge, a swim from one of the rocky dollops in the harbor, or under the pounding shower of an inland waterfall. Then the moonlit, tropical night on the beach, with the palm fronds rattling behind them and the sound of the surf booming out where the Pacific surged against the reef. Henry Worth kept a little shanty on the beach, where he lived and where he collected his *bêche-de-mer*. Lipei Naij moved in with him. It was as simple as that.

For a year and a half they apparently lived this way. There were plenty of breadfruit trees, yams, taro, bananas, and pineapples for Lipei Naij to collect, and there were hogs killed by the natives and given to the white visitor for the couple's simple meals. The harbor was rich in *bêche-de-mer*. There was the jungle to explore, dark, silent, and dripping, writhing with vines and filled with wonders. Outside the jungle, in the little clearings where the creeping vines had to be hacked away constantly, along the paths that wound their way down the volcanic mountain to the shore and across the glistening slope of the beach, the sun was white-hot and blistering—but nothing to a man who had stood in a whaleship's crosstrees. And the steady, sighing trade winds kept the temperature down in the low eighties, though never below the sixties at night. Nearly every day a short, sharp thunderstorm came rolling across the sky until it seemed to break up against Ponape's peak and send cooling waves of showers swirling down across the island. Thatched roofs steamed as the day's heat was soaked away; rivulets danced downhill past the feet of playing children. Then the clouds lumbered out over the open sea, and the late afternoon sun broke through. The peak seemed to rise higher into the heavens, the waterfalls poured down the mountainside, the multicolored plants looked as if they were swarming down the mountain too, as they waved in the breeze and scattered their sparkling pearls of water before them. And when the sun dipped lower, toward the horizon of the Pacific, the delicate outline of the jungle was etched against the sky. Dusk seemed to last only an instant—then darkness and silence descended on Ponape. Only the whisper of the lagoon, the surf out on the reef, and, sometimes, the faint, echoing and re-echoing call of a shell trumpet relaying some message across the island, as Henry Worth and his island girl lay on the still-warm coral sand of the beach of Ponape.

Like so many other Pacific island girls, Lipei Naij could be expected to share this idyl with her white lover for only a little while. Then—into the arms of the next man who came ashore from the next whaler. But this time the pattern was broken. Evidently something more than the usual, normal attraction drew them together, something that made Henry Worth see only Lipei Naij among the swarm of native girls forever hanging around the beach where the whalemen came ashore, something that made Lipei Naij's black eyes focus only on the tattered, sun-bronzed

figure of Henry Worth. Even in the Pacific island atmosphere of the quick and easy liaison this something could happen.

It did. And it never faltered. Apparently Henry Worth did not ask Lipei Naij to marry him; he simply accepted her into his shanty and she accepted him as her lover. To any of his neighbors home in New England he was a worthless beachcomber, a whaleman who might have become a mate or captain but who had failed. To Lipei Naij he was her master. The question of success or failure did not concern her.

Henry Worth did, however, try to make more of himself than a scavenger of the beach. He got some financial help from a passing New Zealander, and set sail on a trading expedition among the nearby islands. The venture failed. It was eleven months before he returned to Ponape again—eleven months during which hundreds of crisp-blond whalemen splashed ashore on the island and set the native girls giggling and weaving in among them. All but Lipei Naij; when Henry Worth returned, again with nothing to show for his efforts, she was waiting for him.

Their existence picked up where it had been interrupted, in the shanty, along the jungle trails, on the moon-bathed beach of the lagoon. For eight more months they lived their languid life together. Then Henry Worth set sail again, in another attempt to make something more of himself than a collector of *bêche-de-mer*.

This time the failure was not his fault. His destination was a reef 300 miles to the west; a wreck lay there, loaded with copper waiting to be salvaged. The wrecking company managed to get

some of the prize aboard, but then a storm swept down on them. They could not beat back against it to Ponape. The little sloop was driven to Guam. Henry Worth had $30 coming to him as his share of the salvage, but dysentery and exposure had made him so sick that almost all of the money went for medical care. ". . . so here I am," he wrote to his family on the Vineyard, "hard up without a cent." But he added, in what had become a refrain: ". . . am waiting patiently for something to turn up . . ." The only thing that turned up was a berth on a schooner to Shanghai, nearly 2000 miles across the Pacific. There was no job there, nor any ship to Ponape, so he stayed aboard the schooner, sailed back to Guam, and finally, a year and a half from the time he had left, he got passage home to Ponape and Lipei Naij.

Again she was waiting for him. Again they moved into the shack on the beach. But now, almost before they realized it, their relationship had become a different one. The slow transformation Lipei Naij had worked on Henry Worth had, in the crucible of storm at sea, finally changed him. This time, and apparently for the first time, he did something few whalemen on the islands had ever considered for a moment. He asked Lipei Naij to marry him.

She refused.

Her reasoning could only be the reasoning of an island girl. Lipei Naij had become a Christian; this in itself was not strange on Ponape in 1880; in the wake of the whalemen missionaries had come here as to most of the other islands of the Pacific. The "Boston Men," they were called, and they fascinated the natives even more than the whalemen had. The Boston Men had come with the singing and "storytelling" of their religion, and with piles of free clothing. Aghast at the nakedness of the islanders, the missionaries urged them to wear clothes, free clothes, shirts and trousers for the men and plain, sacklike "Mother Hubbards" for the women. To the natives these garments were much more decorative than shell necklaces and beaded G-strings, and they were delighted with the dressing-up, the preaching, and the hymn-singing of the Boston Men. That was about as far as it went with most of the islanders, and they became easy but not very devout converts.

Again Lipei Naij was the exception. She became a Christian with the same complete abandon with which she had become Henry Worth's mistress. To her islander's mind there was still nothing wrong with her sharing Henry Worth's shack on the beach. As a Christian, however, she could not commit the sin of marrying him—for the simple reason that he was not devout enough to be her husband.

But Henry Worth's transformation had gone farther than he or she had thought. He listened as she told him how she had prayed for him while he was out on the ocean in his ship, how her prayers had been answered directly by the white man's—and her—God. Perhaps it was the force of this openly embraced faith, this consuming belief. Perhaps it was the storm itself. Perhaps it was nothing more than the lonely thinking a man can do while sailing across the open reaches of the Pacific. Whatever it was, Henry Worth was ready to become as devout a Christian as she.

So Henry Worth and Lipei Naij were married in the little mission church on Ponape; and when the mission ship *Morning Star* came into the harbor shortly thereafter, he was baptized, as his wife had been before him.

Meanwhile, back at Martha's Vineyard, Henry's father had come to a sad and belated conclusion: despite his son's optimistic accounts of each new trading deal as it came along, despite the repeated assurances when each venture failed that "something will turn up," Henry's father realized that the young man was kidding his parents and, more important, kidding himself. Maybe if he came home and found a berth in another Vineyard whaleship, he could get a fresh start. Maybe then he would be able to work his way up to a position of command and respect. He had sailed away so many years ago with such high hopes, with every reason to expect that he would be able to work his way "from hawse hole to cabin," like so many other responsible Vineyarders. Charles Worth felt sure that if only he could have a long talk with his son, he could set the boy on the right path again. Henry did not have to return to sea. Work could certainly be found for him in his father's carpenter shop; and when the father was old enough to retire, the son could carry on. It would not be easy to give up the proud, early hopes that his son might someday be a whaling captain; but there was nothing demeaning about being a good carpenter, either; and it was a sight better than being a human shipwreck on some Godforsaken coral island. So Charles Worth wrote a kind but stern letter to his son. Henry had been away from the Vineyard long enough; it was time he stopped fooling around among the islands and returned home.

The letter struck some chord in Henry. His soul-searching was reflected in the reply he sent home—"I do not know what to do . . . I may be mistaken, but hope you will all pray for me that I may be directed aright, for I am often worried about it . . ." Nevertheless, he decided to stay. For he had made two decisions that would change his whole life. First, he had married Lipei Naij. And second, he had decided to become a missionary himself.

He wrote his father of these decisions. And he also sent home a souvenir of the islands that must have brought an exotic breath of Ponape into the New England household of Charles Worth. It was a letter from the new Mrs. Henry Worth. With it was Henry's translation of her painstakingly composed greeting to the father-in-law she was not even able to visualize, much less meet.

Good day Sir Father [Ran mau Main ai Papa]
Here am I Elisabeth the girl that is married to your son Henry. I do hope that you will not feel very bad because he does not return to you, for I trust you will meet together some time in Paradise for he is a Christian now . . . There are lots of foreigners

*who want to give Henry work trading for them, but we do not
wish it, for we are trying to work for Jesus. We wish God to give
us a good work in this coming year, we also wish it to continue . . . I like to hear about you all. I now send my regards to
you all, and if we never meet in this life we will hope to in the
next, now I have written this for you to see how we write and
spell in Ponape.*

I remain yours [Ari Iet naum n'ai],
Elisabeth Worth [Elisapet Worth].

For Henry Worth, as for any whaleman, marriage to an island
girl was an unprecedented thing, far more than a grateful and
affectionate gesture. Some whalemen went through mock ceremonies with island girls; but practically none were bona fide
Christian marriages. The whaling skippers who kept their native
wives in their second homes did not take the chance of actual,
bigamous marriages to them. Mrs. Henry Worth was Henry's
wife just as surely, and legally, as if she had married him in the
church in Edgartown, Massachusetts.

But by now it was obvious to Henry Worth that Lipei Naij
was more than a simple, love-hungry child. In fact it was through
her influence alone that Henry made the even more surprising
decision to become a missionary. During all those years when he
had been drifting about the Pacific, he had occasionally taken on
the trappings of religion. Every once in a while, in his letters
home, he had recounted how he had returned to God; but each
time it had turned out to be a reaction to some binge, some fight
with his skipper, some remorse over the fruitlessness of his empty
existence. Each time it had lasted only for a few days, or even a
few hours—until he had gone on the next binge, precipitated the
next argument with his skipper, wandered onto some other beach;
then the Bible passages he had been quoting in his letters were
forgotten.

This time he lost himself completely in his "work for Jesus,"
as his wife had described it in her direct way. And this time it
took. For nearly ten years he held to his promise, evidently by
far the longest period in which he had kept to any kind of unin-

terrupted work. He did attempt now and then to carry on some more trading. But the job he always kept before him was his missionary work. This, as he explained to his father, was his home now. Here he lived with his wife and preached the word of the Lord to the islanders he had come to love. There were still those nights on the warm beach at Ponape, when the lagoon lapped at their feet and the jungle stirred like a live thing behind them and the moon rose, fat as a sperm whale's head, over the ocean out beyond the reef. But there was hard work, too. With his wife he translated the Bible into Ponapean; together they converted the songs of the islands into hymns. And the one that became closest to their hearts was entitled *"Nan en jap kajalel ia mia . . ."*—"There's a land that is fairer than day . . ."

Somehow they picked up and outfitted a tiny ship, which they converted into a floating church, sailing in and out among the drowsy islands of the Carolines, preaching to all the natives who would listen to them, handing out the much-prized skirts and blouses and "Mother Hubbards," telling the timeless stories of the Bible, and singing their hymn of God and Ponape, "There's a land that is fairer than day . . ." For the first time in his adult life Henry Worth was able to give up smoking and chewing ("I know it was God that helped me, for I never could stop myself from using it . . ."). And for the first time Henry Worth was a happy man, because he was a useful man.

Once he wrote home suggesting that he return for a short visit, bringing Lipei Naij with him. But his father, probably better able to judge the situation than he, persuaded him not to. Lipei Naij might be Henry's wife in the South Seas; she might even be the one who had saved him from becoming a human derelict. But the New Englanders would not understand this. So Henry Worth stayed out there with his wife.

Sometimes, though, it seems that the Lord is unkind even to those who serve Him well. Henry Worth never wrote about it, but from the whalemen who visited Ponape came the story of what happened to Lipei Naij. She and Henry had one child—the account does not say whether it was a boy or a girl. They were still preaching to the islanders when an epidemic, probably malaria, swept Ponape. Many died, as usual with these nineteenth-century epidemics. And among them were Lipei Naij and her child. They were buried, as befits good Christians, in the little graveyard by the mission church.

More than half of Henry went with them. The tiny ship's cabin was now large and empty. The shack on the beach had the aching silence of death. There were no longer the happy shrieks of the child making countless discoveries along the beach; nor the soft melody of Lipei Naij, going about her work and crooning, "'There's a land that is fairer than day . . .'" The effect of her stayed with him for a while, even beyond the grave. But time in its slow sureness washed away the influence for good just as it gradually dulled the pain of the loss.

Little by little Henry gave up his missionary work. In 1890, twenty years after his original departure from the Vineyard, he came home again. He hung around for a while. He considered shipping aboard a whaler once more. But with Lipei Naij gone he seemed unable to make up his mind and stick to it. Little is written about this visit home, but it is easy to picture the solitary figure walking along the island beach, the lone man picking his way among the spindrift, standing at the water's edge just above the long wash of the surf line as the wind whipped his trousers and he shaded his eyes against the sunset to look out across the gray, cheerless waters of the Atlantic and imagine a sunset across a blue lagoon.

The memory pulled him back, the memory and a dying spark of his promise to Lipei Naij that he would continue to "work for Jesus." He was heard from in San Francisco, where he was trying to collect enough money for another missionary schooner. He got the money—those were the days when Americans gave freely for missionary work in the South Seas—and again he set out westward across the Pacific, westward to the land that is fairer than day.

Ponape was not the place he had left. The searing breath of empire-building had blighted much of the work of the missionaries and, besides, the Boston Men were striving desperately to keep their converts while Spanish monks worked to change them to

Catholics. This kind of conflict, between two groups who said they worshiped the same God, was incomprehensible to the Ponapeans, and the island was swept by a religious guerrilla warfare. It was just the challenge that, in earlier days, Lipei Naij would have used to bring out the best in Henry Worth. But where the island girl had waited for him so often on the hillside overlooking the passage through the reef there was now only the quiet graveyard by the mission church; in it were the two mounds, one so small. Henry Worth climbed the hillside, stood before all that was left of those well-loved, hard-working days, looked out across the lagoon, the reef, the Pacific rolling beyond, and then made his last farewell. He never returned.

His life had come full circle. Soon he was before the mast again. His deterioration was swift. As once more he followed his purposeless course around the world, his father received brief snatches of news from him in Feodosiya, in Genoa, in Rio Grande do Sul, in Montevideo, in Alexandria. Once he wrote that the German Government had acknowledged his claim to a piece of land on Ponape. Perhaps he could return "and settle on it and make myself a comfortable home . . ." But in his heart he knew he could not.

He was an old man now, and old men were not wanted by the shipping clerks. But he had received some help when he most needed it—from the Masons. The rewards of Christianity were still coming to him. He realized this. He still preserved what vestiges he could of his religion, "with Psalms and spiritual songs, etc., and have been kept from the evil, praise the Lord for all his mercies to me who am so unworthy." Then he wrote from Liverpool, from an old sailors' home. That was where he died.

He had written it in one of those last letters, and there is no doubt that he thought of it again on his deathbed in the old sailors' home. His heart, he said, belonged back in Ponape—where once the land was fairer than day, and where once a native girl transformed a decaying beachcomber into a useful man of God.

9. Exiles, castaways, and ten men on the lam

Henry Worth was only one among hundreds of whalemen who exiled themselves on the islands of the Pacific. His island wife was out of the ordinary, but his experiences as a wandering beachcomber were not. Most of the whalemen who jumped ship on one island or another did so only as a temporary arrangement; they had had enough of a bloodthirsty first mate, or they were hypnotized by some tropical paradise, or they formed a brief, fervent attachment to some native girl. Within a few weeks, though, most of these whalemen had tired of the beach and were shipping before the mast again, on the next whaler to come into port. It was a respite, an idyllic vacation; nothing more than that.

But there was a particular class of whalemen who were on the beach for good. They could never ship aboard another whaler, no matter how the unchanging, seasonless life of the islands sapped their spirit. Whatever they had left at home, whomever they thought of, dreamed of, they could not return. They could not even send a message home. And, far from signing aboard another ship, they had to be constantly on the lookout in order to take off for the interior and hide out as long as any ship lay in the harbor. They were castaways in every literal sense of the word—men who no longer had a country, men who no longer could live their own lives. And they had no one to blame but themselves.

These men were the mutineers.

Up until the twentieth century it was the axiom of every forecastle that the one capital crime was mutiny. Master and mate could get away with anything, including murder. Even the foremast hand was frequently able to desert one ship, languish on the beach until the next whaler touched the island, and then sign on for another cruise, with no questions asked. Refusal of duty, even insubordination usually meant only "a taste of the cat." That was no fun; but the whaleman thereupon continued doing his duty, usually with no loss of rank or prestige.

Not so the mutineer. No matter how far he fled, no matter how he tried to cover his tracks, no matter in what hidden corner of the world he tried to lose himself, he was relentlessly tracked down and caught. Shipowners and governments had seen to that. Mutiny had always to be treated as an object lesson; otherwise discipline aboard ship would degenerate into chaos. So no expense or time was spared in searching every watery cranny of the globe, if only to make an object lesson of one mutineer. And the penalty for the crime was usually death. But the cost could not be measured in terms of the single mutineer; it was measured in terms of the countless thousands of rebellious hands who, mindful of the penalty, reconsidered the price and stopped at the threshold of mutiny itself.

Yet the harshest punishment could not prevent mutinies. So maddening was the treatment of the crew by some whaling officers, and so violent and unthinking some of the whalemen themselves that there were mutinies—only a few actually, but enough to add one more deadly danger to the hazardous business of whaling.

Still, almost never did the mutiny succeed. Many times the rebels did manage to take the ship. But only then did they realize what they had done to themselves. From the moment of the uprising a mutineer had snuffed out his life as he had known it. If he ever returned home, it was to prison and the hangman; if he somehow evaded capture, he plunged himself into a wandering, hopeless oblivion.

In the Yankee whaling fleet of the nineteenth century there were two mutinies which, more than almost any of the others, served only to make the lesson a more compelling one.

The trouble had been brewing aboard the New Bedford whale-ship *Junior* for five months. Mainly it was because of the first mate, a man named Nelson, a tough, salty veteran who believed that "belaying-pin hash" and a "taste of the cat" were the only ways to make a crew behave. Nelson had put a great many cruises behind him and had a reputation, among owners and skippers, as an excellent whaleman. Among the hands he had a different reputation, and aboard the *Junior,* that cruise in 1857, he lived up to it.

The *Junior's* owners had left some casks of bread and salt beef aboard, old provisions shipped during the last voyage and never used. Captain Mellen could guess without going near the meat that it was unfit for human consumption, even in a whaler's forecastle, and planned to use it as feed for hogs when they brought some aboard. It was Mate Nelson's opinion, however, that if the stuff was good enough for hogs it was good enough for foremast hands. So was the bread. The *Junior* was Captain Mellen's first command; Mate Nelson had had more experience than he. So the captain let the mate have his way.

The bread came up green and moldy. The meat was so rotten that it pulverized when touched and stank of rot. It was served to the men. Right after supper a delegation came marching up out of the forecastle and to the quarter-deck. The captain and Mate Nelson met them there. The delegation wanted to complain

direct to Captain Mellen that the food would bring them all down
sick. And they had chosen a spokesman for the occasion. His
name was Cyrus Plummer.

He was a harpooner. Judging by his previous record, he was a
troublemaker. After one cruise in the Arctic his captain had had
him shipped home. There was a rumor that on another cruise he
had tried to desert with a whaleboat and its crew. From the time
Mate Nelson and Cyrus Plummer were shipped aboard the
Junior, the course for disaster was set.

All that was needed was the sequence of brutalities by Nelson,
followed by the vengeful little huddles forward on deck, led by
Plummer. They came in rapid succession. Shortly after the episode
of the spoiled food a storm smashed down on the *Junior,* carrying away most of her deck gear and sending her crew scurrying
about on her bucking yards as they fought to shorten sail. Amid
the din Nelson yelled an order at one of the hands; the man could
not hear him. Nelson grabbed him and flung him against the
bulwarks with such force that the man's skull was nearly frac-
tured. Again the muttering group gathered around the anchor
windlass, and again Plummer was the ringleader. Then came the
climactic incident between the two antagonists, the one everyone had been waiting for and dreading.

The *Junior* had by now run down across the Atlantic and
rounded the Cape of Good Hope. She was working her way
across the Indian Ocean, her course set for the bowhead whaling
grounds above Japan. It was a sparkling, warm November afternoon, and Cyrus Plummer was at the wheel. Looking up for a
moment, he noticed an albatross circling the ship. Like any other
sailor he became fascinated by the wheeling glide of the great
bird, the way it seemed to drift along on the wind currents in-
definitely without moving a wing. As he watched the hypnotizing
spectacle, he did not notice the wheel edging over in his hands,
until the ship had fallen slightly off her course and a sail started
its warning *slat-slat-slat.* Plummer immediately came to and was
on the point of bringing her back on course, when the barked
command came from Nelson: "Mind the wheel, there, Plummer.
That the best you can do?"

Plummer, just about to mind the wheel, let her stay where she was.

In half a dozen quick strides Nelson was across the quarter-deck. With a whistling haymaker he caught Plummer full on the jaw. The harpooner let go the wheel and lit into the mate. Nelson went down, taking Plummer to the deck with him. As the two thrashing bodies fell, Plummer's head smacked against the wheel-post. Half-conscious, he sprawled on the deck, shaking his head groggily while Nelson scrambled to his feet. With his copper-toed boots the mate went to work on his recalcitrant harpooner, kicking at the ribs and trying to smash them or puncture a lung. But the noise had brought Captain Mellen racing up the companionway, and the struggling, cursing mate was hauled bodily away from his gagging victim.

Next morning, as Plummer and everyone aboard ship knew it would, his punishment came. Striking any officer aboard ship, no matter what the provocation, was insubordination. The captain, a holstered pistol hanging conspicuously on his hip, gave the assembled crew a lecture on discipline, and then directed the second and third mates to seize Plummer to the rigging.

A tarred rope yarn was knotted about each end of the harpooner's thumbs and made fast to the rigging, hauled up so that the two thumbs supported nearly all of Plummer's weight. The captain turned to Mate Nelson.

"Mr. Nelson," he directed, "twenty lashes."

Every man winced, swallowed hard, and shuddered each time Nelson, swinging his full weight behind it, whipped the rope's end against Cyrus Plummer's bared shoulders. The harpooner's back turned redder, then darker, as the skin welled and finally split open under the blows. Plummer, clenching his teeth on a bit of his torn shirt, refused to cry out, which made Nelson lean harder with each stroke. Even at the end the only sound on the deck of the *Junior* was the swish of the rope's end, the squashy plop as it laced into the jellylike mass of flesh, and the soft patter of blood on the planks. Only when it was over, when Mate Nelson leaned, panting, against the tryworks and the other two mates cut Plummer down, did the men start their muttering again. As they gathered up the quivering, sobbing harpooner and carried him to his bunk in the steerage, the muttering grew louder and more ominous than ever.

Whether this was when Plummer planned his mutiny or whether he had been planning it all along no one knows. But he now began to perfect his plans; and he now had the sympathetic backing of most of the crew. Nearly all of them appeared willing to desert with him at the next port. When he openly proposed mutiny to a few of them, however, they backed off. All of them knew the penalty, and all of them knew how seldom anyone ever escaped the ceaseless, inevitable pursuit. Few of them were ready, even after the provocation of Mate Nelson, to give up their homes for life.

Plummer was, though, and he finally managed to convince nine of his shipmates. That was because he had an alluring plan. He had got the idea on an earlier cruise; then a whaleman had told him about Australia. Most of the country was deserted, the man had said, and anyone could live there the rest of his life without being discovered. There were little towns where an outlaw could get provisions, but where communications were so bad that no one would ever know anything about a mutiny or mutineers. Not only did Australia have the isolation of Pitcairn Island, but it had a lot more conveniences.

And it had gold. Plummer's shipmate had told him that in the wild, unexplored wastes of Australia there was gold for the scooping up. That had done it for Plummer. Ever since, he had been planning to get ashore on the deserted coast line of Australia, go after some of that gold, then slip unobtrusively into Melbourne or Sydney and settle down to enjoy his wealth. Now his plans had taken a different pattern. First he would get his revenge on the bullying mate and on the captain, who seemed to let Nelson run the ship as he pleased. Then, with his followers, Plummer would take a whaleboat ashore—for adventure, gold, and later, when things had blown over, the high life of the wide-open Australian cities.

The trouble was that Cyrus Plummer had not kept up with developments in Australia. And he did not know the geography of the coast line well enough. The spot he selected for his escape was Cape Howe, on the southeastern tip of the continent. In 1857 it was one of the most deserted locations on earth, a wild bush inhabited only by outlaws, savages, and the chain gangs of Australia's penal colonies. Plummer could not have selected a worse time, either. There were nearly 100,000 convicts building roads through this bush in the 1850s; periodically a few broke away and escaped across the open countryside. The result was that around Cape Howe in 1857 any stranger was arrested first and questioned later.

Not knowing this, Cyrus Plummer went ahead with his carefully laid plans. With a twisted sense of irony he chose Christmas night for the mutiny. Surreptitiously he collected or noted the ready location of cutting spades, knives, and whaling guns, murderous blunderbusses used for firing bombs into a whale's thick hide; for these guns he gathered powder and big lead balls. With four men picked from the nine who had cast their lots with him, Plummer crept below, into the officers' cabin, a small wardroom off which were the doors to the cabins of the captain and mates.

At a prearranged signal Cyrus Plummer got his revenge. In the uproar, the billowing clouds of choking gun smoke and the thundering of bodies against the bulkheads, the command of the *Junior* was wiped out. Plummer himself took care of Captain Mellen, shooting him and burying a hatchet in him for good measure. One of the others killed the third mate.

But the second mate and First Mate Nelson were still alive. They had barely escaped, however, and were too wounded to keep Cyrus Plummer from climbing back on deck and announcing to the hastily assembled crew: "I am master now."

For the next five days, while the bodies of the captain and third mate were dumped overboard and the wounded and shackled second mate tried to navigate at Plummer's order, Mate Nelson hid out in the hold—starving, sipping at a crack in a water cask for his only nourishment while his strength slowly drained away with the blood from a deep knife wound in his shoulder. Finally one of the crew found him, and he was dragged onto deck. Exhausted and faint, he waited for Plummer to take his revenge.

But, strangely, Plummer did not touch him. In fact, when a whaleman started to beat up the mate, Plummer stopped him. Nelson, the new skipper announced, would navigate the *Junior* to a point off Cape Howe. Then the ship would be left to him and the loyal remainder of the crew.

Recovering from his surprise, Nelson took the navigating instruments and charted the course. And on January 3, 1858, the *Junior* backed her mainsail twenty miles off the long, broken coast of Cape Howe. Plummer had the two mates brought before him. He and his followers were leaving now. There would not be enough crew left for the ship to continue whaling, and in any case all the gear had been tossed overboard. But he wanted the mates to promise that after his two whaleboats had pulled away for land, the ship would be headed for New Zealand, and not any port in Australia.

With no alternative the mates promised. And in a gesture that seemed a little eerie considering the circumstances Plummer made the two men swear on the ship's Bible, then kiss the Book. They did.

Over the side went everything the mutineers could not use. Down the falls went the two whaleboats. The ten men dropped into them. At Plummer's command they cast off.

For more than an hour, standing in the stern of his whaleboat, Plummer held a spyglass to his eye and watched the *Junior* as she braced forward, fell off on the weather tack, and slowly crept away toward the horizon. Then a smoky haze blotted her out for the last time. A chill loneliness settled upon them. Plummer sat down and sang out an order, and the oars grabbed at the water in practiced unison as the two whaleboats headed for the rapidly disappearing shore.

They could not sail the distance because of head winds. Heavy clouds were forming where the haze had just hidden the land. Plummer had already made his first mistake; he had set out in the afternoon, leaving only a few hours of daylight for the row to shore twenty miles away. Now the winds increased, still head-on, and the growing storm swept the two whaleboats even farther out to sea. Almost before they knew it they were in the midst of a full gale, with the boats pitching through foaming waves, gear and provisions banging over the side, and the men scrambling among themselves to get a good hold and hang on for their lives.

Unable to do anything but ride with the storm, Plummer and his lieutenant in command of the other whaleboat fought to keep their little craft under control. But in one smashing series of waves the boats were swerved broadside into the trough, and the next sweeping wall of water boomed down on them and swamped both boats. Flailing away with the bailers and heaving most of the gear overboard, the men managed to save themselves. The thoughts of them all, as night fell and the storm seemed to in-crease and marble-topped mountains of black water thundered past and under them, must have gone back to the deck and the dirty but safe forecastle of the whaleship *Junior*.

But like most Pacific storms, this one soon blew itself out. The scared, exhausted men sprawled about as they could in the bottoms of the whaleboats and rested. Then at dawn they started the laborious row toward land, which now lay fully thirty miles away and was only a dim outline on the clearing horizon. Huge, heaving swells from the storm lifted them high enough, though, so they could get a good look at the coast every now and then. The oarsmen bent to their long job.

It was late afternoon when they finally drew near land, picked out an island just off the shore of Cape Howe, and dashed along the top of a comber to bump onto a sandy beach. The place they had picked was wild and desolate, all right, just as Plummer had hoped. Not a sign of human life was anywhere, not even a camp-fire. But after they had stretched their aching legs on the beach for a moment, they were surprised to see a naked native ma-terialize from the bush along the shore of the island. He was an old man, and with signs he and the mutineers managed to converse. For a gift of some tobacco the native agreed to guide them across the strait to the mainland. The boats came close to swamping again in the rushing tide rips of the channel, while sharks swarmed around them, devouring each other as the men shot at them. But Plummer and his followers made it to the beach. A canoe appeared from nowhere and came pitching expertly across the channel to take the old man home. The mutineers dragged their boats above the high-tide mark and set up camp with the few belongings they had left.

That night, their first ashore, was not a pleasant one. The beach was so wild and barren that it was as if they had left the world behind them. Inland, against the sky, mountains cut off their view. The shrill calls of birds and the sharp screams of strange animals came to them from all sides of the land. It was summer below the Equator and drought had parched all the countryside. Here and there the dark sky was lit up by patches of dancing bush fires along the base of the mountains. Every man was exhausted by the long haul in the whaleboats; but few slept well that night on the Australian beach.

The bright morning brought new hope, which quickly disappeared. The thin scrub was no protection from the blinding, blistering sun. Exploring parties went out into the brush and returned with nothing—no fruit, none of the animals that had screamed at them through the night, no water, nothing. Where were the rich harvests of the forest Plummer had told them of, where the natives to trade with and the dark-skinned women to take into the brush, where, in fact, the gold? Here was nothing but sand and stunted bushes and twisted bracken. A sickening feeling of desperation began to infect the mutineers. The little supply of water and food they had taken from the ship and managed to preserve through the storm was nearly gone already. Where would they find more? Had they cast themselves on this lonely shore only to die of thirst and starvation?

So what was the next move? In the gloomy consultation held on the simmering beach Plummer announced that the only thing to do was to go up the coast in the whaleboats. Somewhere in that direction he felt sure there must be the beginnings of the mountain roads that would lead them to Sydney. But now the ranks split. Seven of the ten mutineers agreed that, as one of them put it, "I'm hungry and thirsty, but I'm not ready to hang yet."

No vote was taken, however. The ten men agreed to separate as they wished. They divided into three groups. Plummer and three still-faithful followers climbed into one of the whaleboats, pulled out until they were half a mile offshore, and headed north. Two of the men who stayed behind headed west along the beach, away from Sydney, planning to turn inland after they had put a few more miles behind them. The remaining four set out straight inland, aiming for what looked like a break in the hills to the northeast.

These four men, walking single file and pushing their way through the tangled brush, ran into trouble from the start. At a pause in the march one man put down his gun; when he picked it up he let out an agonized yell. He had dropped the gun on a huge snake, which had stabbed him in the arm when he reached down again. He took out his sheath knife and gashed a wedge-shaped piece of flesh away where the skin was already swelling around two red dots in his arm. While he lay on the ground, sobbing in pain, his shipmates took turns sucking the poison from the wound and spitting it out. After an hour of this he was able to stumble along as they went on inland. All that day they kept moving, every man suffering from the hot sun and thirst; the taste of blood had made their mouths dry, and the water was gone. By nightfall they found a ravine; it was dry, but when darkness fell dew formed on the leaves of the plants and bushes. They sucked it until the thirst was more bearable, then pushed on again. The next day, though, nearly made them give up. The land grew even more rugged, the hills more precipitous. There was still no water, and all they had left to eat were a few bits of ship's bread. At night they managed to dig some roots from under rocks and suck a little moisture out of them. Next day they had all but decided to beat their way back to the beach when they came upon a brook. Every man ran to it, flopped full length, and drank until he could feel his stomach skin stretch. Then they lay on their backs and rested in the flickering shade. After they had got back on their feet and gone on a few more miles they found some berries. Thus sustained, they had their first good sleep since they had left the *Junior.*

But the next day was one of such horror that they were sent plunging back down the mountainsides in full flight, their painful climb all in vain.

Although they had seen not a sign of other human habitation, they were in the bushmen's country. It was only by fantastic luck that they had not yet been discovered and attacked by savages. The first they knew of it was a chorus of shrieking cries only a few hundred yards away.

Ducking for cover and working their way cautiously in the direction of the yells, they came suddenly on a scene that terrified them even after the blood bath aboard the *Junior*.

A small band of naked natives had been surprised by another and was being slaughtered as the whalemen cowered in the bush nearby. Women and children, dashing for cover, fell with spears quivering in their backs. Men who were caught alive were tied to trees, and while fires were lit at the victims' feet the victors gouged out their eyes. One was flayed alive.

The mutineers watched this scene only for a few minutes. Shaking at the thought of being discovered by savages like these, the four men lit out for the coast much faster than they had come. They had nothing to eat or drink that day, and terror alone kept them moving, crashing through the underbrush and dodging among the boulders as they fought their way back to the sea. Because they were running west, they came out on the other side of the cape, so they made it in a day and a night. When they reached the tide flats they found some clams to fill their knotting stomachs. Then they lay on the shore to recover from their exertions and their fright.

Plodding along in the loose sand, they made their slow way back around the point to where they had started. There they sprawled on the ground and considered their dilemma. Inland were barren mountains and sadistic savages. Up the coast was Sydney and police who were probably looking for the *Junior* mutineers by now. Where to go? What to do next? In fact, how to keep alive? It was as if some mocking fate had lured them to this little strip of beach, with screaming savages on one side and thundering surf on the other, there to let them slowly die. Again the thoughts of the mutineers must have gone back to the security of the ship they had so impulsively deserted.

Caught in their dilemma, the four mutineers could only think of returning to the island where they had touched when they had first landed in their whaleboats. Plummer had taken one of the boats when he had gone on up the coast. The other lay where they had concealed it in the brush behind the beach. Now they uncovered it and started to shove it across the sand to the water's edge—when one of the men let out a yell.

Up the coast and around a bend a column of smoke rose into the air, smoke that could come only from a steamer running along the coast line. All four men stood together and studied it. They realized that it was too close to the shore to be a merchant vessel; it must be some kind of coastwise steamer. Was it a government boat on a regular patrol? Or had news of the *Junior* mutiny reached Sydney? And were the police out looking for them? Whatever the smoke meant, the four men knew they must not be seen. The sand flew as they dug in behind the first line of bushes. Then they lay low and watched.

An open, thirty-foot vessel rounded the bend and chugged by them, flying a British customs flag at the stern. The men aboard were studying the beach as they went slowly by. Then the steamer swung out toward the island and disappeared behind it. The mutineers started to climb out of their holes, then quickly slithered back into them. The steamer had not appeared on the other end of the island. Apparently she had put in there. The only sounds were the surf breaking on the beach and the wind whistling across the sand as the four men waited.

Then the steamer appeared again, headed straight for the beach. In the bow was the same old native who had guided them ashore four days before.

With no time to run for it the mutineers huddled lower in their pits and cursed to themselves as the boat came nearer. Off the sand bar she stopped. A canoe was put over the side. Two of the officers climbed into it. So did the native. The canoe plummeted through the surf and ground onto the shelving shore. The native led the two officers straight to the whaleboat.

Yet the four mutineers were not discovered. For some reason the officers did not detect fresh signs of activity on the beach. They concluded that the whaleboat had been left here four days before and that the mutineers had fled inland. The officers knew that part of the country well enough not to pursue the men into the bush. They apparently figured that the savages could be counted on to do their work for them. Nevertheless, they took with them as evidence a whaling gun left behind in the boat. On its stock was burned the name "JUNIOR."

The canoe was hauled aboard, the native was dropped on his island, and the steamer chuffed out of sight. The men in their sand holes watched her disappear, waited to make sure she would not surprise them again, and finally crawled out into the open. They went down to the water's edge. The steamer could not be seen; by her smoke they could follow her course around Cape Howe and off west on her patrol. Now they were able to agree on what to do next. With escape inland cut off and government steamers patrolling the coast line they had no choice. They would take their whaleboat up toward Sydney. Since there was no refuge for them in the wilderness, they would have to take their chances with civilization, hoping to slip into the city unnoticed and lose themselves in the crowd.

But they never made Sydney. They had hardly gotten out on the sea when around Cape Howe came another government steamer. Although this one was larger, she held close to the shore line like the other; evidently the two steamers passed each other near this spot on their regular patrol of the coast. This time there was no escape, no time to get ashore and hide out. The government boat quickly closed the distance and, as the men made the oars bend in their desperate race, the officers sent a shot across their bow. The mutineers swung in toward the beach, hoping they could run for it even though they had been discovered. In only a few minutes the whaleboat grounded and all four men jumped—into quicksand. Up to their shoulders in water, with the sand already sucking at their waists, they could do nothing but hold onto the side of the whaleboat while a punt came over from the steamer and plucked them out of their trap. A few hours later all four were in the Melbourne jail.

Of the ten mutineers of the *Junior,* now only six were still free.

At about this time the two men who had set out together had found the going just as hard in the brush country inland. They had picked their way along the shore for two days, followed a creek inland, and plunged ahead into the unknown toward the mountain ridges. Their food was nearly gone by now, too, but one of them set some snares and caught a few rabbits. Carefully providing for the harder days ahead, they saved most of the catch, wrapping it in leaves and carrying it over their shoulders in a piece of shirt. They found a low pass through the mountain ridge, got through, and found themselves on the edge of a desert. A large bird caught in another snare added to their provisions. But then they had bad luck.

Walking through some low bushes, one of the men noticed pods that looked exactly like peas. He scooped some up, broke open the pods, and ate the pealike pellets inside. Within an hour it seemed as if knives were going through his stomach, and he was vomiting continually. While he tried to lie still in the hot, speckled shade of a scraggly bush, he and his companion took stock. They had been gone five days, had gotten through one mountain range, and made some progress toward the next. But the land, instead of getting richer as they went inland, was getting more barren. Their catch of rabbits and one bird had dwindled to only enough for another day, and they had seen no sign of game in the last forty-eight hours. After this experience they would not dare eat any berries they came on. It looked as if they were going from bad country into worse. They decided to cut back for the coast.

The trek back nearly killed them. They could not find the pass that had let them through the mountain range, and the course they took led them over even more rugged terrain. Their snares caught nothing. They found only enough water to keep them alive. Once, in a clump of tiny trees, they came upon a sight that, at this moment of their misery and dejection, turned their blood cold. It was a heap of withered bones, the remains of some wandering castaway who, like themselves, had floundered about in this arid waste until he could no longer go on and had simply died where he lay.

They too could go on no longer that day. After some rest they would still be able to stagger forward toward the coast; but, each one must have thought to himself, for how long? How many more days would it take them to reach the shore? Would they still find no food, no water along the way? Even if they reached the coast, what would they find there? Certainly nothing to eat or drink. That night, as they lay near each other and blessed the cool darkness and watched the flickering light of the brush fires north along the mountain range and listened in vain for the distant murmur of surf, both men must have thought, like their four companions before them, of the comfort and security of the whaleship *Junior.*

And maybe these two men thought also of the *Essex.* Had they heard the story of the *Essex,* of her survivors who, like these two, were dying of starvation, of the ones who lived through the long open-boat voyage by cannibalism? No doubt they had; the *Essex* story was known in nearly every whaler in the nineteenth century. But whether the two mutineers recalled that famous thirty-seven-year-old tragedy or not, one of them had begun to consider a means of survival for himself at the expense of the other—murder and cannibalism. In his weak, half-mad condition, he was able only to make a sudden, clumsy attack and he was quickly subdued. For the rest of the night there was no sleep for either man, each one huddling against a rock watching the other and waiting —and each one knowing that if he let himself drop off to sleep it would be his last.

By dawn both men were haggard, wild-eyed, and barely able to walk. But after forcing themselves forward for a few hours they came to a slimy pond where two long-dead fish floated on the surface. Fighting off the nausea, they ate the fish and slurped up a little of the water where they could push the green slime out of the way. They managed to keep this food down, and in fact it strengthened them enough to keep them going all that day and through most of the night. Some time before dawn they came out onto sand and heard the sound of the sea breaking just ahead of them. In the darkness they could see the ocean only as a glimmering black carpet heaving under the starlight, with fringes of foam edging the curved beach.

Neither man could stay awake any longer. Even the fear of death was not enough. Both collapsed on the sand. Both slept.

The hot glare of the sun woke them. They surveyed their beach and found that it was a tiny cove bounded by towering rock ridges projecting out over the sea. One of the fugitives looked back toward where they had come, then jumped to his feet and let out a yell as he started running.

Over the brow of a hill back of the shore came a group of white men. There were at least a dozen of them. They were armed. And they were obviously following the tracks made by the two mutineers.

Searching frantically for some hiding place, the two men spotted a small cave in the rocks and ducked into it like a pair of rabbits run to ground. They lay in their tiny warren, sobbing for breath and peering back over an edge of rock to watch their pursuers fan out across the cove. They had found a place to hide for the moment, but only now they realized that in so doing they had trapped themselves. Back of them was a granite face so sheer they could not climb it. In front of them was the ocean. To the left was a steeply climbing path that led only to a precipice, hundreds of feet over the sea. To their right was a path, the escape route they had just taken. Now it was cut off by the posse that was systematically combing the rocky ledges, slowly but surely working closer and closer to the one in which they hid.

As the pursuers came on toward them, one of the mutineers quit right there. He had been too long without enough food and water and he had stumbled through too many miles of brush and mountain and the fight was gone out of him. He lay down and waited for them to come and get him.

But not the second mutineer. He took the only chance remaining to him. Breaking out of the cave and running as fast as he could make himself go, he half sprinted, half hobbled up the rocky hill to the precipice. The posse spotted the gaunt figure immediately, charging up the hill, a black shirttail flapping out behind him. One of the pursuers took up the chase, firing as he ran. The mutineer cleared the crest and streaked for the edge of the cliff. But at the brink he stopped. Below him the precipice dropped straight down for hundreds of feet. There was no foothold or handhold on its sheer side. At the bottom clumps of black rocks pointed toward him, the sea swirling and snarling in among them.

The fugitive turned and started inching back toward his pursuer. He came bent over, his hairy arms out and his hands reaching like claws. His chest heaved under the torn black shirt, and he mumbled and growled as he advanced. The man who had once been a whaleman aboard the *Junior* was now merely an animal at bay, a hunched, maddened creature silhouetted against the sea atop the wind-swept point of rocky land.

The vigilante raised his gun and took careful aim. But before he could fire, the mutineer had stopped, spun around, and started what this time was a suicidal dash off the precipice. The shot echoed and re-echoed among the rock ledges of the hill. The mutineer's legs went out from under him as if his knees had hit a wire. The bullet had caught him neatly in the thigh. He plunged forward on his face, lay still for a moment, then started flopping over, the blood spattering the rocks under him. Still he made for the precipice, rolling over and over and hunching himself along on his elbows until he had almost reached the edge. But before he could make it, his pursuer had caught up with him. There was a brief flurry as the two wrestled on the brink of the cliff, and then a second member of the posse jumped on the fugitive. Still kicking, wrenching, and sobbing, the mutineer was dragged back down the hill to the beach where his companion already lay trussed like a pig.

The vigilantes had received news of the *Junior* mutiny, and a warning from the patrol boats that the mutineers were hiding out along the coast. So the posse had gone out for a day or two of hunting. The brace of captives was taken back to a town near Melbourne, where they were promptly tried and convicted of mutiny. At the time the U.S. Consul in Sydney, Howard Whittier, was in Melbourne on business, and word reached him that the

mutineers had been brought in. On horseback he raced for the town, but he was too late. When he arrived, the two emaciated bodies had just been cut down from the gallows.

Of the ten mutineers now only four were still free.

Cyrus Plummer, the leader of the *Junior* mutiny, did not know what had happened to his former shipmates in the wild bush. But he knew that his had been the right decision. With his three remaining followers he had made the whaleboat voyage up the coast without being spotted by the government steamers. Now the four remaining fugitives followed a convict-made road from the coast toward Sydney. Ducking off into the brush cover whenever a coach, dray, or tramping band of convicts went by, the mutineers reached the outskirts of the city without arousing any suspicion and without any of the hardships the other two groups had experienced.

Pausing to reconnoiter before going on into the city, they came upon a roadside inn. Taking the chance that no one had heard of the mutiny, they calmly walked in, had supper, and took rooms for the night. Again Plummer had guessed right; the innkeeper had apparently heard nothing about any mutinies, and was long since accustomed to putting up groups of American whalemen who had deserted to go prospecting for gold.

But as the fugitives were climbing the stairs to their rooms, the inn was suddenly held up by a bushranger who started to line up the inn's customers and search them for gold. The Australian troopers were apparently hot on the bushranger's trail, because they burst in only a few minutes after him. For a wild few minutes the place was flooded with gun smoke and bullets nicked the walls around the mutineers as they crouched on the balcony over the tavern. The bushranger was wounded, manacled, and lugged away. The troopers paid no attention to the other customers; they were not looking for mutineers, yet.

Early next morning Plummer and his three shipmates settled their bill and headed down the main thoroughfare into Sydney. As they made their cautious way into the city, Plummer decided to visit a tavern, take a private dining room, hide out there for a few hours, and see what information he could pick up from the barmaids or the tavern keeper. Somehow he had to find out if news of the mutiny had reached Sydney yet. If not, he and his men could move freely into the city and proceed to lose their identities. But if the police were already on the lookout for them, the job would be enormously more complicated.

Again his decision was a wise one. A few guarded remarks were enough to elicit the information that news of the *Junior* mutiny was spreading fast. Despite his promise Mate Nelson had lost no time in bringing the *Junior* into Port Jackson, Sydney's harbor. The search for the fugitives would soon be on. But strangely, despite this warning, Plummer made a foolish mistake.

The combination of the liquor and barmaids did it. As the four men hid out in their little room and tried to make their plans, they drank more and more. And probably because they had brought a good bit of money with them and were spending it freely, the two barmaids waiting on them became increasingly friendly. Plummer's three followers were in a stupor by afternoon, and Plummer himself was beginning to get expansive under the provocation of one of the barmaids. As she told him lurid stories of the daring and bravery of the bushrangers she knew, Plummer finally was unable to resist the temptation to brag a bit himself. He was, he announced to the girl, considering a little bushranging too. He should have realized what the girl was up to when she expressed her doubts that a man as kindhearted as he could kill anyone. But the liquor had dulled his instincts of caution by now. Making a great conspiratorial show of it, he nuzzled her soft white ear and whispered into it that he was Plummer of the *Junior.*

The confidence had its desired effect, Plummer thought, little realizing that the girl had suspected this from the start. In his doltish condition it took him a few minutes to realize what he had done—and, more important, what had happened almost immediately thereafter.

Suddenly it dawned on him that the girl he was fondling was not the one to whom he had whispered his secret. The other barmaid was not in the room.

The realization brought him to his feet, chilled and almost sober. He tried to shake his companions out of their lolling stupefaction. They were too far gone; they could not even understand what he was shouting at them. Leaving them sprawled across the table, singing and bubbling in the spilled booze, Plummer ran to a window in the front of the tavern. As he had guessed, the barmaid was coming down the street, followed by a policeman. Plummer raced across the room to the back window. It looked out on a yard. He jerked the window open, skinned out, dropped to the ground, and ran for a fence at the end of the yard. As he climbed over it he saw a policeman coming along the alley on the other side. The place was already surrounded.

But there was just this one officer covering the back of the tavern. Before the policeman could get his gun clear, Plummer dropped him with one smashing right and lit out across the field.

He reached a long barn and skidded around behind it. There he ran into a man leading a horse. While the startled groom froze in his tracks, Plummer grabbed the reins. The horse reared, yanking the groom off his feet. Plummer mounted and was away. There was a patch of woods nearby, and Plummer made for it, letting the scared horse run full out. Once among the trees, he reined in, slid off, and let the horse gallop on without him.

But although Plummer had made his escape, the barmaid had done her job well. The police easily scooped up the other three fugitives and lugged them off to jail.

Of the ten mutineers now only one remained free.

Cyrus Plummer stayed under cover in the woods until nightfall. Then he made his way back into another section of the city. First he found a barbershop, where he had his beard shaved off, the black, bushy beard that he had been growing ever since the *Junior* had left New Bedford half a year before. Without it he bore practically no resemblance to the harpooner who had led the mutiny, to the fugitive the police were now on the lookout for all over Sydney.

Feeling more secure, Plummer made his way to the waterfront and its dives. There, as he hoped, he made the acquaintance of some enterprising characters who were completing plans to rob a gold-laden ship sitting at anchor in the harbor. Plummer's luck was with him; the conspirators had just come to the conclusion that they could not bring off the job safely without having a good seaman along with them. Plummer was careful this time to say nothing about the *Junior;* but he established himself as a seaman and was promptly cut in for a full share. It turned out to be a quick, simple job. Less than twelve hours later he was richer by some $15,000 worth of crude gold.

At this point Cyrus Plummer could well congratulate himself. It had all worked out exactly as he had planned. He had had his revenge on the officers of the *Junior.* He had landed his men safely on the Australian coast, and had led his three faithful shipmates to Sydney without so much as a hungry day or a scratch. It was their own fault that they had drunk themselves into such a blind daze that they could not break for it when the police closed in on the tavern. As for the others, the ones who had elected to stay out in the bush, whatever their fate, they had asked for it. Now he, the leader of the mutiny, had reached Australia as planned. He had not only made a fortune for himself, as planned, but he had accomplished it almost immediately and with fantastic ease. Already he had enough money to flee where he liked, to whatever country or wilderness he preferred. In fact, if he chose not to hide out until it all blew over, he could probably get away with staying right here in Sydney. His beardless face was so good a disguise that he doubted if even a former shipmate of the *Junior* would recognize him without a close look. As he sauntered up to the doorway of the tavern he had left the night before, happily contemplating a gigantic breakfast after a good night's work, Cyrus Plummer was enjoying the pardonable pride of a successful man.

But what he did not know was that there was a peculiar law in Sydney in 1858. Because of the frequency of robberies like the one in which he had just participated, an ordinance had been passed requiring a license to dig, or even carry, gold; which meant that anyone found to have crude gold on his person and no license was immediately suspect.

As Plummer strode across the tavern he took a piece of his newfound gold from his pocket. It slipped from his hand and fell to the floor. He bent over, recovered it, and when he straightened up again he found a stranger standing in front of him. The man had an official look about him. And he held a revolver in his hand.

"If you'll come along to the magistrate's office, mister," the stranger said politely, "we'll ask you a few questions. And if you're all right, there's no harm done."

10. The almost perfect mutiny

Cyrus Plummer tried to mutiny and then escape; and he failed. In one of the remotest and wildest areas in the world vigilantes combed the shore for the mutineers; police and even barmaids tracked them down in the cities. It happened that ringleader Plummer did cheat the gallows after being caught. Brought back to the U.S., he stood trial. He pleaded innocent and in fact attempted to turn the court proceedings into an investigation of Mate Nelson. He was found guilty and, although most of the other captured mutineers got off with long prison terms, Plummer was sentenced to hang. Then, as sometimes happens with mass sentiment, public opinion became aroused against capital punishment for Plummer—so aroused that at length his sentence was commuted to life imprisonment by President James Buchanan. Yet even though Plummer escaped the full penalty, shipowners and skippers could console themselves that the lesson remained:

even in such a daring flight as Plummer's not one of the band went uncaught.

But suppose they had. Suppose, too, they had found a way to survive in the Australian wilderness, or had been able to filter unobtrusively back into one of the big cities. Then what? Probably the acute homesickness that becomes a physical ache; destitution that borders on madness, simply because of the cruel, final knowledge that they could never go home. Oil-smeared, foul-smelling New Bedford wharves would become, in the mind's eye, a sparkling harbor with just the right scent of greasy luck in the air. Vermin-filled waterfront boardinghouses would seem, to such a man at such a distance, exotic bagnios. They could never go home. The comforts of any foreign city, no matter how metropolitan, would be nothing more than those of raw frontier towns, because they could never go home. A palm-thatched hut on a tropical island, overlooking the most spectacular panorama of sea and sky, would only make these men think of a plain white house on a muddy cowpath, because that was home and the tropical island was not.

And imagine the thoughts of the world's most famous mutineer, Fletcher Christian of the *Bounty*, as he sat on the ledge outside the little cave he visited regularly on Pitcairn Island. From the ledge, perched high over the surf, he could look out across the Pacific, with nothing but the endlessly pulsing ocean between him and the horizon. On this forgotten piece of rock he and his followers had successfully found the perfect hide-out. But they had cut themselves off from all hope of ever returning home. The things Fletcher Christian thought of in solemn contemplation on his rock ledge were different from what the *Junior* mutineers would have daydreamed about and longed for; and yet they were the same thing—home. Much has been made of the circumstances that seemed to cast Fletcher Christian in the role of the hero. And the romantic legend that has come down from that famous mutiny conveys the impression that for a while at least the fugitives led a pleasant, self-satisfied life with their native wives on their lovely green island. None ever went home. Despite the legends the real evidence indicates that if Fletcher Christian and his followers could have had it to do over again, they would not have turned on Captain Bligh.

There was a man on Nantucket Island, Massachusetts, who realized this, even at the beginning of the nineteenth century. He was Captain Mayhew Folger, the sealing skipper who had come upon Pitcairn Island and discovered the mutineers' hideaway nineteen years after Christian and his men had seemed to disappear from the face of the earth. In the few hours Folger stayed on the island he saw enough and heard enough to grasp the fact that, indeed, mutiny always fails.

There was another man at Nantucket, a much younger man, who knew the story of the *Bounty* mutineers. Like nearly everyone else in the little town he had heard it all from Captain Folger's lips, in the long winter evenings by the fire when an occasional youngster is given the cherished privilege of sitting on the outer edge of the circle while the captain spins this yarn or that, while the wind whistles by the eaves, the surf pounds against the beach outside, and raindrops hiss on the crane in the big fireplace.

Did the young listener hold his breath when the captain told of his conversation with the last remaining mutineer, when he described the tears that glistened on the leathery face of the white-haired exile at the mention of England after all those years? Did the youthful, imaginative mind go out across the Pacific to a lonely piece of land set in the midst of a huge ocean, visualizing the bitter, recriminatory homesickness that always lived like a load on the heart of the old fugitive? Maybe home did not mean so much to a young man already itching to sign on for his first voyage to the whaling grounds halfway around the world. But it must have meant a great deal more within a few years.

For Samuel Comstock went to sea at fourteen, and by the time he was nineteen he had served on three cruises and had become a harpooner. He was a good whaleman. He was one of those nineteenth-century Yankees who seemed born and bred to whaling and thoroughly enjoyed it. Certainly whaling suited him better than the life he had left at home under the strict hand of his Quaker schoolmaster father. Yet even a home that does not suit a young man's temperament looks a lot different when he is many thousand miles and a year or two away from it. And a nineteen-year-old is a nineteen-year-old whether he has rarely left the family farm and is frightened even by the nearest city or whether he has matured himself by sailing around the world and working his way into a position of honor and responsibility. So there can be little doubt that Samuel Comstock thought often of the rolling moors of Nantucket, of the white fences and the spring gardens and the particular sound of the surf off the South Shore. At the same time, though, he was apparently beginning to think of mutiny.

Like many an accomplished nineteen-year-old, Samuel Comstock was an arrogant young pup. He was a good whaleman, yes, and he knew it. He was short, but muscular and handsome, with a quick, flashing smile that charmed some men as much as it did most women. And he had an explosive, violent temper. Because of his mercurial personality, his swaggering walk, and his proved ability, he found himself in a dangerous, isolated position—dangerous because of an unwritten rule aboard whaleships.

The officers of a whaler lived aft and of course had the run of the ship. The crew lived forward in the forecastle and were not supposed to go aft unless ordered. In the middle, literally as well as figuratively, lived such semiofficers as harpooner Comstock. They bunked amidships in the steerage; they were neither mates nor crew. Like the officers they could go where they wanted on the ship. Like the crew they had little or no authority to order a man about. But the most important element in the unwritten rule was that these harpooners, these men in the middle, were neutral. Amid the stern discipline of the whaleship feeling usually ran strong between officers and crew. But no matter what the conflict, no matter how recalcitrant the crew, no matter how brutal the officers, the harpooners were expected to mind their own business. For Samuel Comstock this position was complicated by his personality and ability. While the officers tended to dislike his arrogance, the men of the forecastle regarded him as a demigod. It happened, though, that this situation fitted perfectly into his plan.

How carefully he worked out this plan in advance is hard to

say. By the time the whole bloody thing was over, though, it was obvious that he had plotted far more than an ordinary mutiny. There was a pattern to it that indicated Samuel Comstock had thought a long way ahead of revenge and murder, even ahead of escape from the globe-circling arm of maritime law.

Something, no doubt an incendiary combination of his arrogance and the condescending treatment from the officers, gave him a fierce hatred of the captain and mates of the ship. On the hot, quiet days when he stood at the masthead, supposedly watching for whales but actually nursing this hatred and laying his plans, he had apparently pondered the stories of other mutinies and learned their lesson. He had visualized the plight of Fletcher Christian, sitting on his rock shelf and looking out across the waters that rolled around the world to England; thus he had learned Christian's lesson too. And it apparently began to dawn on Samuel Comstock that there *was* a way to lead a mutiny, escape the law, and, yes, even return home within a few years. It would be a complicated procedure and it would require meticulous timing and intricate conspiracy. But if all the details were planned well enough in advance, and if he could keep his wits about him through it all, it could work. When he had it plotted out, Samuel Comstock could pride himself on having devised, for the first time, the perfect mutiny.

Whether it all came to him in one or two lonely watches at the masthead on that fourth cruise or whether he had been refining the idea and working out the details over a number of years no one knows. Certainly he had felt the urge to rebel against the authority of the ship on other voyages. His maddening self-assurance and his flashing temper must have led to many a brush with the officers above him. But he did not go so far as mutiny—until he sailed as harpooner under Captain Thomas Worth.

Worth was master of the whaleship *Globe,* and he took her out of Edgartown harbor on December 15, 1822. Already the sand bar that was later to strangle Nantucket's whaling business was building up across the island's harbor mouth, and many Nantucket whalers now fitted out at Edgartown, on Martha's Vineyard, across the south. Those first few days of the *Globe's* whaling cruise must have made the crew uneasy. Superstition did not rule the life of the sailing man quite as much as legend made out; yet sometimes there seemed to be early signs when a voyage was fated to go wrong. Two years earlier the men of the *Essex* had had their warnings, from storm and murderous whales, before the last big beast finally stove in her bow and sank her. Now the signs appeared aboard the *Globe*. First came an ordinary enough accident; hardly was she out of the harbor when the cross-jack carried away, and the *Globe* had to go slatting back into port. Next day she put out again, ran straight into head winds, and was forced to sit them out in Holmes's Hole, even nearer the mainland than Edgartown. On the third day the wind had hauled around, and the *Globe* finally dropped land astern. Then, twelve days out and in the midst of the Atlantic, a winter gale came smashing down on the ship and her men. For two days it threatened to pound the *Globe* to pieces, and only the skilled hands of veteran whalemen at the helm, such men as Samuel Comstock, saved her. All the way down the Atlantic, around Cape Horn, and up the Pacific the lookouts sighted whales only twice. Clearly, for those who could read them, the signs were there. The cruise of the *Globe* was headed toward disaster.

Did Captain Worth sense this? Was he harsh, even brutal, because the cruise was not going as it should? There is no evidence that he had any hint of what was to come. It would have been difficult to imagine, anyway. And for that matter, *was* he brutal? Even today you can get an argument on Nantucket Island, or on Martha's Vineyard, Worth's home, by assuming off-hand that Samuel Comstock's mutiny was motivated by the captain's brutality. There is evidence that Worth ran a taut ship, all right. But did he deliberately feed the men spoiled food, thrash them unnecessarily, even try to maroon troublemakers, leaving them to starve on a barren island? A few historians say so. Others deny it. Whatever the case, the most complete contemporary account that has come down to posterity defends Captain Worth. Some of the crew did complain about the food during the dreary months on the Japan Grounds. And their protests brought little satisfaction from Captain Worth. Possibly one reason for his anger was that the mumbling delegations coming aft were led not by a member of the forecastle but by Harpooner Samuel Comstock. This man, Worth must have realized, was going to bring trouble to the *Globe* before the voyage was over. And whatever the argument about his brutality, no one will plead that Captain Worth was an especially mild-mannered man himself. So the conflict was set almost from the start.

Other officers aboard the *Globe* had a taste of Comstock's violent temper and brooding hatred. Nathaniel Fisher was third mate, a tall, powerful man. One day when the officers and men of the *Globe* were gamming with those of another Nantucket whaler, the *Enterprise,* Comstock livened up the festivities by challenging Fisher to a wrestling match. Fisher soon began to get the best of him, whereupon Comstock let go with his fists. Fisher could have had Comstock flogged for that; instead, with two or three well-directed blows, he sent the harpooner sprawling on the deck. Comstock climbed back to his feet, wiping the blood from his jaw and showing no more fight. As he went off he glared at the officer and muttered, "I'll have my revenge, in time." From the black malevolence in Comstock's eyes Fisher could see that he meant it.

Why was Comstock constantly looking for trouble? Was he simply showing off? It was in his nature, and on this cruise his younger brother George, who idolized him at first, was signed aboard for his first voyage. Or was it because Comstock was working the crew—and himself—slowly up to the pitch of a long-planned mutiny? Whichever his reason, the situation aboard the *Globe* was developing as if he had planned it that way from the first day out.

There was only one missing element. So imagine Samuel Comstock's delight when, after the cruise off Japan, that element was suddenly provided for him. He needed a little band of followers to help him carry out the actual mutiny. Evidently the men who had groused about the food were not angry enough for outright rebellion. But when the *Globe* dropped her anchor at Oahu, six of these men found the Sandwich Islands too inviting. In their place Captain Worth shipped the only new hands he could find.

They were six of the most disreputable, the surliest—and the most rebellious—hands he had seen in all his years of whaling. But their true colors did not show until the *Globe* was well out on the Pacific again. By that time it was too late. The bloody climax was already close at hand.

The *Globe* was running down toward Fanning Island, just above the Equator, when one morning the second mate, John Lumbard, bellowed down into the forecastle for the hands coming on watch to get a move on. One of the men who had shipped aboard at Oahu was Joseph Thomas, a lazy, filthy, sullen beachcomber. Thomas made it a habit to linger over his breakfast as long as he possibly could. This morning he snarled up the forecastle companionway that he was still eating. Aboard a tightly disciplined whaleship, as Thomas well knew, such an answer was calculated to drive an officer mad with rage. And because some of the other crewmen had taken up the same jeering trick, Captain Worth had started coming by the forecastle himself at about this time; his shouted command was usually enough to make the men change their minds and get to work. Not this time. Mate Lumbard rapped the scuttle and sang out for the watch. Most of them came tumbling up. Captain Worth's command brought the others out in a hurry—all except Thomas, who carefully kept the mate and skipper waiting for a minute or two before he sauntered insolently on deck. Worth confronted him.

"And what, might I ask, has happened to *your* hearing?"

Thomas yawned. "Hadn't finished my breakfast." He turned and started to amble aft.

"Thomas, I'll knock you to hell," Captain Worth shouted at him, "if you don't come out of the forecastle quicker the next time you're called."

Thomas swung around. "You'll pay for it if you do," he snapped.

That did it. Captain Worth took three quick strides and let go a roundhouse right. Thomas ducked, slipped by the captain, and ran forward. Worth did not chase him. He went to the fife rail, unfastened a length of two-and-one-half-inch rope, and tested it against his hand.

"Mr. Lumbard," he called. "Bring that man aft."

Wriggling, gouging, kneeing, Thomas was dragged to the waist of the ship. With no more ado the other mates assembled the entire crew. Joseph Thomas was seized to the rigging and his back was bared. The entire preparation took only a few minutes.

Captain Worth surveyed the men gathered before him. "There are some among you," he said, "who have been asking for trouble ever since we left Oahu. Thomas more than anyone else. You will now see what's in store for anyone who tries to get away with insubordination aboard this ship. Mr. Lumbard, fifteen strokes."

Joseph Thomas' insolence had melted away. Already, as he hung by his thumbs and tried to balance on tiptoe on the swaying deck, he was whining softly to himself. As the lash whistled through the air and smacked against his bare shoulders, he yelped and swore. The skin of his back turned red, then purple, then tore under the lash, and he groaned, then cried, then cursed, then screamed until, with the last plopping blow, he was yowling and spitting like a wounded animal. When he was cut down he collapsed on the deck, sobbing and blubbering in his own blood.

Standing amid the crewmen and listening to them mutter all around him, Samuel Comstock studied their twisted faces. He knew that now the time had come.

All the rest of that day Comstock made his final preparations, edging up alongside one man here, another there, and outlining his plan for the mutiny. Luck was with him. Not only were the half-dozen men he selected still hot with anger at the flogging they had witnessed, but their whispering messages were lost amid an unusual bustle aboard the *Globe* that day. They had spoken the whaleship *Lyra,* and while captain, mates, and foremast hands had their gams no one noticed the conspiratorial meetings of Comstock and his new followers. By nightfall, as the last of the *Lyra's* boats went bobbing back, the order was once more hissed from man to man:

"We take the ship tonight. At midnight."

"Take ship tonight. Midnight. Pass it on."

"Take the ship at midnight."

"Tonight. Pass it on."

"Midnight."

Yet still neither the captain nor any of the mates had an inkling of the plot. Ordinarily on a whaleship the size of the *Globe* the boat steerers and their crews took the after-dark watches, dividing up the night between them. On this night no change was made in the routine. So a little before midnight the watches changed. Samuel Comstock and his boat's crew took the deck.

Among the crew was Comstock's younger brother George. It was his trick at the helm. Leaning on the big wheel, twining his arms through the spokes and watching the stars' reflections dance on the sea, George kept her a good full before the gentle breeze, and let the night sigh past him. As unsuspecting of what was to come as any of the officers and most of the crew, he noticed not a thing out of the ordinary. At midnight, when his duty at the helm was up, he picked up the rattle kept by the binnacle for signaling his relief.

Suddenly a heavy footfall sounded near him and a voice barked:

"Drop that!"

In the pale glow of the binnacle light George saw the face of his brother Samuel. With the features dimly outlined from the light just below his jaw Samuel Comstock's face looked the personification of evil. George froze in shock and fright.

"Make the least damned bit of noise," whispered his brother, "and I'll send you to hell." Then George saw what Samuel had in his hand. It was a razor-sharp boarding knife.

Dumbly George watched his brother lay the knife on the workbench near the cabin gangway. The mutineer came over near the wheel and lit a lantern at the binnacle. Taking it with him, he went slowly and silently down the companionway to the officers' messroom.

Off this small center room, with the bulwarked table and the fat stump of the mizzenmast rising through it, were the cabins of the captain and mates. As Samuel Comstock stepped softly into the room, three of his confederates slipped in from the steerage forward. So far the plan was working with perfect timing. One of them carried a heavy ax which, by prearrangement, he handed to Comstock. Two of the three stationed themselves at the two doors to the officers' cabins; First Mate Beetle had one to himself and the other was shared by Second Mate Lumbard and Third Mate Fisher. Then each man waited while Comstock set the lantern on the table and gently shoved open the door to the stateroom of Captain Worth.

He had memorized the room well, so that even in the dark of midnight he would be able to slip across the stateroom to the tiny cabin which contained the captain's bed. Everything still went as planned; the door did not even squeak. The silence was broken only by the creak of the ship and the *wash-wash* of the wake.

But then came the first hitch. It was one of three split-second occasions in which Samuel Comstock's perfect mutiny almost failed.

It was a steaming, torrid tropical night. So Captain Worth, after trying in vain to sleep in his cramped, airless cabin, had slung his hammock in the larger stateroom and crawled in. Only the slight luminosity from the sea glowing in the stern ports outlined the swinging figure in the hammock a moment before Comstock blundered right into it. With a whistling gasp, he jumped back. The figure in the hammock did not stir, only swung slowly back and forth with the roll of the ship. Comstock took a firm grip on his ax and lifted the weapon as high as he could raise it in the low-ceilinged room. He timed the roll of the ship and tensed his hold on the handle. Then he brought the ax crashing down.

Captain Worth did not have a chance to cry out. There was the thudding, crunching sound as the ax struck. The hammock swung away but did not break. The figure in it stiffened. Comstock swung once more. The captain's head rolled off the edge of the hammock and hung there, suspended by a tendon. Something hot and sticky splashed Comstock in the face and saturated his shirt. It was blood.

Comstock spun around and ducked out of the stateroom into the center messroom. There the lantern still sat where he had left it on the table. In its dim light Comstock could see that Silas Payne, the man he had appointed his lieutenant, had swung open the door to the first mate's cabin. Comstock scooped up the lantern as he ran around the edge of the table. When he reached the doorway he saw Payne lunge at the bunk with a boarding knife. But here came another of the moments in which the perfect mutiny almost failed.

Comstock had got there too late with the lantern; or rather Payne had not dared wait, assuming the captain might cry out any second. In the darkness he had missed his target. Mate Beetle was only wounded. He came to life immediately, shooting out of his bunk as he stammered, "What! What! What!" Still half asleep, already dripping blood, Beetle watched as the two mutineers closed in on him. More by reflex than shrewdness, he started to whine and plead, desperately trying to gain time. "Payne! Comstock!" he shouted loud enough for the other officers to hear, "DON'T! DON'T! Haven't I always . . ."

For the moment it worked. Comstock stopped, savoring his revenge, watching the mate cringe before him. "It's a damned good time to beg now," he sneered, "but it's too late."

This second was all Beetle needed. In a well-timed leap he was at Comstock's throat. Both men went down. Standing by with his boarding knife and watching the thrashing pair, Payne could do nothing, for fear of sticking Comstock. The lantern bumped on the deck and went out.

But Comstock was saved by Captain Worth's blood. Beetle had just fastened his grip on his attacker's throat and had begun to throttle him, when Comstock shook himself like a dog and Beetle's now gory fingers slipped loose. The harpooner rolled away. Payne grabbed the ax and handed it to Comstock. As Beetle tried to scramble to his feet, Comstock got to his knees, swung once with the ax, and crushed the first mate's skull.

Now two of the officers were dead; but two remained. They were in the cabin next to Beetle's, and they could not possibly have slept through the last minute or two.

But Comstock had to take a chance anyway. The lantern had gone out in the scuffle; trying to finish off two men in a little cabin in the dark might lead to the same kind of blundering that had helped Beetle almost turn the tables on them. So he told the three mutineers in the messroom to keep the second and third mates barricaded in their cabin while he went on deck to relight the lantern.

Out in the open it was as if nothing had happened below. The stars glimmered off the water. The pin-point lights of the *Lyra* could be seen off to starboard. A clear, clean breeze hummed through the rigging. Comstock paused only a moment, then ran for the binnacle, the lantern bumping against his side.

At the helm, the rattle still by his feet, was George Comstock. The boy's hands were clenched on the spokes of the wheel. The ship was still on course. But as Samuel Comstock leaned over the binnacle to relight his lantern, he heard the soft, muffled sobs.

"What are you crying about?"

George tried to fight it back and failed. "I'm afraid," he wailed. "They'll hurt me too."

To Samuel Comstock, fresh from the blood bath below, this cowardice was contemptible. Any little affection he might have had for his brother was gone in that moment at the helm of the *Globe*. George Comstock was no longer Samuel's brother, if indeed he ever had been.

"I'll hurt you," was all he could think of snarling, "if you talk like that." He ran back to the companionway.

In the messroom the other mutineers were still keeping watch on the mates' cabin. Not a sound came from the other side of the door. Comstock went into the captain's stateroom and grabbed two muskets from the rack. Fixing a bayonet on one and loading both, he prepared the last assault. This time it would be made with guns. Using an ax and boarding knife had almost upset everything the last time. Now he ordered his men away from the door and fired through it in what he judged to be the direction of one of the bunks. The blast in the little room blinded them momentarily and made their ears ring. Then, from the cabin, came a faint groan. Still Comstock waited.

Third Mate Fisher broke the silence. "I'm shot in the mouth," he yelled through the splintered door. "I'm shot in the mouth."

Comstock's answer was: "Open that door."

Handing the empty musket to Payne and taking the one with

the bayonet, he trained it on the door. A full minute passed, and then the door suddenly banged open. Comstock lunged at the blurred figure as it jumped back into the cabin.

But he forgot the doorsill. It caught him in the toes and tripped him neatly, sending him headlong onto the deck inside the cabin. Lumbard pounced on him. Comstock slithered away and fought to his feet. When he stood up he found himself confronted by Fisher and Lumbard. Fisher was spitting blood from what was left of his jaw; but he was holding the musket and pointing it straight at Comstock's heart.

The other mutineers started to crowd into the cabin, then caught their breaths and stopped in their tracks. A tense silence dropped on the scene. Again Comstock could hear the ship's timbers groaning and the Pacific lapping along her sides as mutineers and officers stood facing each other, each waiting for the other to make the first move. Again Comstock's perfect mutiny hung in the balance.

Fisher, holding the musket and pointing its bayonet a few inches from Comstock's chest, could see over the stocky harpooner's shoulder into the bloody faces at the door. He could not tell how many of them were armed, how many others were waiting in the messroom for him to fire the single shot from the musket before they rushed in on him, their hatchets and knives flashing. That there were only three others, that their courage would undoubtedly dissolve if Comstock fell Fisher had no way of knowing. And the flow of blood from his smashed jaw seemed to be increasing. Already his knees were weak.

Comstock sensed the third mate's hesitation. Softly, smoothly, he started talking. The ship, he assured Fisher, was all but taken. The captain was dead. So was the first mate. The rest of the crew, Comstock lied, was behind him to a man. The remaining officers didn't have a chance, he said. He paused. But, he added after a moment, he might be able to save Fisher's life. The crew was pretty angry. Their blood was up. They would still listen to him, though. If he could point out to them that the third mate had voluntarily surrendered, Comstock was sure they would let him live. Fisher, Comstock said, was smart enough to see the sense in that. But . . . he couldn't hold them back much longer.

Fisher said nothing. He kept the gun pointed at Comstock. Every man held his breath. Standing beside Fisher, Second Mate Lumbard opened his mouth to speak, then closed it. He was just about to say something again when Fisher made up his mind.

He handed the musket over to Comstock.

Sucking in his breath, Comstock grabbed the musket, shoved Fisher back against the bulkhead and turned on Lumbard. As the second mate clumsily tried to dodge the sharp bayonet in the tiny room, Comstock forced him against the edge of his bunk. There was a whistling, wheezing groan. The bayonet had gone to the hilt in Lumbard's stomach. Comstock yanked the musket back as the second mate crumpled, his hands pressing against his belly and blood trickling over his fingers.

Comstock backed away from the second mate, studied the thrashing figure for a moment, and then, as if he had almost forgotten there was another officer, wheeled to face Fisher. The third mate was still backed against the bulkhead, his clenched fingers scratching at the wood as if he were fighting to keep himself on his feet. He said nothing as he faced Comstock, but even in the gloom of the cabin his face looked like the belly of a mackerel and the blood slobbering down his smashed chin made a vivid contrast. Comstock stood silently facing him. The only sound in the cabin, above the ship noises, was the retching groan of the dying Lumbard and the murmuring bubbles of air as Fisher panted through the blood in his mouth.

Did any twinge of conscience bother Comstock at this point? He had given his promise to let Fisher live, and in return Fisher had handed back the gun. Did Comstock feel that he faced any kind of moral dilemma? Apparently not. Probably it was because there was no room in his perfect plan for an officer to be living at the end of the first phase. Despite three fleeting moments when the whole thing almost went awry this first part of the plan was at the verge of success. All that remained was for him to finish off this last man. The ship would be his. But more important than any rational consideration was the fact that Samuel Comstock was now gripped by a kind of insane blood lust that was about to break loose in a wild frenzy. At the moment, though, his voice was calm as he said to Fisher, "You've got to die."

Fisher did not plead or whine. The scratching at the bulkhead stopped. His shoulders drooped. He seemed to relax with hopeless finality.

"All right," he said in a last gesture of bravado. "If there's no hope, at least I'll die like a man." He searched Comstock's face once more. It was set as before, except that by now the jaw had begun to shake. Fisher turned and faced the bulkhead, his back to his murderer.

Comstock raised the musket and aimed it at Fisher's head. The bayonet was almost touching the back of the third mate's neck.

The blast was as if the little cabin had exploded. The acrid smoke stung Comstock's eyes. Through his tears he could see the body of Fisher flop in the corner like a rag doll.

Comstock stood for a moment surveying his carnage. His legs were spread wide and he still held the musket to his shoulder. The bayonet pointed at a smeary splotch of blood and brains on the bulkhead where Fisher's head had been. Now Comstock's jaw was twitching convulsively, and his shoulders started to shake. He had done it. He had had his revenge. The ship was his. The mutiny, the first part of his carefully laid scheme, had gone just as he had planned it.

But it was as if the full meaning of what he had done had not really penetrated his mind until now. Only at this moment of triumph did all the months of plotting and waiting and nursing his revenge come welling to the surface. The cold, solid demeanor was suddenly gone. In this moment Comstock was a man completely out of control. Twisting the musket, bayonet down, and holding it as he would a spade, he drove it again and again into the still-quivering body of Mate Lumbard.

"I am a bloody man!" he screamed. His body shook and he stumbled drunkenly as Lumbard's body rolled away from the bayonet and the blood smeared the deck under his feet. "I have a bloody hand!" Comstock shrieked. "I will be revenged!"

The sight, the scent, and the taste of blood drove him berserk. He ran crazily through the ship, the aroused crew scattering before him as he clambered on deck and glared madly about him before racing from side to side. Then, almost as suddenly, the madness subsided, transforming into a growling, sadistic malevolence.

"Bring up the captain!" he yelled. The other mutineers, eying the bayonet on the musket Comstock still held, skittered below and came bumping up the companionway with Captain Worth's body. At Comstock's direction it was laid out on the deck. A boarding knife was driven into the corpse at the bowels and hammered up until the point protruded at the neck where the head, still hanging by a tendon, rolled with the swing of the ship. Comstock gave his command; the body was hoisted to the rail and dumped over the side—no brief, muttered words consigning the captain to the deep and to God, just a heave over the side. Along the rail the crewmen watched as the splash washed away across the surface of the sea and what was left of Captain Worth disappeared forever.

At that point Comstock suddenly remembered the *Lyra.* She was somewhere off to starboard in the darkness, though no lights could be seen now. But at her helm someone was waiting for the long-overdue light that, by prearrangement, was to be hoisted as a signal for both ships to tack. Comstock ordered the light to be set—but for the *Globe* to be kept as she went. Seeing the light, the *Lyra's* helmsman would swing her over onto the other tack, and the *Globe,* staying on her course, would rapidly leave her astern. To make sure, Comstock ordered all sail set. There was a bustle in the rigging while reefs were turned out and topgallants set. The *Globe* slowly gathered speed before the light wind.

The next body to be brought on deck was that of First Mate Beetle—all in the proper order of precedence, according to the meticulous plan. The corpse was dragged up the companionway, hefted to the side, and dumped over. Another splash, as the crew watched, and another officer was gone from the *Globe.*

When the bayoneted body of Second Mate Lumbard was brought on deck, one of the men discovered the man was still alive. But over the rail he went. Somehow, though, despite his wounds and loss of blood, Lumbard had enough life left in him to grab hold of the plank-sheer and hang on there, blubbering and gasping as he begged Comstock for one last bit of mercy.

Comstock strode over to where the clawlike hands still clung to the ship and life. Lumbard's head was out of sight from the center of the deck and, as most of the crew stood and watched in fascinated horror, the voice of the mate, whining and spitting blood, seemed to come bubbling up from the depths of the sea. Comstock stood at the rail for a minute while the mate kept up his wail. Then there was a last shriek, cut off by a splash, as Comstock crunched his sea boot down on Lumbard's fingers and let him drop.

The body of Third Mate Fisher was already on deck, and it quickly followed Lumbard's. Then someone yelled from near the helm. A faint flash of phosphorescence and a thin sound of splashing could be heard astern. Lumbard, the fantastically indestructible Lumbard, was apparently trying to swim after the ship. Comstock roared for a boat's crew to lower and go after him, and this time make sure he was dead.

The men started toward their boat. They did not argue. Going out into the blackness to kill a swimming man was a fearful assignment; staying on board to face the wrath of Samuel Comstock, though, was worse. Then, if any of the crew had had a second thought, Comstock realized it at the same time. He yelled at them again. No boat would be lowered. He must have caught his breath at the thought; here, at the successful climax of his mutiny, he had almost given it away. The men in that boat could have made for the *Lyra* and either caught her in this light breeze or at least gotten close enough to signal her lookout at dawn.

There would be no giveaway now, though. All the officers were gone. And if Lumbard was battling for a few more moments of life, he would not battle long. The sharks, already attracted by the blood, could faintly be detected, rolling in the white wake of the *Globe*.

With the mutiny done there was no doubt of Samuel Comstock's absolute command, for the time being at least. One look at the white faces of the crew watching him and at George Comstock, weeping like a little boy, was enough to show that whatever word

Samuel Comstock spoke was law, through fear alone. But now, he realized, although the mutiny was over, it meant success only for the first phase of his well-laid plot. Part two would be a different kind of struggle, a longer one in which he would have to keep his command of the ship, in which he would have to dominate the rebellious crew while he charted and followed a course to the group of islands he had selected. Most of the crew, he had already calculated, would follow his lead because they were terrified by him. But what about the remaining few? What about the half dozen who had been in on the actual mutiny with him, the ones who had kept an eye on the ship while he was in the officers' cabins doing his grisly work, the ones who had been down there with him? They had followed him easily enough in the heat of the moment when it was kill or be killed. Would they acknowledge his command from now on? How long before they realized that only the stab of one knife or the report of one musket could give *them* the command? That was what Comstock would have to be on the alert for every moment from now on, throughout the voyage to his islands. Until then he could not start on part three of his plan, in a way the most important phase of all.

But there was no time for plotting and thinking; he had done all that incessantly through the long months since leaving Edgartown. Besides it was going just as he had planned it. So Comstock, looking about him and seeing the entire crew watching and waiting for his next move, kept the initiative. Immediately he appointed Payne his first mate. Then he ordered the officers' cabins washed down. The remaining edible food was broken out. All whaling equipment was thrown over the side. There would be no more whaling, only flight. Dawn was breaking as work aboard the *Globe* got back into routine and the new captain prepared to move into his cabin. The breeze had freshened and the ship was plowing along as if she too were concentrating on flight. Nowhere on the horizon could any sign of the *Lyra* be seen.

All that day, while Comstock slept off his bloody orgy and Payne ran the ship, the crew went about their jobs, still trying to believe what they had heard and seen. Even though everything aboard had been washed completely the air, even the odor, of death still hung on the ship. It was only slowly that the men began to recover from their stupor and wonder about the future that had been thrust upon them. Where was the *Globe* headed? The crewmen could not tell because the course was changed every hour or so; obviously only Comstock and Payne knew their destination, and possibly even Payne did not know yet. What would happen to them when they got wherever Comstock was taking them? Comstock was apparently not going to tell what his intentions for them were. As it turned out, it was just as well they did not know.

It was soon apparent, though, that the *Globe* was going to be run differently from when Captain Worth was in command. They sighted one of the Marshall Islands, whereupon Comstock had her steered for the land and a boat was sent ashore for fresh provisions, something his predecessor had rarely done. But when the natives came out in their canoes, climbed aboard, and a few tried to purloin something from the ship, Comstock opened fire on them, something Captain Worth had rarely done either. One of these natives managed to scramble into his canoe and start away. A boat was lowered in chase. As the whaleboat drew up on the canoe, the native turned, held up his hands, begged forgiveness, and offered the only treasure he had, some scraggly beads, in return for his life. He was shot. His canoe was left drifting while the boat returned to the ship and way was made again out onto the Pacific.

At another island Comstock had the ship brought warily in near land, where he had her lie and wait. The natives paddled out and came aboard. They had some fresh coconuts and fish, which they readily traded for a few trifles Comstock offered them. None of them was caught swiping anything from the ship. So they were allowed to return to shore. That night, by Comstock's order, two canoeloads of native women were brought out to the *Globe*. Immediately the whaleship became a riotous, floating bordello. Not until late in the morning were the women dumped back in their canoes and sent ashore. Life aboard the *Globe* was different from the regime of Captain Worth.

So was the living terror. Apparently Samuel Comstock was one

of those rare men with no conscience whatever. His partners admitted openly that they did not sleep well, so guilt-ridden were
their nightmares. Comstock's answer was that when Captain
Worth appeared in *his* dreams, he threatened to kill the old man
a second time. Nevertheless, while Comstock felt no guilt, he appeared to be inundated by fear of the example he had set, and
by the realization of how easily the same thing could happen to
him. Now the quick-smiling, arrogant young whaleman was gone.
Comstock was suspicious, jumpy, brutal. He collected, counted,
and locked up anything aboard ship that could be used as a
weapon. He made every hand move into the after quarters, where
he or his confederates could overhear any attempt to plot a
countermutiny. He slept little, always on watch for fear he would
be struck down just as he had struck down Captain Worth.

His new ship's articles were read to the crew. Any man who
saw a sail and did not report it would be put to death. Anyone
who refused to fight off a ship would die too. ". . . and the
manner of their death, this: they shall be bound hand and foot
and boiled in the trypots of boiling oil."

Comstock's terror rapidly bred terror, which soon engulfed
the ship. So it was only a matter of time before the first victim
of this spreading fear would be claimed. He was William Humphries, a Negro steward. And poor, frightened young George
Comstock happened to be the agent of his death.

It was George Comstock who stumbled on Humphries as the
steward was loading a pistol. In answer to George's questions
Humphries could only stammer that he had heard something that
had made him fear for his life. George now faced a cruel dilemma.
If he went to his brother with his information, Humphries would
probably not live another twenty-four hours. But if he did nothing, if he did not report what he had seen to Samuel, an attempt
might indeed be made to retake the ship. It might succeed. And
although he was apparently not accepted into the company of
the mutineers, George could guess what would happen to the
brother of the head mutineer in the slaughter that would follow.
Besides, if he kept his mouth shut and if Humphries were then
found out, Samuel might also discover that his brother had

shielded the steward. George Comstock's insides still turned to water when he thought of the things he had seen and heard just a few nights before. He went to his brother and told him.

Samuel Comstock and Silas Payne were in Humphries' cabin in seconds, and the pistol was grabbed away from the quaking steward. Next morning a "trial" was held. Humphries was summoned before the mutineers and, while the rest of the crew looked on, was asked a few questions. The steward readily admitted that he had had the gun. He gave as his only excuse that he had been scared out of his wits by what was going on about him and had stolen the weapon for self-protection. Comstock interrupted his explanation: "It appears that William Humphries has been accused of a treacherous and base act, in loading a pistol for the purpose of shooting Mr. Payne and myself. Having been tried, the jury will now give in their verdict, whether guilty or not guilty."

The jury consisted of four men selected by Payne and Comstock. Their quick verdict: guilty. Humphries was dragged forward, seated on the rail under the studding-sail boom of the foreyard, and relieved of his watch. A cap was pulled over his eyes. A rope was made fast around his neck. The other end, run through a block on the yard, was let down to the waist of the ship. Every man of the crew was ordered to take hold.

Comstock stood by the ship's bell, ready to give the signal. Calling across the deck, he asked Humphries if he had anything to say. "You have," he added, "fourteen seconds to live." Still horrified at how fast everything had happened and how rapidly death was approaching, Humphries gasped, in muffled tones through the cap, "Little did I think I was born to come to this——" The bell rang, the men heaved, and the heavy knot choked him off. He did not jerk his feet once, but swung slowly from side to side as he rose to the studding-sail boom out over the sea. The body swung up there for a minute, then started to revolve. Comstock ordered the rope cut. Down Humphries came, and then the rope caught in the rigging. The body splashed into the sea, but the tangled rope kept it sloshing alongside, twisting around and around, mocking Comstock as he looked over the rail. With a cursing shriek Comstock ordered the rope cut away and a runner hook attached to the body. For some minutes, while the crew worked to free William Humphries for his salt-water grave, everyone was too busy to notice the white terror on the face of Samuel Comstock.

For two weeks the *Globe* creaked along, now in one direction, now another, while Comstock tried to confuse his crew and at the same time follow a general course to the island group he had selected. No more men were strung up to the yardarm, but every man lived out each day in fear he would be the next. Despite the better food, despite the fact that no one had to stand the dreary watch at the crosstrees it was the atmosphere of a death ship. The regime of Comstock and Payne was brutal in its own way, and it was terrorizing; no one knew when the unpredictable new skipper would explode into a rage and make someone pay with his life the way Humphries had. But it is a tribute to harpooner Comstock's seamanship that in the trackless ocean, with all that weaving north and south, the *Globe* reached her destination, more than 1000 miles away, in fifteen days after the mutiny. One night the red-hot sun sank into nothing but endless water on all sides. Next morning a man furling sail out on a yardarm looked across the sea, dropped the gathered end of the sail, and bellowed, "Land! Land!"

"Where away!" came from the deck.

"Off the starboard bow! There! Land!"

Comstock was already climbing the rigging. "Can't make it out. Where'd you say?"

The man perched on the yardarm almost lost his balance as he swung on the footropes and tried to point with both arms. Then Comstock saw it.

Mili Atoll sits so low in the ocean, almost as if it were a pudding floating on the swells, that it cannot be seen from a deck only a few miles away. It is a big atoll, more than a hundred miles in circumference. Its dozens of tiny sandspit islands form, with the outer reef, a rough circle surrounding an enormous green bay, dotted here and there with islets. On the few charts which showed it at the time it was known as part of the Mulgrave group (Marshall Islands); its present-day name is closer to what the islanders called it then: Milei Atoll. As the men of the *Globe* hung like so many birds in the rigging and watched the atoll draw near them, the little islands gradually seemed to rise out of the sea and take shape before their eyes. Some of the protuberances were nothing more than coral sandbanks that looked as if they had been exposed by low tide. Others were slightly larger, but barren and baking in the equatorial sun. There were a dozen or more that had patches of green underbrush and tall, waving palm trees. That meant water and food. It also meant natives.

What kind of natives? This low-lying little group of islands had probably never been visited by whalemen, maybe not even by any white man. The atoll was off the regular routes the whaleships usually followed, and it snuggled down into the Pacific so that they had almost passed by it themselves. So, if they were the first whalemen to touch here, how would they be received?

They were not long in finding out. As the *Globe* swung about parallel to one of the outer islands, far enough out to keep clear of the projecting reef, the canoes swarmed across to meet them. With enormous relief the men found their hosts friendly, awed by the sight of the big ship and delighted with the visit. Apparently there had been one or two such ships in the area before, but so long ago that no intelligible account of them could be gotten from the sign language of the natives. These islanders wore their long, jet-black hair piled high atop their heads and, except for sashes hanging fore and aft, wore nothing but loincloths. And their teeth, the teeth of those who had not been chewing betel nut, flashed white with their uncontrolled laughter as they studied their visitors' clothes, the bushy beards, and the heavy sea boots. When Comstock signed to them that he would like fresh food, they promptly guided one of the *Globe's* whaleboats through the reef to the shore, loaded it with coconuts and fish, and returned with it to laugh even more loudly at the spectacle of the whalemen clumsily hacking open coconuts.

That night Comstock kept the *Globe* offshore, and the next day he coasted along the reef, looking for the island best suited to his purpose. That afternoon he found it.

The island was long and narrow. It was green, which meant that it would support life, for a while at least. Despite its vegetation it lay so low that a lookout sailing by only a few leagues away would miss it entirely. The shore was jagged with coral, ideal for breaking up the remains of the ship once she burned to the water's edge. And the water near the beach was still and deep enough so the ship could lie safely at anchor while they stripped her.

Now Samuel Comstock was ready for phase three of his perfect mutiny.

The scanty evidence being what it is, there is little beyond a passing remark made by one or two of the participants to indicate what indeed were Comstock's intentions now. But what evidence there is suggests that it was more than mutiny alone, more than wild, unplanned flight to a lonely island, there to rot out the rest of his life. What he had apparently figured out long since was a way to kill the *Globe's* officers, get rid of the ship, and still be able to return home in a few years.

So the vital part of his plan now was the susceptibility of the natives. If he could get on their good side, if he could win them over to him by making liberal presents of provisions and equipment (not including anything usable as a weapon), the time would come when he could lead them in an attack on the rest of the crew. Then, as simply as that, he would be the only survivor. He would erect a signal tower and sit back to wait. It might take years, but sooner or later, with more and more whaleships crisscrossing the Pacific and with the *Globe* long overdue, his signal would be discovered. He could show his rescuers the remains that had been taken ashore from the ship. He could tell them, in gruesome detail, how the natives had first accepted their visitors, then had risen up and killed all but him. He would return to Nantucket, not only safe from the law, but a hero as well. It would indeed be the perfect mutiny. It had gone so well thus far that Samuel Comstock, standing on the deck of the *Globe* and studying the beach before him, must have congratulated himself on his shrewdness—and his luck.

It was at precisely this point that his luck began to change. All during the two weeks since the mutiny Silas Payne, his first mate both in the killing and the remainder of the voyage, had been showing signs of rebellion against Comstock's harsh, suspicious discipline. Now that they had reached land safely, Payne made it obvious that he no longer felt bound to regard Comstock as master.

They anchored the ship, constructed their rafts, and floated their provisions and equipment ashore. A tent was set up on the beach, and Comstock established his headquarters there, leaving Payne in charge of the ship. Hour by hour Payne directed the loading of the rafts and watched them being floated ashore, to be unloaded by another crew under Comstock. But each time the empty rafts returned to the ship one or another crew member reported to Payne that Comstock was handing out material to the natives. From where he stood on deck Payne could see the islanders swarming around the landing operations; their village was only three miles from the beach. Then Payne noticed a sudden commotion. The islanders were doubled up in raucous mirth; they were pointing at two of their men who were prancing about in trousers, jacket, and even the cap of a ship's officer.

Payne swore and slapped the rail. He strode along the deck to where a loaded raft was being pushed off.

"You, there!" he shouted down to the man propelling the long whaleboat oar. "You tell Comstock for me to stop giving away the ship's supplies to the damned natives. He's even giving them our uniforms. Tell him if he doesn't stop it I'm coming onshore and make him stop."

The man nodded mutely and went on pushing the overburdened raft toward the beach. Payne watched it bump against the coral and Comstock and his men jump to unload it. The man on the raft could be seen talking to Comstock. Then the harpooner straightened up and looked across the water to where Payne stood on deck. They stood there staring at each other for a full minute, so far away that they could not have made themselves heard but feeling each other's glare as if they were in a small room. Comstock turned and spoke to the man on the raft.

When the raft bumped against the *Globe's* sides Payne was waiting for the answer. A little reluctantly, but a little pleased too at a sign of falling out between the two leaders, the man repeated his message: "He says you're to come ashore. Commands it, he says. 'Tell Mr. Payne,' he says to me, 'Tell Mr. Payne I command him to come on shore immediately.'"

Payne was already striding across the deck to the cabin gangway. Clattering down into the captain's cabin, he wrenched open a chest, took out a revolver, and stuffed it in his pocket. In a moment he was back on deck and swinging down a rope onto the raft. Provisions were still being loaded, but Payne turned and barked at the man leaning on the long oar. "Take me onshore!"

When Payne jumped off the raft onto the beach, Comstock had disappeared into the tent. Payne went in after him, and immediately every whaleman on shore contrived to find work as near as possible to the tent, straining their ears to catch some of the fight. The argument droned on in low, inaudible mutterings, then increased in pitch and sound as anger rose in the two men. Finally everyone on the beach could hear Comstock fairly shout, ". . . and if any man wants anything further of me, I'll take a musket to him!"

The answer from Payne was a quick, hot "That is just what I want!" There was a moment's silence, and Payne said, "I'm ready."

Another pause. Then Comstock said in a level, measured voice: "I'm going on board once more. After that you may do as you please."

The whalemen scurried back about their work as Comstock came striding out of the tent and down the beach to the raft. The man was still leaning on his long oar. Comstock jumped aboard the raft, turned to him, and commanded, "Take me out to the ship." The man shrugged his shoulders and started pushing the raft off the beach.

Payne was still in the tent when Comstock returned. The harpooner-skipper was now wearing a cutlass, swinging against his legs in a scabbard. He trudged through the coral sand up to the tent opening, stopped there, and called:

"Payne."

Payne came to the flap. He said nothing.

The two men stood eying each other for half a minute. Then Comstock spoke. "This," he said, patting the cutlass at his side, "shall stand by me as long as I live." He turned and marched off, across the beach and inland, toward the low-lying native settlement in the distance. The whalemen looked at each other, shook their heads in bewilderment, and went back to the unloading.

Payne stood in front of the tent and watched Comstock go off, his feet slipping in the loose coral sand, the scabbard slapping against his legs, until he reached firmer ground. He picked up stride, straight along the path that led through the low, scraggly brush to the island village. When the retreating figure had disappeared, Payne went down the beach to hurry up the dawdling men.

The work went on through the afternoon and, just before dusk, everyone on shore squatted down to eat. Then one of them looked up, choked, spat out his food, and exclaimed, "Jesus!"

Coming down the beach toward them was a large straggling crowd of natives. As they came nearer, the whalemen could see Comstock in the lead. Every one of the *Globe's* men was on his feet by now, watching Comstock and the natives as they came up to the camp. No one spoke. The whalemen could hear the crunching sound in the sand as the islanders approached. Payne estimated that there were at least fifty of them. But they carried no knives or spears. They made an odd little tableau, like a missionary and his converts out for a walk. Without a word Comstock led his band by the camp, on down the shore, and then off inland again, doubling back toward the village.

Payne watched them file up another of their sandy paths. And apparently at that moment it dawned on him—the whole plot, the masterful design Comstock had so obviously worked out for his perfect mutiny. Only Payne's interference had put a crimp in the scheme that had been working so well. Of course that was why Comstock was giving so many lavish presents to the natives, and making so sure that they were gifts from him alone. Of course that was why he had proposed himself for the more arduous shore party and Payne for the loading out on the ship. Payne could only wonder how many muskets Comstock had already handed out to the islanders who had been flocking about the beach tent. That explained why he had flared up so suddenly at Payne's complaint against his handouts. And it cleared up the mystery of his abrupt departure. He had taken with him only his knife and cutlass. Why? To allay suspicion. But even now he was probably gathering his grateful natives around him, showing them how to use the muskets, inciting them to follow him in one overwhelming attack on the whalemen's little beachhead. That attack, Payne realized, could come at any time.

The camp on the beach went into a flurry of excitement as Payne hastily prepared his defenses. Orders were yelled up and down the shore; the raft went scurrying out to the ship for all the firearms aboard and extra hands to use them. As a knot of men gathered around him, Payne explained the danger. Every man appropriated a knife or lance or cutting spade, meanwhile looking anxiously toward the slumbering settlement across the little island.

Darkness fell swiftly on the encampment; but in the last dusk no sign of the natives or Comstock could be seen. Payne selected the sharpest-eyed men of the crew, gave each one a loaded musket, and cautioned him that he must keep a better lookout than he ever did at the masthead. He then ordered everyone else to keep near the tent and stay put. The sentries, he said, would shoot on sight anyone who approached the camp.

The little group of whalemen bedded down on the beach, trying to sleep while the sentries trudged around and around them. Overhead the stars sparkled at them in the brilliant tropical night. The soft wash of surf on the shore murmured to them. Every few minutes a coconut palm back of the beach rattled in the stillness, or the raft scraped on a bit of coral, and one of the guards stopped, lowered his musket, listened for a minute, then resumed his endless pacing. Midnight came, with no sound from the village. Slowly the night gave way to the first thin streaks of dawn; still not a sound came from the village. Out across the water the masts and spars of the *Globe* took form and were silhouetted in the red glare of full dawn. The sun was about to burst above the horizon when one of the sentinels stopped, peered toward the village, then ran for the tent.

"He's coming!" the guard yelled into the tent. "He's coming! Comstock!"

Within seconds Payne and three of his confederates came tumbling out of the tent, all carrying guns. They caught sight of the figure of Comstock, still almost a mile away, just as he passed behind a large, sprawling clump of brush. From there he would have to turn and make his way along the shore line toward them, and as he did so he would probably be hidden by the brush until he was less than a hundred yards away.

The three men looked at Payne. He nodded. All four kneeled, facing the spot where Comstock would appear. They checked their muskets and waited.

It seemed like a great deal more than the few minutes it took Comstock to close the distance. Everyone was up, first watching the four men who knelt in front of the tent, then watching the path where Comstock would come from behind the brush. Down the beach, from the opposite direction, a hungry sea bird wailed mournfully.

Then there was a blur behind the brush and the head of Comstock appeared. As he strode quickly toward them, the rest of his body came into view. He was in the act of drawing his cutlass from the flapping scabbard when he saw the waiting whalemen. He stopped, his eyes sweeping the group until he saw the tent, the four men, and the four muskets leveled at him.

Instantly he was whining as he ran toward them.

"Don't shoot me!" he cried. "Don't shoot me! I won't hurt you!"

All four muskets fired almost simultaneously.

Comstock brought up short. The scabbard swung between his legs and tripped him. He teetered for a second, then fell forward, face down in the coral sand. Payne dropped his gun, scooped up an ax, and ran to where Comstock sprawled on the sand. With one swishing, crunching blow he nearly severed the head from the body.

As the whalemen ran up to the bleeding corpse, the last nerve quivers were running down Comstock's arm. The cutlass was still clenched in his hand. It had indeed stayed by him the rest of his life—less than twenty-four hours.

At Payne's command the burial was swift but complete. The body was sewed up in a canvas as if for burial at sea. Then it was lowered into a five-foot grave on the beach and the cutlass was laid alongside. The sand was dumped back over the canvas shroud. Payne read a few words from the ship's Bible. A musket was fired over the damp, sandy mound. It had taken Samuel Comstock more than a year to work his revenge on Captain Worth. In only twenty-two days the captain had been avenged.

The perfect mutiny had failed.

His grave is still out there today, on the edge of the constantly moaning sea, just above a dirty, uneven line of seaweed, broken shells, and leaping sand fleas. In unbroken, endless rhythm the waters reach up toward him, then roll back into the swells of the Pacific. His skull and the cutlass were dug up later; but the rest of his bones still lie, whitened and forgotten, under the coral sand. A huge black rock once marked the grave, and the sea spray sometimes made it glisten like a shiny, ebony symbol of death. The rock may long since have been washed away by some sudden tropical typhoon. But the scuttling of the land crabs, the crying sea birds, and the groaning murmurs of the sea still make their dirge across his neglected resting place. It is a lonely, forsaken shore; and Samuel Comstock has no epitaph save that of his Quaker schoolmaster father, given 128 years ago. When the *Globe* came back across the Pacific and the news reached him in Nantucket, he wrote to a relative: "Oh Samuel, Samuel! Heaven-forsaken Samuel!"

11. The boy with hair like the sun

There is an irony in Samuel Comstock's death; the irony is that his plan for the perfect mutiny was very nearly fulfilled without him. This is how it happened.

As soon as the brief burial service was over, Silas Payne proclaimed himself commander of the little force. He decreed that there would be no more unloading from the ship that day. The only duty was to stand watch, two men at the encampment to make sure the natives took nothing more and six men to guard the ship.

Payne was well aware that few of the crewmen regarded themselves as mutineers and that most of them were waiting and watching for a chance to escape. So he went out to the ship and ordered one of the hands to bring ashore the two binnacle compasses. He knew the *Globe* could not be navigated without them and, more important, he knew the six ship watchers knew it. But he made the mistake of not inspecting the two compasses brought to the beach. One was from the binnacle; but the other was the hanging compass, that ingenious device of the whaleship that was usually suspended in the captain's cabin, swinging over his bunk so that merely by opening his eyes the skipper could immediately tell that the ship was still on the course he had set. Payne had left this one aboard, since it would be useless to the man at the helm. But what he did not discover was that some one of the six ship watchers had substituted the hanging compass for one of the stationary ones, and the other binnacle compass still stood by the helm where it had been all along.

That very night it was put to use. Payne and everyone else ashore except the two men on watch had turned in soon after dark. At ten o'clock one of the patrolling guards looked out to sea and thought he spotted a moving blur in the dark that looked suspiciously like a sail. The offshore wind made it impossible for him to hear anything beyond the waves at the shore line. But he went down to the water's edge, peered out to where the ship had lain at anchor at sundown, then came racing back toward the tent, yelling into the wind:

"THE SHIP'S GONE! THE SHIP'S GONE!!"

Payne erupted from the tent and ran, stumbling and cursing, over the coral sand to the edge of the beach. He was quickly followed by the rest of the men. The sharpest-eyed among them could not make out any sign of the *Globe*. There was an undertone of mumbling among the men, but none spoke his real thoughts: now they had a chance. It would take months, possibly a year. But now their situation would be reported and a rescue ship would come for them—if only those six men could manage the great, clumsy ship and sail her to some port without wrecking her on one of the countless reefs and shoals of the Pacific.

The effect of this development on Payne and the four others who had participated in the mutiny, though, was just the opposite. Now, instead of rescue, the hangman's noose loomed before them. As Payne trudged back up to the tent, he still clung to his only hope. The wind was strong, he muttered, and the ship had probably dragged anchor. By morning they would be able to see her; she would be only a little farther out. They would go after her and bring her back near shore. When he had disappeared into the tent, the others looked meaningly at each other. But still no one dared say aloud what he was dreaming about an hour or so later.

Payne may or may not have been able to get back to sleep that night. He was up at the crack of dawn, standing at the water's edge, shading his eyes, and sweeping the horizon. There was nothing to be seen, nothing but two floating gulls and a raft that had been alongside the *Globe* and was now drifting slowly out onto the Pacific. Either Payne had not slept or he made his plans while he searched the empty expanse of ocean; because he immediately set the men to work on a new project. Two whaleboats lay where they had been pulled up on the beach. One, Payne ordered, was to be broken up and its wood was to be used in building a raised deck on the other. This enlarged boat would then be seaworthy enough to take them out onto the ocean in search for another island refuge. Payne's explanation was that the natives might force them to leave this island. At the time he thought he was lying. He was not.

And he did not realize, yet, that the castaways were engaged in a race against time. At first the natives were quite as friendly as they had been when the whalemen arrived. But the atmosphere changed rapidly, and the islanders were quick to change with it. Payne did not treat them as Comstock had; no doubt he did not feel any obligation to, since he realized that with help probably coming he and his four followers would have to push off in a few weeks for another island. When natives came visiting with their little "gifts" of breadfruit and coconuts, they received few "gifts" in return. When they nosed into the tent, they were driven out in a cloud of profane abuse. When one or two of them helped themselves to something they found lying around—no crime in their village—they were shouted at, sometimes threatened or manhandled. Yet more and more whalemen went coursing through the native village, shoving islanders out of their way and helping themselves to whatever they found. It had taken the whalemen practically no time to discover that, despite Payne's assumption a few days earlier, Comstock had not dared to provide the natives with guns. So one of the favorite pastimes of most hands was to take a musket or two into the village and fire it off, just to enjoy the terrorized reaction of the natives. The approach of a band of white men from the tent village on the beach always became the signal for the natives to hide their food and belongings—and especially their women.

It went on like this for nearly a week, and the islanders seemed to accept it with no thought of retaliation. But there were two among the crew who behaved themselves. Both were young men, barely out of their teens. One, William Lay, of Saybrook, Connecticut, became attached to an elderly couple. The other, Cyrus Hussey of Nantucket, struck up a friendship with a distinguished-looking old man, not knowing he was one of the chiefs of the atoll come over from another island to view the strange white visitors. From their new-found friends the two young men discovered that the natives were hurt and angered and were already meeting to determine their revenge. But when this information was passed along to Payne, he refused to take it seriously. There was not the slightest indication he could see that the islanders were anything but awed and subdued by their powerful visitors.

In fact, Payne and his new first mate, John Oliver, went on a little woman-hunting expedition of their own. They had no difficulty finding a couple girls—there were still some who were fascinated by the white men—and bringing them back to the tent.

But by morning Payne's woman had crept away and returned to the village. With a howl of rage Payne determined to go after her. He and two of his fellow mutineers armed themselves and went to the village. The sight and din of the guns was enough to send the whole settlement scattering again, and the woman was quickly found. Payne dragged his now unwilling companion back to the tent and there, as an object lesson to the islanders who had followed him silently and at a safe distance, he thrashed her and locked her in irons.

The knot of natives standing outside the circle of the encampment watched, expressionless. Then they went back to the village.

Next morning one of the whalemen discovered that the tool chest had been broken open and rifled. A hatchet, a chisel, and some other tools were gone. Again a group of natives appeared near the camp, simply standing there and watching. Payne went to one of them and demanded that the tools be returned immediately. The man went off toward the village. The others made no move.

By nightfall the man Payne had upbraided was back, carrying a broken half of the chisel. Payne decided another object lesson was needed. At his orders the emissary was bound and flogged. The man did not even moan.

Nor was there a sound from the natives who still stood and watched at the edge of the camp. They wandered off, one by one, when night came. But at dawn they were back. None of them made the slightest threatening move. It was an eerie, menacing thing, and the effect rippled through the camp like a current, setting every man on edge. And now the number of natives seemed to be increasing.

Payne evidently decided he had to keep the offensive. He selected four men to go to the village, taking the bound native with them as a hostage. They were to find the hatchet and the man who had stolen it. For some reason Payne gave the men guns and powder but no musket balls. Whether it was because he was afraid of arming four of the crew it is difficult to tell now; the excuse he gave was that the sound of the guns would be enough to awe the natives and that therefore musket balls were unnecessary.

It was a tense little group that walked into the village. The sand street appeared to be deserted, but the four men knew that black eyes were watching from every hidden peephole in the grass-thatched huts. The islander with them, silent, impassive, his hands bound behind his back, refused to lead them to the culprit, if indeed he knew who it was. In fact, the hostage moved along with them as mutely as if he could not hear a word they spoke to him.

So the whalemen started a systematic search of the huts, flushing a fluttering group of islanders from under each grass roof as they strode in. The square gradually filled with natives until most of the village was assembled in a sullen audience. When finally the hatchet was found, lying openly on a mat in one of the huts, not a mutter came from the villagers. One of the whalemen tried to talk to the natives who had rushed out of this hut, hoping to determine which one had taken the hatchet. Again nothing but blank stares. It began to look like part of a well-planned conspiracy. The four men decided to waste no time getting back to the beach. Keeping their hostage with them, they started down the trail. As they looked back, they saw that all of the natives were following them.

The four knew enough not to break and run. Instead they stopped and turned to confront the mob. The islanders came on, to within a few hundred feet, then stopped too. With only the sound of the trade wind whirring through the brush and beach grass around them the two groups faced each other—the four men ranged in a row, their legs widespread and their chins jutting in an attempt to look indomitable, and the hundred or more islanders studying them, it seemed, as if calculating when to strike.

No one in either group moved, not even the black hostage who had so far made no attempt to break and rejoin his people. The tense little tableau lasted nearly ten minutes, with the whalemen not daring to turn their backs and continue on their way. But the natives showed no signs of returning to their village. The heat of the sun—and the suspense—began to soak the shirts of the four white men. Then came the first move from the islanders. Someone behind the front row of shiny black figures stooped and picked up a rock. Another followed his lead, and another, and another. The whalemen looked at each other and moved their muskets to be ready.

The first rock flew, so effortlessly that none of the four saw it until it struck. The thud was clearly audible as the rock caught one of the men over the right eye and nearly knocked him to the ground.

The other three immediately raised their muskets and fired. At the sound, the islanders quailed. But this time they did not retreat. While the whalemen tried to reload, a shower of rocks descended on them. The natives' accuracy was deadly; each of the four men was hit by half a dozen rocks at once and the hostage, now breaking to join the others, was not even grazed.

Demoralized by the silent, breathless suspense, frightened by the sudden and accurate rock-throwing, the whalemen retreated a few paces until they were behind a clump of brush. Then they turned again to face their attackers. But it was too late.

Only later did they realize their mistake. If they had stood their ground, they probably would have kept their supremacy on the island. Even at that point the natives held their white invaders in fearful awe, still half convinced that these men were supernatural in some way and that any open attack on them would bring swift and terrible retribution. That first flying rock had been a kind of feeler, and only the size of the mob had kept them from backtracking at the sound of the gunfire. The shower of rocks had been thrown in desperation, and if the whalemen had stood their ground and fired once again, the islanders probably would have gone scuttling back to their village, sure that they could not overcome their now unwelcome visitors—except possibly by stealth. And of course if the muskets had had more than useless powder in them, if only one or two islanders had fallen after that first discharge, the outcome would have been different.

But no natives had fallen. And, more important, the great white men had retreated. They could be made to run. This the islanders had discovered for the first time. In the instant every one of the more than a hundred black throats swelled with a blood-chilling, exultant war whoop.

It burst upon the four men like a thunder squall. Blanching in terror, they broke and lit out for the beach as fast as they could go. They ran amid a torrent of thudding rocks, and the shrieking war cries increased until the whalemen were sure the savages were upon them. Then a rock caught the slowest of the four neatly in the knee. He went down. Before he could even roll away, the first dozen of the natives were all over him. The other three whalemen heard his cry and looked back just as an islander mashed his skull with a boulder. They redoubled their speed.

Behind them the rest of the natives still came, still shrilling their bloodthirsty yell.

The three survivors made it to the encampment. At the edge of the beach settlement the pursuing natives stopped.

The terror of the fleeing men quickly spread through the rest of the camp on the beach, especially as they watched the natives gather in a menacing council of war. There was silence from the huddled mob for a minute or two, then shouts, then more war cries. Some of the natives streaked off for the village. They were quickly back with spears, knives, and crude but vicious-looking shark's-tooth swords.

Payne meanwhile was gathering his own men in a semicircle and distributing all the guns and ammunition he had. His plan was to maneuver his armed semicircle of men forward until they surrounded the built-up whaleboat, which at the moment lay between them and the savages. Then, when the attack came, they would fight as they could, and if they had to retreat they would take the boat with them, backing slowly toward the sea. But before he could get his men organized, the natives made their first move. It was as if they had exactly guessed his strategy. They fell upon the boat and started to demolish it.

Payne acted quickly and with considerable bravery. Putting down his musket, he walked straight toward the natives, alone and unarmed. The islanders stopped as they saw him come toward them. An elderly, dignified-looking man, obviously one of the chiefs, strode forward to meet him. The two met halfway between the armed camps. The chief sat down on the sand and motioned Payne to sit beside him. Payne sat.

The white mutineer and the black chief talked together earnestly for a few minutes, and then both rose and joined the rest of the waiting natives. There was another huddling council meeting, this time without the shouts and war cries. Around the tent every man listened to his heart thump as he watched and waited.

The meeting, with two or three chiefs and Payne holding forth in the middle of the big circle, took almost an hour. Finally, however, the ranks broke and Payne came striding back toward the tent. As the jostling men crowded around him, he described the terms of the surrender he had just made. There would be no battle. But he had given every article of equipment, provisions, even the tent, to the islanders. And he had promised that from now on the white men would submit to the rule of the natives. In return, no whaleman would be killed.

Thus Payne demonstrated as much ignorance of the island mentality as he had in abusing them earlier. Once the white men had made their first retreat, once they had shown that they were vulnerable, they had no chance. And the promise to let them live was nothing more than a gesture of macabre native humor.

Payne barely had time to explain the conditions when the natives moved forward to help themselves. It was all too sudden; the whalemen had no time to prepare themselves for it. And they probably did not realize that the first sign of resistance would be regarded by the islanders as a signal for the massacre.

There were at least two natives who could see what was about to happen. They were the couple who had been befriended by young William Lay. Instead of joining in the looting they did a startling thing. As the other islanders happily set about overturning cases, dumping barrels, and tearing down the tent, the old man and woman picked their way through the melee, came up to Lay, took him by the arm, and literally dragged him away from the milling crowd.

Lay was surprised and frightened. When the couple squatted on the sand and pulled him down between them, he tried to break away. They held him fast. He asked them what they were trying to do. They said nothing. He squirmed and thrashed. They simply tightened their grip on his arms.

At that moment the beach seemed to erupt with screaming war cries. The shouting, cursing voices of wounded whalemen rose above the din. Lay looked back over his shoulder just in time to see the massacre at its height.

It took less than ten minutes. Evidently some outraged whaleman had been unable to stand by any longer, had lost control for a moment and struck a native. That touched it off. In unison the islanders turned from their looting and set upon the whites. As the victims lit out in every direction, the savages swarmed around them and cut them down. Two fleeing whalemen got within ten feet of Lay when they were knocked sprawling; their skulls were smashed with rocks. Another tripped, fell, got to his feet again, staggered toward the water, and fell again; before he could get to his knees, an old woman ran a spear through his belly. That was all Lay got a chance to see before the couple shoved him flat and spread themselves over his squirming body. A blood-lusting native tried to shove a handspike into him but was driven off. Lay was about to suffocate when the couple jumped up, dragged him to his feet, and ran down the beach, with Lay sprinting alongside them. Taking a quick look back over his shoulder, he could make out little more than a swarming, weaving chaos of black bodies dancing in and out among the twisted, disemboweled bodies that had been his shipmates.

The path the two natives took went down the beach, then cut back toward the village, along a bay, and across a causeway of coral. Its sharp points cut Lay's bare feet; but his two guardians would not let him slow down. They ran and prodded him along as if his life depended upon it; undoubtedly it did. So Lay stumbled and hobbled alongside his tough-footed friends, the drops of blood from his lacerated feet making tiny reddish smears on the blue surface of the lagoon eddying about the causeway.

In the village they made straight for the old couple's hut, and Lay was abruptly shoved inside. There he waited, listening to the high-pitched babble as a crowd formed outside. There he heard the shrill excitement of the village as the savages came triumphantly back from the massacre at the beach. While the screaming natives ran back and forth across the narrow opening, Lay could only edge farther back into the gloom of the hut and wonder what would happen to him when, inevitably, he was found.

He did not have long to wait before the old man came into the hut, took him by the hand, and gently led him out. As Lay stood blinking in the sunlight and trying to guess what was to be done to him now, he suddenly made out a particular group of natives approaching the hut. They were surrounding a white man, and escorting him rather than forcing him along. The man was Cyrus Hussey, another of the whalemen from the *Globe*.

While the natives gestured, argued, and gibbered around them, the two men tried to talk to each other. Hussey had been sure that no one else had survived the slaughter; he was as startled as Lay to find there was another besides himself. His native friend had saved him in much the same manner as the old couple had protected Lay. But, each survivor asked the other, what had they been saved for? What did the natives intend doing with them now? Despite the knowledge of words and phrases the two men had already learned from the natives, the pandemonium around them was so great that they could make nothing out of the wild palaver. Then, abruptly, they were separated; Lay was ushered back into the hut and Hussey was taken to the other edge of the village. Obviously the natives were not going to let their two survivors plot any revenge together. Each in his own hut, William Lay and Cyrus Hussey spent that night watching sleeplessly, wondering, and still reliving the gory scene back down on the beach.

So it was that two young whalemen from New England, William Lay and Cyrus Hussey, lived more than a year and a half among the savages of Mili Atoll in the Pacific Ocean. And in all that time they never quite recovered from that day and night of massacre and terror. They owed their lives to the kindness and consideration they had shown the natives. But they knew the islanders well enough to realize that morals and principles were not the same out here, and gratitude alone could not be counted on to protect their lives.

They were not mistreated, though. They were fed as well as any of the natives, on breadfruit, coconut, and fish. They went along on expeditions after these fish, sometimes netting them, sometimes chasing schools of them into the shallows and spearing them. The two boys joined the community feasts, with fish steamed in pits on hot stones and eaten with large quantities of ship's bread from the *Globe*, which had quickly become the island delicacy. The white visitors were permitted to watch the native dances, 300 half-naked women wiggling, jumping, and screaming in crescendo while the men provided accompaniment on their only musical instrument, a booming drum. The spectacle of all these savages racing about and trying to outyell each other in mounting hysteria sent chills down the spines of the young whale-men.

But no one attacked them, and in fact it developed that the white visitors were the occasion for the celebration—natives had come from all the islets of the atoll to wonder at the white skin, the light hair and the curious clothes of the young men, and the hilarious way they ate with tools.

In many ways it was a pleasant existence—exploring the little outcroppings of the atoll, taking lazy afternoon siestas in the grass huts, leisurely gathering breadfruit and coconuts, swimming in the translucent waters of the lagoon, drifting on its calm surface and fishing or racing a half-dozen miles across its sparkling waters to visit one of the other islets in the circle.

Once they even went off to a mock-heroic "war." High Chief of the atoll was a grizzled old man named Luttnon, who appeared to be feuding constantly with his brother. In some kind of flare-up the brother killed a few subchiefs, and promptly fled to an island they called Alloo. Luttnon, apparently deciding this had gone on long enough, decided to attack Alloo and finish off his brother once and for all. The main reason for this decision became obvi-ous when Lay and Hussey were sent for—Luttnon was giddy at the thought of what havoc he could wreak among his brother's troops with the white man's gunpowder. Could Lay and Hussey prepare a few muskets for the expedition? They explained that they were sorry, but they had no more gunpowder. That was no problem, Luttnon answered. He had plenty, salvaged from the camp on the beach. On inspection this turned out to be a small box containing some powder mixed with mustard seed. When Lay and Hussey explained that it was useless, Luttnon, who was High Chief after all, politely but firmly ordered them to make it work.

The two boys did their best to separate the powder from the mustard seed, and prepared half a dozen musket charges; but they set off for the beachhead with great misgivings. They need not have worried, however. By the time Luttnon's war canoes reached Alloo, the mysterious but efficient inter-island telegraph had warned his brother. He had decamped. The attacking party sailed in pursuit but could not catch him. So, after knocking about Alloo for two days, overturning and smashing things, Luttnon's army went home and the war was over.

As the months passed the boys were accepted as part of Mili Atoll. Yet even then, as long as they were among the natives, there was an ever-present, nagging fear on both sides. The islanders separated the two men from the start, first at each end of Mili village, then by moving Hussey to another of the circle of islands. They crossed paths many times during their stay, but rarely were they allowed to talk together for more than a few minutes; the natives did not want them plotting any mischief. They were forced to give up their shirts and trousers, to wear only skirts or loincloths, and to go barefoot on the sharp coral. And the islanders could not understand why the young men refused to have their ears bored and stretched. The few books, including a Bible, that the boys had rescued from the mess on the beach, were destroyed by the natives, who could not read them and therefore feared them.

The mutual suspicion was constantly there, on the part of black and white alike. Every once in a while it flared into the open. One day, six months after the massacre, a tremor of excitement and panic swept the atoll. Rounding a point, guarded by 300 natives, William Lay saw the cause of it: a full-rigged ship, standing in toward the shore and shortening sail as she came. Quickly both whalemen were whisked away and hidden. All that day and night they sat and waited, watching in vain for a chance to slip away and escape to the ship, praying desperately that a shore party would land on the atoll and rescue them. They were besieged by questions from the islanders: was this their ship that had sailed away, now returning to look for them? Was it another ship from their country across the ocean, preparing to attack the atoll and take the white men home? Or was this a second whaler, calling on the atoll as the *Globe* had? Would its sailors now set up another camp on the beach, mistreat the natives again, and set the scene for another massacre? Lay and Hussey could only answer that they did not know. Neither had had a close enough look at the ship to make any guess about her. And as the islanders' fear and suspicion mounted, the young men had to pretend that they too were afraid of this strange visitor. For both of them, each in his separate hideout, it was a night of fearful suspense—watching armed savages moving restlessly about them, listening to the hushed murmurs of the little councils of war every few minutes, and frantically trying to plan some way to make themselves visible when the visitors from the ship came ashore next morning.

But the visitors never did come ashore. Evidently afraid of this unknown island and its unknown inhabitants, the captain sailed on that night. Next morning not even the ship's topsails were in sight. Lay and Hussey never did find out what ship it was that came so close to rescuing them. And it took a few days for the islanders to relax their vigilance over the young white men they had so nearly lost.

Another incident was a great deal more dangerous. In fact, the two young whalemen came so close to death that only the prestige—and the heartfelt pleading—of two native chiefs saved their lives. These two chiefs were Ludjuan, who had adopted Lay, and Lugoma, foster father of Hussey. They saved the boys' lives at a meeting of all the chiefs. Lay and Hussey were nearby when it happened, but of course were not allowed to be present. As in most such secret meetings, however, a full description of it was all over the island within a few days. Lay and Hussey had learned the language well by now, and from all the reports they heard they were able to reconstruct the meeting at which they had almost been sentenced to death.

It started with a mysterious plague that swept the island. The disease seemed to concentrate on the young people, swelling their arms and legs and faces and blinding them. Whenever one died, the traditional moaning and crying could be heard across the lagoon all night long.

Gradually the feeling grew that the white boys were responsible for this. The religion of the islanders, if it could be called that, was a simple and negative one. Their one god was Anit, an evil deity who must be constantly appeased. The Mili islanders had no god of good to thank for blessings, only Anit to blame for

THE BOY WITH HAIR LIKE THE SUN 273

calamities and to fear. So most of the chiefs reasoned that Anit was displeased by the presence of the two boys on the atoll. If they were sacrificed, Anit would be satisfied and the plague would disappear. Lay and Hussey went with their masters to the chief island, then had to wait on the beach while their fate was decided. As they waited and prayed, the meeting of the chiefs of Mili Atoll was convened.

Unhurriedly they assembled in the hut of Head Chief Luttnon. No greetings were spoken, as was the custom. The chiefs simply sat down on the tapa mats and stared at each other in stony silence. In the circle, his face to the door of the hut, sat the Head Chief. He said nothing. The silent circle sat for a few minutes, with no sound save the trickle of the lagoon over the coral nearby and the rustling of the palm fronds overhead. Each man was pre-occupied with his own thoughts.

Finally one chief was moved to speak: There will be no warriors, he said. He spoke in a low, singsong monotone. The disease is striking all the young people. Soon there will be no more warriors left. If an enemy should attack us now, he said, we could not defend ourselves.

Another chief spoke, in the same low singsong, as if part of some native chorus: Before the sun sinks each time on my island, he said, the disease has struck another young man. It swells their legs and then it swells their arms. And then it swells their faces until they cannot see.

Another chief chimed in: It is the will of Anit.

All the chiefs bowed their heads, while another said: It is the will of Anit, the Great God.

Then the silence again.

Finally the Head Chief spoke what was on everyone's mind: Anit's evil, he intoned, is upon us. It is come to us because we let the two white boys live.

It was spoken as a statement, but it was meant as a question. The tempo of the chorus picked up as some of the chiefs nodded and muttered agreement and others moaned, *Reab, reab*—it is false.

In the tradition of such meetings the preliminaries had been taken care of, and each chief who now spoke would address the circle in the manner of an orator. An old chief took a deep breath and launched into his soliloquy:

We welcomed the great ship and the white men, he said. They treated us well then. The man they call Com-Stock was friendly and gave us many gifts. Then the white men killed the man Com-Stock. And they were not our friends any more. They frightened us with their fire sticks. They took our women and beat them. The man they call Payne. He came into our village and beat our boys. We waited. Then we killed the white men who were not our friends. Anit was pleased. We had good fishing. And we had no disease. Then Anit found the two white boys alive. Some of us took the white boys into our homes. We fed them and kept them from dying. Anit was unhappy to see us do that. Then came the sickness and death. Anit is angry. We must kill the two boys. Then Anit will be happy again.

The old chief dropped his head on his chest, exhausted. Another promptly took up the argument:

When the two white boys are sacrificed, he murmured, Anit will drive the disease away. Then there will be no more dying.

Across from the Head Chief sat a chief named Ludjuan. The grass sides of the hut had been pulled up to let the breeze waft through, and from where Ludjuan sat he could look off across the lagoon to the beach where the white men had been killed. He could recall the scene so vividly, seizing the white boy and keeping him away from the flying spears and stones, his wife lying down across the boy to keep him safe. Then the dash down the beach and across the coral, which had cut the boy's feet so badly, and to the safety of their hut in the village. The boy called himself William Lay, and he had been kind to Ludjuan's wife when the other white men had been so cruel. Ludjuan had tried to return this kindness. He had sheltered, fed, and protected William Lay. When the boy had been caught stealing coconuts at night, Ludjuan had kept the other natives from punishing him. Once, during a famine, the boy had even taken a taboo coconut from the new grave of a warrior. But Ludjuan had explained to Lay that this would make Anit very angry, and when the boy had promised never to do it again, Ludjuan had once more protected him from punishment.

Lay had become a good worker and a good fisherman. And Ludjuan and his wife had come to love this kind young man.

The other chiefs were using argument, Ludjuan realized. They were appealing to reason. Those chiefs who had not yet made up their minds were beginning to agree with the ones who wanted to kill the two boys. It was time to use some reasoning to protect them. Ludjuan spoke:

No, he said, Anit does not punish us for letting the white boys live. Anit is angry, but he is angry because we killed the other white men. They were unfriendly, but they did not kill any of us. We killed all but two of them. We covered the beach with their bodies. We put spears through them. We crushed them with stones. Anit did not want that. He is angry with us for that. He will be more angry if we kill the only two men who lived. We are now paying Anit for what we did. If we care for the white boys, Anit will let us live. He will drive the sickness away.

Ludjuan saw that some of the chiefs were still silent. They were waiting for him to say more, still not convinced. He had kept his best argument for the last:

The great ship, he said, as the murmuring protests died down. Do not forget the great ship. Before the white men were unfriendly to us, the great ship sailed away. Maybe five, maybe six men went with it. They took it away to their big island across the ocean. The great ship lives at a very big island. There are many more great ships at this big island. And many more white men. And big fire sticks in their great ships. You saw what the white men's fire sticks did. The great ships have rows of fire sticks in their sides. They can knock down all our trees and burn all our houses. Many of these ships will come here. If the two white boys are still alive, the white men sent by their Head Chief will not kill us. We can sell the white boys to them for many beads, food, maybe fire sticks. Then we will win all our wars with the other islands beyond where the sun goes down.

I know all this, he added proudly, because my white son told me.

As Ludjuan stopped, he thought some of the chiefs were on his side. But not enough of them were, and the chorus of *reab, reab* sounded like a dirge for the two white boys. Another chief took up the old refrain, to a moaning background accompaniment: We had no sickness. Then the great ship came. Now we have sickness. Two of the white men are still here. Anit is punishing us because two of them are still alive. We must kill them. Then the sickness will go away.

Throughout the meeting one old chief had not opened his mouth, although everyone had glanced in his direction now and then to be ready to listen to him when he was moved to speak. Now he signified that he would speak. The dirge stopped.

Lugoma was one of the most powerful of the chiefs. He ruled his own tiny atoll of reefs and islands within Mili Atoll. At the meeting he sat at the right of the Head Chief. Lugoma deserved his importance in the council. He was one of the smartest as well as one of the strongest of them all. During the meeting he had listened carefully to each chief's speech and had noted how the tide was running against the white boys. He realized that argument was getting nowhere. In this meeting the white boys could not be saved by an appeal to reason. Lugoma must take hold of their emotions. He knew how sentimental the Mili islanders were, so quick to laugh or cry. An appeal to their emotions was the only way to save the lives of the white boys.

He too was emotional when it came to the white boys. Lugoma was the "father" of the second one. Cyrus Hussey, the boy called himself, and Lugoma loved him like a son. The boy was open-faced and pleasant, and he had a sparkling eye. He worked hard, was a good fisherman, and he was the only boy Lugoma had ever seen who liked to help the women with the meals. But what endeared him to Lugoma most was his hair—fine, silky hair. It was long now and gathered like the islanders' black hair at the top of his head. But it was such hair as had never been seen on Mili Atoll before—golden hair, like the sun in the sky.

Lugoma straightened, cleared his throat, and surveyed the circle. Every eye was on him.

Yes, he said, Anit punishes us because we killed. If we kill more, Anit will punish us more. Then Lugoma changed tack without pausing. His voice took on a plaintive, pleading tone. Look, he said, at my boy. He is a laughing boy, a happy boy. He is a good fisherman. He was kind to us when the other white men were unfriendly. That is why I saved him. He has been a good worker. On each island, wherever he goes with me, everyone wants to see him. They want to touch him, laugh at his talk through his nose, stare at his long, silky hair like the sun. I have saved him from the spears. I have taught him to fish, to eat with his hands, to change to our clothes. My women bathed him when the red came to his skin. Now his skin is dark, almost like ours. He speaks the words we do. He is one of us. But his hair, his hair is not. It is more golden than ever. It is hair to wonder at. It is like the sun over the waters of the lagoon. He lives as my son. He has saved my life by working hard to catch more fish when the breadfruit and the coconut and, yes, even the rats have gone. He is of my family; and his hair is like the sun in the sky.

Lugoma paused and looked about the circle of chiefs. None spoke. He went on:

Can any of you, he said, sitting here, believe that these boys brought this sickness to us? Can any of you look at them and believe that? The sickness will go away. You do not have to kill these two white boys.

Lugoma was shaking now. But he turned and looked straight at the Head Chief.

Anit spare me, he said, but I say it. Yes, you can kill the white boys. But—he paused—you must kill me first. His voice dropped to a whisper. You must kill me first. Then you can kill my boy. My boy with the hair like the sun.

Lugoma's chest heaved. His head drooped. There was silence. No moans, no mutterings of Anit-says-kill. When Lugoma looked up, he saw the glisten of tears in the eyes of the Head Chief and most of the others in the circle. In the silence he could hear again the wash of the lagoon on the coral and the brushing palm fronds over him.

It was decided with nothing more said. The Head Chief did not speak. Nor did any of the others. Finally, one by one, the chiefs rose and wordlessly went down the beach to their canoes. They would wait. They would not kill the two white boys from the great ship.

Near the canoes Lugoma found Hussey and Lay waiting, still closely guarded, still sitting apart. Hussey looked up with pleading eyes, trying to read something in the face of his chief. He rose as Lugoma came up to him. The old chief put his arm around the shoulders of Hussey and stroked his blond hair as they crunched through the coral sand to his canoe.

"You will not die," Lugoma said simply. "We will go home now. My son."

It was June of 1824 when a storm-battered, barnacle-covered whaler came limping into the harbor of Valparaiso. Her sails were torn, her rigging slack, her paint peeled, and only six men were aboard. On her stern the faded and worn letters could barely be made out: "GLOBE, NANTUCKET." With only one compass six men of her crew had brought her three fourths of the way across the Pacific Ocean, 7500 miles through a maze of islands, shallows, and coral reefs to civilization. The American consul, Michael Hogan, had no choice but to put the men in irons after hearing their story of mutiny and murder. Under a new captain the *Globe* was sent home to Nantucket. There the six men awaited trial.

But before the guilt could be properly assessed, other witnesses had to be found. This meant a search for the mutineers' lonely island. It meant sending a warship back across the Pacific. That was no simple project in 1824, but the cardinal principle of the sailing ships of the nineteenth century still was: no mutiny could go unpunished. So far as the survivors in the states knew, all the men except Samuel Comstock, the mutiny's ringleader, were still alive somewhere on a place called Mili Atoll. So, after many delays, the U.S. schooner *Dolphin,* Lieutenant Commander John Percival in command, sailed from Valparaiso. Young George Comstock, from the *Globe,* was aboard as guide.

It was an even more difficult voyage than expected. Provisioned for four months, the *Dolphin* took eleven. At one of the Marquesas Islands she drifted in a calm so near the shore that the sailors could watch the native women gather on the beach and dance and sing their siren songs. When the sailors applauded, the girls swam out to the schooner. The officers had to beat them off with boat hooks when they tried to climb aboard.

On another island, where the men went ashore to fill their water casks, the natives became threatening. The officers drew an imaginary circle around the sailors and called it "taboo." This was probably the first, though reverse, application of "off limits," but the natives respected it. At other islands, probably as a result of visits by whalemen who had taken provisions and "paid with the fore topsail," the natives greeted the *Dolphin* with spears and showers of arrows. Other natives pretended friendliness, then stole everything they could lay their hands on.

So it was a pleasant surprise when, after finally reaching Mili Atoll, they found the islanders friendly and apparently trustworthy. But questions about white whalemen brought only a vacant look and a shake of the head. Commander Percival could not know that the Mili islanders had no intention of giving up their prized visitors, even after nearly two years.

Then, while talking to some natives in a canoe alongside the *Dolphin,* he found what he had come for. Under the canoe's seats, badly hidden, were the lids of some whalemen's chests. Immediate questioning brought the same evasive answers. And insistence brought, for the first time, angry shouts.

For days it went on like this. Every time they were asked about the white whalemen of the *Globe,* the natives only shook their heads and professed to know nothing. But more evidence—spars made in Nantucket, a solitary mitten with a *Globe* crewman's name on it—proved that if there were any survivors, they were on this semicircle of islets. Percival and his officer in charge of the boat crews, Lieutenant Hiram Paulding, did not realize it at the time, but they were playing a gigantic game of hopscotch. The prize was William Lay and Cyrus Hussey, the only two surviviors on the atoll. Every time Paulding headed his boat for one of the islands, the natives quickly whisked Lay or Hussey or both to another island. Percival could not threaten to level the atoll with his guns, because he was sure that the natives would promptly murder whatever hostages they held. So the game kept up. But, as had to happen sooner or later, the natives became overconfident. They moved one of their hostages across the lagoon in plain sight of Paulding's boat.

All Paulding saw was a canoe racing for one of the islands. He turned and went after it, following it to the shore. Just outside the surf line he had his men drop the kedge anchor while he studied the scene on the beach.

There must have been more than a hundred natives on the shore. But what dismayed Paulding more was the sight of every woman and child filtering back among the trees.

Just then one of the men came halfway down the beach. Thirty yards away from Paulding's boat he looked like all the other natives, with his sun-blackened skin, his sashes fore and aft, his hair tied in a knot on the top of his head. But Paulding felt a creepy shiver run through him as the man shouted in English.

"The natives are going to kill you," he yelled. "Don't come on shore unless you are prepared to fight."

Then came an eerie conversation between Paulding and the man on the beach, shouted across the snarl of the surf.

"Who are you?"

"William Lay, one of the crew of the *Globe*."

"Come to the boat."

"The natives won't let me."

"Then run."

"I can't. They would stone me to death before I made it. As we talk, they think I am luring you onto the beach. They won't give me up. They plan to get you on the beach and then kill you all."

The conversation was interrupted by one of the natives, obviously asking what Lay had been saying. Lay gibbered at him for a moment, then shouted at Paulding that he had said he was still trying to set the trap.

Paulding faced a delicate dilemma. He had come to the islands expecting to be attacked, but to be attacked by natives led by mutineers. Was this really one of the mutineers? According to George Comstock William Lay was innocent. But was this Lay? Or was he one of the ringleaders, with his life to lose if he were captured by the U.S. Navy? Even if this were Lay, was he really innocent?

There was only one way to find out. Paulding gave the order to ride the surf onto the beach. Leaping out, he raced up the sandy bank, grabbed Lay, and put a pistol to his chest.

"Tell those natives," he said, "that I'll shoot the first man to make a move. Who are you?"

It was William Lay. Still in his teens, he had seen blood wash the deck of the *Globe*, mutineers murder each other, savages massacre the crew; and he had been held hostage for twenty-two months. Now, suddenly, it was too much for him. His eyes flooded and all he was able to do was stammer, "I am your man," before he broke down in sobbing spasms.

As Paulding stood there, his arm around the shaking shoulders of Lay while his men warily watched the natives, one old man started walking toward them. Paulding faced him, slowly raised his gun, and pointed it at the stooped figure. The old man came on. Paulding pulled back the hammer. Then Lay looked up and suddenly said, "Let him come. Let him come. He saved my life. He protected me."

Ludjuan walked up to Lay and took his arm. He asked the boy something, gesturing to the armed sailors surrounding him. Lay nodded. Another question. Lay answered in Ludjuan's language. The old man stood for a moment looking at Lay, expressionless. Then a tide of grief spread across his weather-beaten face. Tear streaks went down his cheeks. His lower lip quivered. He turned, head down, and walked back up the beach.

William Lay was wiping his eyes and the old chief had come back down to the water's edge, where he stood with the surf wetting his feet, as the boat pulled off from the island. But by the time they were a couple dozen strokes away from the surf, Lay had recovered himself. Now his talk poured out in an interminable stream. It was difficult to make out what he was saying. Only a loquacious, pouring jumble of: "What happened to the *Globe*? Did she make Valparaiso? Are any of her men aboard the schooner? Anybody here know East Saybrook, Connecticut? That's where I'm from. You from East Saybrook? It's near New

London. Falmouth? That's not near East Saybrook. Nantucket? Yes, I know Nantucket. I sailed on the *Globe* from Edgartown, across from Nantucket. Oh yes, you know that already. It was— how many years ago was that?" He had spoken English to only one man in two years, and then only on the few occasions when the natives had let him and Cyrus Hussey come together for a few minutes.

Paulding finally stopped the flow long enough to ask the all-important question: how many others were there on the atoll?

"Only one. Cyrus Hussey. He lives over there." Lay pointed to an island across the lagoon. Paulding headed the boat for Hussey's island.

They glided behind an uninhabited point, rounded it, and saw a little beach. One canoe was drawn up on the sand. There was a row of huts on the lawn back of the shore, under the shade of the coconut and breadfruit trees. The beach was deserted. Paulding had slipped up on it undetected.

As the boat landed, a man came past the trees to the beach, followed by several old women. At the sight of the boat and the sailors the man and the women stopped. Then the women spotted Lay and started shouting at him. They wanted to know, Lay explained, what he was doing in this boat with the white men. The man was Lugoma, the chief who had adopted Cyrus Hussey. Once, Lay said, when the other chiefs had wanted to kill the two boys, Lugoma had dissuaded them by offering his own life first.

It was a peaceful scene compared to the threatening army of natives who had gathered on Lay's island. But Paulding took no chances. Walking up to Lugoma, he held his pistol to the chief's head.

"Tell him," he said to Lay, "that unless he produces Hussey immediately, he will be shot."

The chief recoiled as the gun came up to his face. He barked something at the women, who ran screaming toward the huts.

Around one of the coconut trees, walking slowly as if approaching something he did not really believe was there, came Cyrus Hussey. He wore a piece of blanket tied about his waist. His feet were bare. His skin was burned black like Lay's. And swinging down across his shoulders in ringlets was a long mane of hair, bleached golden blond by the tropical sun. Lugoma turned and watched the boy come down the beach. In the silence they could hear Hussey's bare feet scrunch in the sand. He came up to Paulding and stopped, still staring in wonder, still saying nothing.

"Well, young man," said Paulding, "do you wish to return to your country?"

And the answer, little more than an awe-struck murmur: "Yes, sir. I know of nothing I have done for which I would be afraid to go home."

In the background stood the women. They started to moan, then wail. Lugoma wheeled and shouted at them. They shut up. Then Lugoma turned to Hussey and studied him. He was not going to let himself cry like his women; but he could not stop his eyes from misting, and he had to keep swallowing hard.

"They will not hurt you, my son?" he asked. "These people of yours, they will not hurt you?"

Hussey said no, they would not hurt him. They were only going to take him home now.

The chief thought for a moment, then turned to Lieutenant Paulding and asked a question. Hussey translated.

"He wants you to promise that you will bring me back someday."

Paulding replied softly, "Tell him I will if your mother will let you come."

Hussey smiled and translated. Lugoma nodded, then muttered as if to himself, "Your mother. Yes. Your mother. You go home to your mother."

Paulding reached in his pocket, went to Lugoma, and handed him something.

"Tell him," he said to Hussey, "that this is a gift. For saving your life."

Hussey spoke to the chief, who was fumbling with his gift. "See," he said, "it is what we call a jackknife. It opens out, like this."

Lugoma wiped his eyes, opened the blade, closed it, opened it, closed it again, and looked up at Hussey. His eyes were like brown saucers. A wide smile broke across his face.

As the lieutenant, the sailors, and the two castaways started toward their boat, Lugoma walked over to Hussey. He took the boy's arm, turned him around and looked at him once more, silently, for a full minute. Then his hand reached up and touched Hussey's long, golden hair. His hand was still outstretched when Hussey went slowly down the beach to the boat.

The last Cyrus Hussey saw of Lugoma, the chief was walking up the lonely beach, his head bent over as he slowly opened and closed the blade of his new jackknife, the gift of the boy with hair like the golden sun, the boy he knew he would never see again.

12. "Onshore grounds"

OR PURSUING THE WHALE
THROUGH MUSEUM AND LIBRARY

Only three generations ago you could have stood on a sand hill
on the back side of Cape Cod and counted as many as a dozen
sails against the horizon at any one time. A lot of them would
have been whalers. Heading out from Boston or New Bedford,
their sails would have looked white, their hulls trim, their lines
taut. Rolling home from the sperm-whale grounds along the Equator or the bowhead grounds of the Arctic Circle, their sails would
have been stained dark brown, their hulls mossy with sea growth,
their lines slack and looped on loop. But coming or going, they
would have been an awesome sight—whole fleets of great, fat-
winged monsters plowing majestically across the sea in unending
procession.

You would stand there a long time today without seeing even
a little lumber schooner. The tiny handkerchiefs of private yachts
still go by, many more than there were in the days when man did
not have to traverse the sea amid the stench of Diesel fumes; but

the great ships are all gone. The whalers are extinct. Today's "whaleships" aren't whaleships; they are floating mechanical slaughterhouses. The old ones don't come parading triumphantly into Sag Harbor or Nantucket harbor any more. Most of them lie hundreds of fathoms deep in the Atlantic or the Pacific. The rotted timbers of the *Essex* are 2500 fathoms down in the middle of one of the Pacific's most open stretches. The *Ann Alexander*, also sunk by a whale, molders at the bottom of the Offshore Grounds, not far from the Galápagos Islands. The *Globe*, like many another tough old whaler, served her time well, was sold as a trader, and finally broken up in Brazil.

So they died, the *Acushnet*, which took young Herman Melville out to the whaling grounds and the cannibals of the Pacific, the *Christopher Mitchell*, whose forecastle was once graced by a woman, the *Junior*, where Cyrus Plummer stood his long watches and nursed his bitter revenge, the gallant little *Favorite*, the tough-hulled *Belvedere*, the unsinkable *Pocahontas*, the stinky old *Splendid*. But of them all there is one you can still see, go aboard and inspect; and this is about the closest link you can still form to the great days of the sailing whalers. The *Charles W. Morgan*, her thirty-seven voyages behind her forever, is permanently warped to her berth at the Marine Historical Association in Mystic, Connecticut. Visitors are welcome to wander about her decks, waddle through her forecastle and steerage, and look into the officers' quarters aft. Her deck is usually fitted out with tryworks, cutting spades, harpoons, and other impedimenta of the whaling cruise, and although her whaleboats are no longer swinging alongside, the museum has a completely equipped whaleboat as an example. For the amateur fan of maritime history the Mystic seaport is easily the outstanding one in New England, probably in the country. Besides the *Morgan* there are at least half a dozen other ships berthed at the docks. In the buildings of the museum are more ship models than you can count, every conceivable kind of gear, old prints, figureheads, scrimshaw, and even kits from which you can make your own ship models. There is a unique gift shop, the Seaport Store, in case your wife, like mine, can take just so much maritime history at a gulp. I find that on the average the Seaport Store can be counted on to provide for about half an hour of uninterrupted research; whether or not it is an expensive half hour depends upon how well you have brought up your wife. Children, of course, are usually fascinated by the ships, and care must be taken to keep their little hands away from the rigging, or they will be gone to the topmast like so many scared monkeys; getting them back on deck is no simple matter for an adult whose only experience aloft has been vicarious. But what seems to interest the children even more than the ships is the complete seaport village that is being reconstructed around the museum's wharves, with everything from a church to a grog shop.

There are other museums nearly as rich as the Mystic one in the history and lore of whaling. Another good one if the children are along is the Old Dartmouth Historical Society's museum on Johnny-Cake Hill in New Bedford, Massachusetts. Here is what can be called the largest ship model in the world—or the smallest whaleship, depending on your definition. It is a child-size whaler, built especially for the museum. One of New Bedford's most successful whaling merchants was Jonathan Bourne, and his favorite ship was the *Lagoda,* which he owned for forty-five years. His success with her can be measured by one of her cruises, which brought home a catch valued at $200,755. When Bourne died, his daughter commissioned the Bourne branch of the museum and the "model" of the *Lagoda* as his memorial. To adults it is a graphic example of what the old-time whalers looked like, in every detail; to kids it is a paradise. The Old Dartmouth Museum also has such lifelike displays as a riggers' loft, a sail loft, a whaling merchant's counting room, a whaleboat shop, and a collection of gear so large and varied as to remind you that after the sand bar strangled Nantucket, New Bedford was the whaling capital of the world. William H. Tripp, the curator, has the usual scholar's love of helping anyone who really is interested in whaling and its history.

Thirty miles out to sea from New Bedford, on Nantucket Island, there is a fine old whaling museum as well as a historical museum. But nearly all Nantucket is a museum to whaling. Here, as if preserved under glass for a hundred years, is a whaling center of the nineteenth century. When the sand bar and the discovery of petroleum crippled Nantucket, the island went into virtual hibernation. Not until the tourist business became big enough to support Nantucket did it revive, and the island's chief commodity is history. So the old houses, the sail lofts, the wharves that stood there in Nantucket's golden days stand there now. No textile mills or shore factories have crowded in on them and pushed them down. Nantucket's nineteenth-century loss is its twentieth-century gain. Thousands of tourists go there every summer. Many go for the beaches, the moors, the surf, and the clear, keen air; they go back the following year for something beyond all this—the calming, unhurried sense of living in another century. There is much of the same feeling, and much of the same history, on the island halfway between Nantucket and the mainland; Martha's Vineyard has its own share of the history of whaling. There are those who say Nantucket is "richer in history" and those who give their vote to the Vineyard; but you don't get me into that argument.

There are many other good museums for whaling history, in New York City, in New London, Connecticut, in Sag Harbor, at the end of Long Island, in Boston and Salem, Massachusetts. On a vacation tour through New England, watch the service-station road maps for museums in the seacoast towns; chances are that there is something fascinating in every one.

So much for the lazy man's pursuit of the whale. If you have gone beyond that phase, if you have become a hopeless addict, let yourself go into the written records. Nearly every museum has its collection of logs, journals, and contemporary histories, and they are there to be read; few museums will refuse to let you study a log or old book if you know how to handle one and are sincerely interested. Once you are plunged into this gold mine, you are really lost. Well I remember the day at Mystic when the then curator Carl Cutler showed me the personal journal of a man who had sailed aboard the *Morgan*. While the water lapped and sucked at the old wharves below and gulls cried across the river, I went down around the Horn with the *Morgan* and didn't come back for two days. The story of the *Morgan's* escape from the cannibals in my Chapter 4 came originally from that journal. It was also one of the sources of the story of the girl in the forecastle, told in my Chapter 7. Two years later the same journal, edited by Carl Cutler, was brought out as a book: *Whale Hunt,* by Nelson Cole Haley (Ives & Washburn, 1948). It is one of the best single accounts written about a whaling cruise, and one of the most exciting.

The museum library at Mystic is full of such logs and journals, some almost as fascinating as the Haley account, some dull, but all authentic, contemporary histories. Carl Cutler has retired now, but the museum accomplished the impossible twice by (1) finding a man worthy of taking the helm from Cutler, and (2) luring the new curator away from his native Nantucket. He is Edouard A. Stackpole, who for years was President of the Nantucket Historical Association and who knows more about the history of Yankee whaling than any other man, partly because so much of the history keeps turning out to have been made by one of Stackpole's ancestors. His book, *The Sea-Hunters* (Lippincott, 1953), is the most complete and scholarly history of American whaling, bar none, since the great *History of the American Whale Fishery,* written by Alexander Starbuck in 1878. For the real student of the American whaleman *The Sea-Hunter* is the basic work. My own book is for the amateur and not the scholar. Still, without the more than generous help and guidance of Ed Stackpole, I could not have written it.

In reading the contemporary accounts it is usually best to start with the old books and other printed records. The logs themselves make slow going at first because they were written in longhand. The log was usually kept by the first mate, whether he happened to have a legible hand or not. You will find it surprising, though, how soon you catch on and are reading along at a fine clip, especially after you learn to skim over the interminable remarks about wind and weather so much more important to the whalemen then than they are to the reader now.

The best sources of such reading material are in the museums and the libraries of nearly all the seacoast towns of New England. The files of the newspapers of these towns and cities are usually full of such material too. The New Bedford newspapers, the Nantucket *Inquirer & Mirror*, and the *Vineyard Gazette* are among the best. And the following places are rich in logs, journals, diaries, old books, and contemporary accounts:

> *New York Public Library*
> *Marine Historical Association, Mystic, Connecticut*
> *Old Dartmouth Historical Society, New Bedford, Massachusetts*
> *New Bedford Public Library*
> *Edgartown Public Library, Martha's Vineyard*
> *Dukes County Historical Society, Martha's Vineyard*
> *Atheneum Library, Nantucket*
> *Historical Museum, Nantucket*
> *Whaling Museum, Nantucket*
> *Massachusetts Historical Society, Boston*
> *Harvard College Library, Cambridge, Massachusetts*
> *Essex Institute, Salem, Massachusetts*
> *Peabody Museum, Salem, Massachusetts*

And if you are particularly interested in reading whatever more there is about the stories I have told in this book, here are the main sources, chapter by chapter:

1. The major source for this story, of course, is Chase's account, entitled *Narrative of the Most Extraordinary and Distressing Ship Wreck of the Whaleship Essex of Nantucket*, published in New York in 1821. This is a very rare little book; the rarest copy of all, Melville's own with his notes in the margin, sold for a reported $1600. The New York Public Library has a copy which you can arrange to read, though it cannot be taken out of the building. The Nantucket Atheneum and Whaling Museum also have copies that can be read if handled carefully. The Whaling Museum and probably some of the other museums as well have a book that is not so rare but not so authoritative, either. It is titled *Loss of the Essex*, and it was published, a dozen or so years after the wreck, by the Religious Tract Society in London. It contains an account by Chase (less accurate than his *Narrative* and

probably an embroidered version of the original) and amplifications by Captain Pollard and one of the three men (a Briton) who had elected to wait for help on Henderson Island. Some of the story as told by these two survivors checks with other known facts of the time; other parts of their story do not.

The essentials of the *Essex* disaster, though, are known throughout most of the island of Nantucket. This was not always so. They say that in the first generation after the tragedy many Nantucketers preferred not to repeat the account of cannibalism and murder. Once a Nantucket woman asked the daughter of a survivor about it and received the answer: "Miss Mollie, here we never mention the *Essex*."

For other details not included in the Chase *Narrative* or the to-be-trusted accounts by Pollard and the Henderson Island survivor I have relied on the stories that have come down through the generations of Nantucketers who *would* talk about it long after the shock had worn off. Some of those stories have recurred often enough and from enough different sources to indicate that they are true in essentials at least. And for the atmosphere of the whaleship closing in on the whale I am indebted to two excellent contemporary descriptions of the scene: *The Whale and His Captors*, by Rev. Henry T. Cheever (Harper & Bros., 1850), and *There She Blows!*, by William Hussey Macy (Lee & Shepard, 1877). Nantucket's Whaling Museum has copies of these two old books, and some of the other museums probably do too.

2. The best single source on Melville's years in the Pacific that I have seen is a book entitled *Melville in the South Seas*, by Charles Roberts Anderson (University of California Press, 1939). I wasn't able to find a copy to buy or even take out of a library. But the New York Public Library has one that can be studied in its reading room. Of course there are dozens of good recent books on Melville that include the Pacific islands phase, among them Newton Arvin's *Herman Melville* (William Sloane Associates) which won the National Book Award for 1950, Howard P. Vincent's *The Trying-Out of Moby Dick* (Houghton Mifflin, 1948), Leon Howard's *Herman Melville* (University of California

Press, 1951), and *Herman Melville, Cycle and Epicycle* (Harvard University Press, 1953), by his granddaughter, Eleanor Melville Metcalf. But for the reader who wants to delve into just about every scrap of information of any importance on the subject of Melville there is nothing better than the monumental and brilliant work by Jay Leyda entitled *The Melville Log* (Harcourt, Brace, 1951). Leyda has here gathered all the bits and pieces, assembled them in chronological order, and put them down in the form of a log, enabling you to chart the course of Melville's life all the way from his birth in New York City to his death there seventy-two years later after living with "cannibals" in the South Pacific, traveling through much of the rest of the world, and writing America's greatest novel. There are other sources for the story of Melville's life in the Pacific. It was Professor Wilson L. Heflin of Annapolis who noted, during Nantucket's observance of the anniversary of *Moby Dick* in the summer of 1951, that the man Melville saw in mid-Pacific and thought to be Owen Chase was not Chase at all. The account of Melville's first, eerie glimpse of Captain Pollard, through the oil-yellowed fog of a Nantucket night, was told me by Edouard Stackpole when he was president of Nantucket's Historical Association.

Of course Melville himself was a chief source. The books of his that shed the most light on this period are *Typee, Omoo, Mardi, White-Jacket* and, most important, *Moby Dick*. When *Typee* first came out it was generally regarded as highly romanticized. But then Richard Tobias Greene, the shipmate who deserted with Melville and lived among the Taipi tribe with him for a while, popped up in Buffalo, New York, and confirmed a great deal of the book as plain truth. Melville's novels were fiction and should be treated as such. But in many cases, when the facts come to light, they indicate that, despite the learned protestations of some scholars, the best single source on Melville seems to be Melville.

3. The rogue whale, especially the murderous white whale known as Mocha Dick, appears again and again in contemporary accounts, journals, and logs. There were countless descriptions of the damage done by him, mostly in newspapers and logbooks

of the day. And there are hundreds of scientific studies of the fantastic creature that is the whale; despite that, some seemingly unscientific lore of the animal is sworn to by many whaling veterans who ought to know what they are talking about. I have set down both the most important known scientific facts and the lore that is attested to by competent experts.

An important document in any consideration of the Mocha Dick legend is an article written in 1892 and entitled "The Career of Mocha Dick." The article brings together many of the stories of battles between Mocha Dick and the whalers, and it has been suggested that the whole account is a magnificent fake. Many of the incidents mentioned in the article are apparently substantiated by other sources; yet a lot of "The Career of Mocha Dick" could be the product of a rich imagination. It will be difficult ever to tell because the author of the article is unknown. In any case Mocha Dick was real enough to inspire the imagination of Herman Melville.

4. I have drawn heavily on two major sources for the chapter on the "cannibals" and the *Morgan's* narrow escape. The incident itself, as I have mentioned, is recounted in the private journal of Nelson Cole Haley, which Carl Cutler showed me at Mystic eight years ago. For the basic information on the "cannibals" I am much indebted to a thorough study done by J. C. Furnas, entitled *Anatomy of Paradise* (William Sloane Associates, 1948). Those who know far more about the subject than I ever could claim that *Anatomy of Paradise* is the soundest popular work on the Pacific islanders. For anyone interested in reading more about the islanders I found the following books as interesting as they are informative:

> *The Sexual Life of Savages,* by Bronislaw Malinowski (Readers' League of America)
> *Coming of Age in Samoa,* by Margaret Mead (William Morrow)
> *Growing Up in New Guinea,* by Margaret Mead (William Morrow)
> *The Fortunate Islands,* by Walter Karig (Rinehart)

> *Islands of the Pacific,* by Hawthorne Daniel (G. P. Putnam's
> Sons)
> *Pacific Adventure,* by Willard Price (Reynal & Hitchcock)
> *The Last King of Paradise,* by Eugene Burns (Pellegrini &
> Cudahy)

5. As I said in telling the story of Tilton's walk home from the
Arctic Circle, he delighted many a visitor to the old *Morgan* with
his own account. He also wrote up the adventure as a book, which
was published in 1928 (Doubleday), but is hard to find now except in some of the whaling museums.

Because it did not alter the outcome of his expedition, and because it would unnecessarily confuse the narrative of the account,
I have told the story without mentioning the Revenue Cutter
Service until the end of Tilton's account. Actually Tilton and the
men of the U.S.R.C.S. met when each had got part way along
the coast. But at that point neither knew which would get
through, or for that matter whether either would make it. So the
rescue ship would still have to be sent north, since there would be
no way of knowing whether or not help had come to the isolated
whalemen at the Arctic Circle. Tilton therefore kept pushing
south, and not until long after he had made it did he know that
his odyssey had indeed been in vain. The best account of the
U.S.R.C.S. expedition was written by one of the members,
Lieutenant Ellsworth P. Bertholf. Entitled *The Rescue of the
Whalers,* it can be found in *Harper's* magazine for June 1899.

6. The stories of the whaling and sealing skippers can be found
everywhere, in their biographies, their journals, their ships' logs,
and newspaper and magazine accounts of the day. A secondary
but sometimes richer source is the store of memories of their
children and grandchildren, which means Nantucket and the
Vineyard and Sag Harbor and Mystic and all the other towns
and cities that once sent fleets of whaleships down around the
Horn. There are, however, two very good collections of biographies about whaling captains which are easily obtainable. One,
entitled *Whaling Masters,* is put out by the Old Dartmouth Historical Society, was a Federal Writers Project and is printed by

the Reynolds Printing Company, New Bedford (Reynolds, by the way, is a specialist on books about whaling; ask them for their list of publications and try to resist ordering them all). The other collection of biographies is entitled *New London Whaling Captains*, by Barnard L. Colby, was originally a series of articles in the New London *Day* and has been brought out in book form by the Marine Historical Association at Mystic.

In this chapter I mention the method in the apparently mad meanderings of the whaleships in the Pacific. There is an excellent description of the whaling grounds in the bulletin of the New York Zoological Society, Vol. 34, No. 6, November-December, 1931. Also, in his classic history, *The Sea-Hunters*, Edouard Stackpole gives a more extensive description of the whalers' seasonal visits to each of the whaling grounds.

It is Stackpole, too, as I point out in the chapter, who determined that Christopher Burdick and not Nathaniel Palmer discovered the continent of Antarctica. But for an excellent description of Palmer's explorations in the area, written before the Burdick log was found, read Alexander Laing's book *Clipper Ship Men* (Duell, Sloane & Pearce).

As every reader of any book about the sea knows, the Pitcairn Island story has been written about for a century and a half. Captain Bligh of the *Bounty* wrote his own account after he returned to England, and for the scholar it is of course the most authoritative. But the famous team of Charles Nordhoff and James Norman Hall has done the whole story full justice in their trilogy: *Mutiny on the Bounty, Men Against the Sea*, and *Pitcairn Island*. The chief source of the dramatic meeting between Captain Folger and the sons of the mutineers is the captain himself, in his logs and in the recollections of the friends whom he told of his experience. Many contemporary accounts piece together to give the complete story.

Of the sociological and anthropological studies that have been made of Pitcairn Island the one I liked best (of the ones I read) was by Harry I. Shapiro, entitled *The Heritage of the Bounty* (Simon & Schuster). But the most fascinating theory on Pitcairn and the mutineers that I have encountered is contained in a book published last year in England: *The Wake of the Bounty*, by C. S. Wilkinson (Cassell & Co., Ltd.). In an absorbing piece of literary detective work Mr. Wilkinson takes up the evidence and puts it together in such a way as to indicate (1) that Fletcher Christian went home from Pitcairn Island; (2) that he hid out for the rest of his life in England; (3) that through Wordsworth, a friend of the Christian family, he met Coleridge; and (4) that Fletcher Christian was the model for Coleridge's "ancient mariner."

An undeniably intriguing theory, and one I have neither the space nor the competence to discuss at any length. But the theory depends upon three basic suppositions. The first is the weakest: that all or most of the mutineers could have sailed away from Pitcairn on one of the many whalers cruising the Pacific at the time, booking passage for England and paying with *Bounty* currency for silence. This supposition is weak because there *weren't* many whalers cruising the Pacific at the turn of the nineteenth century. The *Essex* went down in 1820, more than a quarter of a century after the settling of Pitcairn; and the lonely plight of the drifting men in the *Essex* whaleboats is testimony to how few ships there were crisscrossing the Pacific in those early days of whaling. And anyone who suggests that money would buy the silence of a whaler's forecastle doesn't know whalers' forecastles. The money would be accepted, all right. But sooner or later, and certainly sooner than late, the whole thing would leak.

The second supposition is a strong one if true: that no evidence of the death of Christian and the other mutineers was ever offered by Alexander Smith, the sole survivor at the time Folger discovered the hideout. Although I haven't seen the answer to this one, certainly a scholar of the subject can determine whether or not any such evidence has ever been discovered.

The third supposition is the most fascinating of all: that Peter Heywood, a crewman of the *Bounty* who had been tried and pardoned for his part in the mutiny, was walking along a street near the docks in Plymouth, England, one day nineteen years later, when he saw a man ahead of him who looked familiar. The man turned and faced Heywood, turned again quickly, and ran off. Heywood was convinced that the man was Christian. That supposition, unless Heywood can be proved as mistaken or a liar, must be accepted as the strongest one of all.

So much for a very intriguing theory about the mutiny aboard the *Bounty* and its aftermath. If you like further reading, there is a project well worth some detective work in the museums and libraries.

7. The stories about the men, their lives aboard the whalers, and the yarns they spun came from all manner of sources, ranging from history books to anecdotes that have passed by word of mouth through generations of whaling families and their descendants. Prowl through any whaling museum library and you will come upon at least half a dozen such stories.

8. Accounts of the whalemen's island women are understandably sparse. The picture has to be pieced together from little bits of evidence come upon usually in unexpected places. So there is no way to delve into this as a single subject; it comes out in the general study of the whalemen among the islands. There is an occasional unguarded remark in a ship's log or a journal, a description by a missionary more intent on telling the truth than in wheedling money from his New England backers, a letter home from a whaleman—these can be found only as you go along.

I owe a particular debt in this chapter, though, to *The New England Quarterly* for permission to use parts of the journal of Laura Jernegan, which first appeared in that magazine, and to Henry Beetle Hough for the story of Henry Worth and Lipei Naij. That story I had not known until it appeared in *Whaling Wives*, by Mr. Hough and the late Emma Mayhew Whiting (Houghton Mifflin). In fact *Whaling Wives* is the best single account of the women who went to sea with their whalemen husbands. It was started by Mrs. Whiting and after her death Mr. Hough performed the amazing job of assembling into a readable account all the intertwined stories of all the interrelated whalemen and their wives. Henry Beetle Hough is, of course, the famous

"Country Editor" of Martha's Vineyard and the genial authority on all things pertaining to the Vineyard and its history.

9. There are a number of contemporary accounts of the mutiny aboard the *Junior,* stories in Australian newspapers, descriptions in New England, and especially New Bedford, newspapers, depositions at the trial, numerous magazine articles of the time. But the most complete story gathered from all these accounts, so far as I know, is the chapter on that mutiny in Chester Howland's book *Thar She Blows!* (Wilfred Funk). Chester Howland, the son of a whaling skipper, is one of New England's experts on whaling and has traveled about lecturing on the subject as well as writing on it. I am indebted to him for generous help and advice.

10. In many of the whaling museums and libraries you can find a little volume with the big title: *"A Narrative of the Mutiny On Board the Ship Globe of Nantucket, in the Pacific Ocean, Jan. 1824. And the Journal of a Residence of Two Years on the Mulgrave Islands; with Observations on the Manners and Customs of the Inhabitants,* by William Lay of Saybrook, Conn. and Cyrus M. Hussey of Nantucket: The only Survivors from the Massacre of the Ship's Company by the Natives." This book was originally printed by Lay and Hussey themselves in New London in 1828, and the copies of the first edition are extremely rare. But it has been reprinted once or twice by other publishers and should not be hard to find in one of the later editions. It is the most authoritative single contemporary account of the *Globe* mutiny. But it is by no means the only one. Samuel Comstock, the leader of the mutiny, had two brothers who told their own accounts. One, entitled *Samuel Comstock, the Terrible Mutineer,* was written by brother William, who had not been along on that fatal cruise of the *Globe;* it was published in Boston and New York in 1840. The other account was by brother George, who had been at the helm of the *Globe* while Samuel carried on his mutiny below decks. Its title: *Narrative of the Mutiny, Capture and Transactions On Board of the Ship Globe of Nantucket.* It is still in manuscript form in the Whaling Museum at Nantucket. To these sources are

added some important depositions, taken from the *Globe* crew-men at Valparaiso and Nantucket; some of these are available at Nantucket, others in the Library of Congress in Washington.

An interesting novel based on the *Globe* mutiny was published in 1952. Written by Louis B. Davidson and Eddie Doherty and entitled *Captain Marooner* (Thomas Y. Crowell), it advances the theory that the *Globe's* master, Thomas Worth, brought it on himself by his brutality and a propensity for marooning unruly crewmen. I do not know of much evidence to support this theory, while there is contemporary testimony to the effect that Worth was no worse than most whaling skippers. As for the theory that Samuel Comstock plotted the perfect mutiny, it is my own. There is no direct statement by him that he planned to lead the natives in a massacre of the rest of the crew; but I am hardly surprised to find no open announcement of it. It seems to me that most of his actions once he reached the atoll support the theory. How else explain his handouts to the islanders and his solitary march across the beach to the native settlement? More important, how else explains the reaction of Silas Payne that he and the rest of the crew should thereupon prepare for an attack? Read the afore-mentioned sources and see if you don't agree.

11. The account of the massacre on the atoll, the life of Hussey and Lay among the natives, and their final rescue comes mainly from two sources. One is their own long-titled book I have just mentioned. The other is a journal kept by a member of the rescue expedition. Lieutenant Hiram Paulding was the officer in charge of the boat that went whisking back and forth among the islets of Mili Atoll in chase of the hostages. His full account, *Journal of a Cruise of the United States Schooner Dolphin,* was published in New York in 1831. It is a rare little book, but some of the museums have copies of it; I know Nantucket's Whaling Museum has. In this chapter I had necessarily to resort to considerable reconstruction based on the spare accounts given by Lay and Hussey. Thus I relied on many helpful books about the Pacific native, some of which I have mentioned in my note on Chapter 4.

Some others appear among the following, a general list of books that should fascinate anyone who wants to read more about Yankee whaling.

America in the Pacific, by Foster Rhea Dulles (Houghton Mifflin, 1932)

Arctic Regions and the Northern Whale Industry, by William Scoresby (2 vols., London, 1820)

A Sailor's Treasury, by Frank Shay (W. W. Norton, 1951)

Catalogue of Nantucket Whalers and Their Voyages, 1815–1870, by Hussey and Robinson (Nantucket, 1876)

Cruise of the Cachalot, by F. T. Bullen (New York, 1898). The *Cachalot* was later identified as none other than the stinky old *Splendid.*

Etchings of a Whaling Cruise, by J. Ross Browne (New York, 1846)

Faery Lands of the South Seas, by Charles Nordhoff and James Norman Hall (Harper & Bros., 1921)

History of Nantucket, by Obed Macy (Boston, 1835)

History of Nantucket, by Alexander Starbuck (C. E. Goodspeed, Boston, 1924)

Incidents of a Whaling Voyage, by Francis A. Olmsted (New York, 1841)

In the South Seas, by Robert Louis Stevenson (Scribner's, Biographical Edition XXII, 1940)

Journal of a Cruise Made to the Pacific Ocean by Captain David Porter in the U.S. Frigate Essex, 1812–14, by David Porter (Philadelphia, 1815)

Japan's Islands of Mystery, by Willard Price (John Day, 1944)

Lowered Boats, by Foster Rhea Dulles (Houghton Mifflin, 1932)

Mid-Pacific, by James Norman Hall (Houghton Mifflin, 1928)

Miriam Coffin, or the Whale Fisherman, by Colonel James C. Hart (New York, 1834). A novel that presents an accurate and flavorful picture of Nantucket during the whaling days.

Nantucket Argument Settlers, by Harry B. Turner (Nantucket, 1944)

Nantucket, the Far-Away Island, by William Oliver Stevens (Dodd, Mead, 1936). The best of the modern histories and guides to the island.

Narrative of the U.S. Exploring Expedition, 1838–42, by Charles Wilkes, U.S.N. (London, 1845)

Narrative of Voyages and Travel, by Amasa Delano (Boston, 1815)

Report of the Secretary of State on the Subject of the Cod and Whale Fisheries, Feb. 1, 1791, by Thomas Jefferson (Philadelphia, 1791)

Sails and Whales, by Captain Harry Allen Chippendale (Houghton Mifflin, 1951). Captain Chippendale, a veteran of the sailing whaleships, got a good look at one of the modern "factory ships" and was so disgusted that he sat down and wrote his book about the great days. After a full life ranging from whaling to authorship Captain Chippendale died last year.

Shantymen & Shantyboys, by William Main Doerflinger (Macmillan, 1951). The best collection of sailors' (and lumbermen's) songs.

South Sea Tales, by Jack London (Regent Press, 1911)

The American Whaleman. A Study of Life and Labor in the Whaling Industry, by Elmos P. Hohman (New York, 1928)

The Cruise of the "Snark", by Jack London (Macmillan, 1922)

The Law of the Sea, by William McFee (Lippincott, 1950)

The Long Harpoon, by Arthur C. Watson (Reynolds Printing Co., New Bedford, 1929). An excellent collection of whaling stories, some of which were originally published in *Yachting* magazine and the Boston *Globe.*

The Maritime History of Massachusetts, by Samuel Eliot Morison (Houghton Mifflin, 1921). A classic for any student or fan of maritime history.

The Nantucket Scrap Basket, by William F. Macy (Houghton Mifflin, 1916)

The Natural History of the Sperm Whale, by Thomas Beale (London, 1839)

The Pacific Islands, by Douglas L. Oliver (Harvard University Press, 1951)

The Pacific Ocean, by Felix Riesenberg (McGraw-Hill)

The Real Story of the Whaler, by A. Hyatt Verrill (New York, 1916)

The Story of Old Nantucket, by William F. Macy (Houghton Mifflin, 1915)

The Story of the New England Whalers, by John R. Spears (New York, 1908)

The Voyage of the Beagle, by Charles Darwin (Everyman's Library, London, J. M. Dent & Sons, Ltd., 1906)

The Whalemen's Adventures in the Sandwich Islands and California, by W. H. Thomas (Boston, 1873)

The Yankee Whaler, by Clifford W. Ashley (Houghton Mifflin, 1938)

There Goes Flukes, by William Henry Tripp (Reynolds Printing Co., New Bedford, 1938)

Three Bricks and Three Brothers, by Will Gardner (Houghton Mifflin, 1945). A warmly human portrait of a whaleship owner, his ships and his family.

Voyages and Discoveries in the South Seas, 1792–1832, by Captain Edmund Fanning (Marine Research Society, Salem, Mass.)

Whaling, by Charles Boardman Hawes (New York, 1924)

Whaling and Fishing, by Charles Nordhoff (Cincinnati, 1856)

Wrecked on the Feejees, by William S. Cary (Inquirer & Mirror Press, Nantucket, 1928). A reprint of a pamphlet written by Cary after his return from a very close brush with death in the Pacific. He was one of the crew of the whaler *Oeno,* which ran aground on Turtle Island in 1825. The whalemen set up camp ashore, but soon one of them precipitated an attack by the natives. In much

the same manner as the Mili islanders with the crew of
the *Globe* the savages of Turtle Island massacred all but
Cary of the *Oeno's* men. Cary lived nine years among
the natives before he was rescued. He wrote his account
after his return to Nantucket, but the manuscript was
lost and not found again until 1887, when it was published in the Nantucket *Journal*. Reprints of it can be
seen in the Whaling Museum and the Atheneum at Nantucket, and the Inquirer & Mirror Press may have a few
copies for sale.

With such books, with this list of whaling museums and
libraries, and with a clear eye and a stubborn disposition you can
now pursue the whale by land as the men and women of the
great days did by sea. You will find the chase made more enjoyable by curators, librarians, and scholars and other experts who
need no more introduction than your enthusiasm, just as I did.
My acknowledgments to such people are many, especially to
Edouard Stackpole and Carl Cutler of Mystic, to Chester Howland of New Bedford, to Henry Beetle Hough of the Vineyard, to
William H. Tripp of the Old Dartmouth Historical Society, to
J. C. Furnas of just about every place in the world but especially
the islands of the Pacific, to Jay Leyda, the Melville expert, and
to Ralph Graves, former nature editor of *Life* Magazine. And I
hardly need add: to my wife, who made every vacation research
trip still a vacation, and to Ann, 6, and Christopher, 1, who made
the writing of the book a real challenge.

To the scholars in the field my apologies for taking liberties
with some of the cherished traditions of whaling. I plead guilty
to using landlubberly words and terms where I considered the
strictly accurate one would be confusing to the amateur. I know
that a "pod" is a saltier term than a "herd" of whales; but I think
"herd" has come to be generally accepted now. The same goes
for "whaler," meaning whaleship and not whaleman; again, I
think modern usage has made an honest word out of it. Where
logs and journals have given varying or ancient spellings of place
names, I have used the modern spelling. Any other way would

be madness, a fact to which a look at a few logs will attest. It is said that the first mate of the good ship *Aurora* was taken to task by the owners, who were particularly exasperated to find that he could not even spell the name of his ship. The mate was indignant. "Look thar," he said, stabbing a stubby finger at a passage in the log. "If O-R-O-R-O-R don't spell 'Ororor,' then what in hell does?" I have also used the word "harpooner" where "harpooneer" was used in the nineteenth century, even by Melville. But "harpooner" seemed to me to be simpler and just as clear. Besides most whalemen didn't use either term anyway; because of the harpooner's double duty at the steering oar during the kill, the whalemen called him "boat steerer." But I have used "native" as the whalemen did—meaning "native of the Pacific." Many an off-islander of the old days, for example, was highly embarrassed by the profane reply of a Nantucket or Vineyard whaleman whom he asked "—and are you a native?"

I hope you have as much fun in the museums as I have had. If it didn't sound odd, somehow, I'd wish you "greasy luck."